For
Nakwan, Nigel,
Janocha, Cimberly,
Enoch, Amber, Carl,
Emma, Simone, Nicolas,
and Jeremy

and to the Memory of
Charlotte Reid,
Herman Reid,
Rosa Lee Spivey,
and Essex Hemphill

ACKNOWLEDGMENTS

What excellence one may find in this work grows out of my uncanny ability to surround myself with remarkably talented individuals and my somewhat less developed ability to learn from them. Great thanks are in order, then, to John Agnew, Mia Bay, Roberto Bedoya, Herman Bennett, Marcellus Blount, Antoinette Burton, Carla Capetti, Hazel Carby, Arnaldo Cruz-Malave, George Cunningham, Michael Denning, Patricia Dixon, Cheryl Dunye, Shelly Eversley, Gerard Fergerson, Frances Ferguson, Brian Freeman, Shari Frilot, Paul Gilroy, Allen Grossman, John Guillory, Philip Brian Harper, Benjamin Herman, Alexandra Juhasz, John Keene, Walter Benn Michaels, Jennifer Lyle Morgan, Jose Munoz, Eve Oishi, Nell Irvin Painter, Carla Peterson, John Plotz, Mary Poovey, Yevette Richards, Paul Smith, Claudia Tate, Peter-Wayne Taylor, Scott Trafton, Gayle Wald, Michelle Wallace, Joshua Wilner, and Larzer Ziff. I most especially want to thank my parents, Robert Pharr, Joanna Bacote and Harold Bacote, and my sister, Daphne Reid Pharr. Much of this work was completed while I spent a wonderful two years as a Pforzheimer fellow in the department of English at the City College of New York. A residency at the Library Company of Philadelphia and a grant from the National Endowment for the Humanities greatly facilitated this project's realization.

Washington, D.C.
New Year's Eve, 1997

CONTENTS

LIST OF ILLUSTRATIONS

Conjugal Union

INTRODUCTION OR, "SPEAKING SWEETLY OF PHILLIS WHEATLEY"

'Twas mercy brought me from my pagan land,
Taught my benighted soul to understand
That there's a God—that there's a Saviour too;
Once I redemption neither sought nor knew.
Some view our sable race with scornful eye—
Their color is a diabolic dye.'
Remember, Christians, Negroes black as Cain
May be refined, and join the angelic train.

—*Phillis Wheatley,* On Being Brought
From Africa to America

This work is concerned most faithfully with questions of history and in particular the question of how one might properly historicize the blackness of Black America, how one might unpack the common sense of that deep tendency within black intellectual life to insist upon black singularity, to conjure that which is pure, unique, that which is decidedly black. I have insisted, therefore, upon the modest assumption that racial and national identity exist within history and are thus permeable and dynamic. The blackness of early national America does not and cannot fit snugly or seamlessly our contemporary realities. The simplicity of this claim belies the fact that it is still quite possible to speak glibly of a Black American literary tradition broad enough to encompass the meditations of both a Phillis Wheatley and an Audre Lorde. Indeed, the rather lukewarm assessment of Wheatley within American and Black American literary and cultural criticism speaks, I believe, to the fact that she, like many of her black fellows in early national and antebellum America, not only displays the traits of an "unfinished" literary training but an "unfinished" racial identity as well.[1] This is not to say simply that Phillis Wheatley has not been properly decolonized. The difficulty is not that she loathes blackness, or her own Africanity, or that of her fellow artist, S. M., whom she bathes in respect and goodwill.[2] Instead, Wheatley's particular idiosyncrasy is that she is not concerned at all with announcing a Black American singularity. What Wheatley remarks in her paean to slavery and Anglo-American imperialism is a conception of her own ontology that is precisely not fettered by geography or race. The "being" of the title is established within the movement between Africa and America, movement that is ordained by the mercy of the Saviour, not the will of the colonizer. Wheatley's work does little, then, to establish black specificity. Nor does it even attempt to address the inherently antihumanistic, antihuman nature of slavery. Instead, she celebrates her enslavement because of the fact that it removes her from a benighted African particularity and places her within an angelic train where all distinction is disallowed.[3]

In attempting this revision of Wheatley's role as (black) literary forebear, I mean to suggest again that the proper role of the historically minded critic is precisely to insist upon consideration of the fact that the blackness of Black American literature exists in a different, if parallel and often overlapping, historical trajectory from the blackness of Black American bodies. The simple fact that Phillis Wheatley was an author of African descent, that she existed within a purportedly black body, should not be enough to secure her status as the originator of the Black American literary tradition. The very obviousness of this claim startles, especially when juxtaposed with the fact that it is taken almost without question that Black American literature is that which demonstrates the impress of the black hand, the black body, even a body, as problematically situated as Phillis Wheatley's. It signals, in fact, the depth of the ideological calculus by which our understanding of the black body is wedded to our understanding of black literature and literacy. Many of the finest treatments of Black American literature and culture are absolutely established on the assumption of a black body that is necessarily prior to any Black American representational strategy. We find, for example, Sterling Stuckey struggling to establish a somewhat tenuous link between a decidedly cosmopolitan intellectual milieu, one that included David Walker, Henry Highland Garnet, Paul Robeson, and W. E. B. Du Bois, and the slave culture of the antebellum South.[4] In doing so he produces a tradition of writing, speech, and performance as Black American precisely by figuring slave intellectualism as an essentially physical and kinetic matter; movement and vocality in the form of the ring shout are nominated by Stuckey as primary vehicles of the culture of Black nationalism. Black American culture emanates from Black American bodies. The Black American intellectual might gain access to the root of his blackness, then, by gaining access to his own body and the (black) truths embedded within. This is while the vehicles through which he expresses racial identity (writing, for example) tend to cover over the "fact" of a specifically black corporeality.

I do not mean simply to proffer already hackneyed charges of essentialism, or ahistoricism, to Stuckey's often nuanced and compelling work and the intellectual tendencies that I take it to represent. Instead, I suggest that Stuckey's interest in antebellum America, and the conceptual tools that he uses to forward these interests, is itself deeply marked by a set of representational and discursive strategies that crystallized in the incredibly dynamic years between 1830 and 1860, when a rather remarkable change took place in the basic structures of American intellectualism. What Stuckey and others have accessed in their work is the fact that during the antebellum period a community of free black northeastern intellectuals sought to establish the stability of a Black American subjectivity by figuring the black body as the necessary antecedent to any intelligible Black American public presence. They did so, moreover, through the production of media, especially newspapers, novels, pamphlets, and a variety of performance forms in which the body of the black was almost constantly on exhibition, in which the intimate details of physical difference were demonstrated with no hint of blushing.[5]

In making this point, I do not mean simply to shock my audience with images from America's barbaric slave past, to shame the collective conscience with the truth of an earlier, rawer racialism. Instead, my focus is on the striking paradox of this phenomenon. The fact of the black body's spectacular display, the many images of a presumably African-derived corporeality, demonstrates an incredible uncertainty as to the status of that body's being. The black of antebellum print culture was hardly a static phenomenon. It was male and female, coal black and perfectly white, bond and free, rich and poor. It could change without much fanfare from the gowns of a mistress into the rags of a concubine. Furthermore, the great gaping mouths, the midnight skin and the impossibly white eyes, and the teeth of the black body that danced across America's minstrel stages forced the question of whether there were any limits to its possibilities. I would suggest that the community of intellectuals to whom I have referred, that first "post-Wheatley" collection of journalists, essayists, orators, and novelists, had necessarily to struggle with the fact of this black body's limitless nature. As a function of both social necessity and philosophical clarity, the black body had to be normalized, turned black. I contend, furthermore, that what has come to be known as Black American literature operates precisely at the site of that body's normalization. Antebellum authors were obsessed with the process of embodiment, with how one might, for example, turn Thomas Jefferson's daughter into a black fugitive.[6]

By marking these facts I hope to place my work alongside that of a number of authors who have come to understand a distinct change in American notions of corporeality during the antebellum era, a change that worked to establish bodies as privileged sites in the (re)construction of American culture. I am indebted in particular to Karen Sanchez-Eppler, who argues that the advent of feminism and abolitionism warped notions of a disembodied, disinterested (public) subjectivity such that formerly excluded persons could enter the public sphere precisely as embodied individuals.[7] My work here is largely to question the nature of that process as it refers to the production of the black subject. Thus, I reject the notion that the black body is some species of the always already and instead look to those technologies that allowed for an ontology of blackness that gains stability precisely through reference to a (black) body. Specifically, I note a sea change in American notions of race, one that involved the disavowal of readily available concepts of racial consanguinity and racial ambiguity. During the antebellum period intellectuals began the arduous, awkward process of establishing the peculiarity of the black body, the distinctiveness that could never be exorcised. I utilize the already impossibly overdetermined notion of black embodiment, then, to refer, not to some demonstrable physical fact, but to a specifically American ideological effect in which race is always produced on a two-dimensional black/white axis.

I have taken my lead from Engels's genealogy of domesticity in which he suggests that, though families are primary locations for the domination and exploitation of women, it is nonetheless women themselves who produce familial structures in order to establish bulwarks against harsher, unsentimental forms of male domination, slavery chief among them. Similarly, I will argue that it was during the antebellum period that the black body came to operate—for blacks—as a primary site in the negotiation of slavery and white supremacy. As the population of free blacks exploded in this country during the first half of the nineteenth century, as they formed themselves into communities and began to articulate a nascent "consciousness," the marker of ultimate difference changed from the condition of servitude to one of race. The fact of that difference, the fact of race, became the primary site for the articulation of a communal consciousness that somehow encompassed the realities of all persons of African descent, but that was indeed not subsumed under an already suspect slave consciousness.

This work relies heavily, then, on a largely unexplored archive of antebellum American writing in which a (free) black subjectivity is championed and demonstrated, in which one is faced with the thorny questions surrounding how to announce a public subjectivity that is also black. What becomes immediately apparent to even the most casual student of these works is the obvious nexus of body and household, the impossibly complicated manner in which homes and families negotiate the production of the black body. It is literally the case that individuals enter black households as white and leave as black. Indeed, the household operates as a remarkable site inasmuch as it marshals all manner of technologies: cleaning, violence, marriage, all to the project of producing black bodies. Thus, antebellum Black American intellectuals were particularly eager to announce the primacy of the household in their self-conscious efforts to establish the black body as rational, self-contained, independent. If one wanted to create a stable black body then one had necessarily to establish a stable black household. Thus, the discomfiting figure of the black body embedded within the white household had somehow to be overcome.

I submit, then, that what disrupts the ontological and epistemological unity of Wheatley, what disallows the assumption that since she is black she must necessarily think and write black, is precisely the fact of her domestication, the fact not only that she exists within an interracial household but also that she establishes and celebrates a supraracial intimacy with its inmates that belies her status as a properly constituted member of a black community, literary or otherwise. To put the matter in the most blunt terms, body and household have become one and the same in this literature. Hence, only the black household, properly constituted, can produce the black body while interracial households produce only anomaly. Phillis Wheatley is able to transcend the fact of her black body so readily precisely because she has transcended the fact of a peculiar black domestication. She has left Africa. Her race has become less a fact than a discursive strategy by which the unstable narrative of her corporeal existence can be negotiated. Thus, as she is brought into the Wheatley household and established there as a (Christian, American) daughter, she disrupts the seamlessness of black ontology. When she puts pen to paper she cannot leave behind the sure mark of the black hand because the blackness of that hand is already so much in dispute.

Hence, it is one of the major claims of this study that the development of the notion of a self-evidently Black (American) literature coincided with the development of the notion of a self-evidently Black (American) body, a body so peculiar, so self-contained as to allow for the production of a Black American community and a Black American culture obviously and indisputably distinct from a presumably white community and culture. At the same time, this (black) body was understood as already a product of specifically black forms of domesticity. Black households produced black bodies that, in turn, reproduced the very households from which they emanated. Once one understands this, it becomes apparent not only why the dominant discourses of the body—race, gender, and sexuality—always stand at the aesthetic and ideological centers of the works that I examine but also why these narratives must be articulated in relation to houses, households, families, and familiarity.[8] This is why I have pointed to Wheatley's interracial domestication in my efforts to disestablish her status as the original author of a noble Black American literary tradition. Wheatley's work disallows the unity of black body and black household, the conjugal union that I argue has been absolutely essential to the production of a Black American literature. Phillis comes to us, then, as a figure who is always somehow improper. It is this unsettling model of (interracial) domesticity that is made obvious by the eighteen gentlemen who introduce and verify Phillis's work, assuring us that she, of course, would never have thought to publish these "products of her leisure moments" if not for the "importunity of her best and most generous friends" (Wheatley 1838, 7).

More striking still is the fact that in the rather strange memoir of Wheatley, written by a relative of her owners's, we find that the young girl was never allowed to associate with the other slaves in the household, but was instead "constantly about the person of her mistress."

> Phillis ate of her bread and drank of her cup, and was to her as a daughter; for she returned her affection with unbounded gratitude, and was so devoted to her interests as to have no will in opposition to that of her benefactress. We cannot ascertain that she ever received any formal manumission; but the chains which bound her to her master and mistress were golden links of love, and the silken bands of gratitude.[9]

Wheatley's bondage ceases to exist as a factor of her body, her blackness. Instead it is the valued product of her domestic ties, those golden bonds of affection. When her memoirist later describes Phillis's refusal to sit at the tables of her free white superiors, she demonstrates not only an understanding of the stark realities of white supremacy but also an acceptance and celebration of the melding of slave and master in which Phillis exists, not so much as a consciousness repressed within itself, but as a consciousness so unconcerned with the purported divide between self and other as to render Hegel's familiar configuration unintelligible. Phillis is no Frederick Douglass, eager to distinguish slave from master, black from white. She is not involved in some pitched battle to establish a black presence in the drama of historical progression. Instead, as she takes a subordinate, if intimate, position at the interracial welcome table, and as she keeps the name Wheatley even after her marriage to a "colored gentleman" who is the recipient of constant hostility within the memoir, Phillis specifically refuses the decidedly modern assumption of a blackness steady in its contradistinction to whiteness.[10]

The work of the self-consciously black architects of Black American subjectivity was not so much to refuse as to rework this calculus. Their struggle was to resist the dissolution of the black body. They sought, through the vehicle of domesticity, to produce a black subject who was not already alienated from her (black) body. They worked, then, to rescue Phillis from her white captors, her white family, and to reestablish her within a solid black body, one so secure in its blackness that it might sustain the certain assault awaiting the black audacious enough to seek public presence.[11]

To suggest that it is through images of the body that blackness entered, and ultimately critiqued, American nationalist discourse is not to say, however, that there was a simple and altogether definable language of the body. On the contrary, the body's inconclusivity, its awkwardness, allowed for the production of a discourse that challenged American racism, if not American racialism, while also turning that challenge in upon itself, producing, as a consequence, a wealth of paradox within early Black American writing, particularly within the novels of the antebellum era. I will maintain throughout *Conjugal Union*, then, an emphasis on ambiguity. In particular, I will not continue to read the many representations of racial crossing within antebellum (black) literature as evidence of a black consciousness turned in upon itself, self-loathing in literary form. Instead, I will argue that the army of mulattos, cross-dressers, and foreign interlopers who march through this literature are significant, not because they have retreated from blackness, but instead have come late, if at all, to normative American processes of corporeality. The great paradox was that the institution of slavery worked not only to subjugate a people but also to blur the distinction between slave and slaver. As Jean Fagan Yellin ably demonstrates, abolitionists repeatedly stressed the fact of racial mixing within slavery's various institutions. The white face that was somehow also black played constantly in the popular imagination of antebellum America where it was met by a number of "foreign" racialist/nationalist discourses, some of which not only accepted but also absolutely insisted upon racial mixing.[12] (See figure I.1.) This drawing of slaves freed by Union troops in Louisiana was reprinted as part of the Union propaganda efforts during the Civil War and its immediate aftermath. It speaks directly to the fear that slavery worked to dirty the distinction between black and white precisely through the (re)production of new (white) slave bodies.

Thus, I will suggest that each of the four novels that I examine—*Clotel*, *Our Nig*, *The Garies and Their Friends*, and *Blake, or the Huts of America*—incorporates a variety of materials and languages in order to produce narratives that at times celebrate blackness and the black body and at others castigate them. Moreover, these novels are themselves embedded within a dynamic process of literary production in which the novel comes to be a respectable cultural form precisely because of the manner in which it incorporates and warps a multiplicity of languages, especially languages of the body.[13] The effect, I believe, is that postbellum America, and in particular twentieth-century America, has had little difficulty recognizing the black body. I make this claim even while I work to demonstrate that the difficulties and vagaries of this particular ideological effect were absolutely apparent to antebellum authors.

In chapter 1, I will dwell on these matters in a more detailed discussion of the prehistory of the Black American novelistic tradition. Therein, I will pay particular attention to the work of David Walker, Maria Stewart, Henry Bibb, and Frederick Douglass, suggesting that these authors set the stage for early Black American novelists by narrativizing the difficulty inherent in attempting to represent the fact of black corporeality through artificial media.[14] Moreover, reading their work allows one to see clearly how the desirous body is always figured in contradistinction to the normalizing family and household, so much so that the black body is always understood as running from the very community that enacts its blackness. The calculus of preestablished desire drawn in opposition to (black) communal norms and necessities is itself an articulation of the constant push and pull involved in the establishment of a stable black

FIGURE I.1 Emancipated Slaves, White and Colored—The Children Are From the Schools Established in New Orleans by Order of Major-General Banks. *Harper's Weekly*, January 30, 1864.

body. Indeed, this motif of running was absolutely central within the aesthetic strategies that were deployed in the production of Black community and remains with us even now.[15]

In chapter 2 I mount a defense of the work of William Wells Brown, suggesting that the excessive nature of his texts does not indicate artistic inability but instead an aesthetic practice in which the project of American republicanism is itself understood as excessive. America contains both the most stable, most successful republican institutions the world has ever seen *and* the most horrible, most rigid aspects of slave society. This fact is so obvious that Brown is forced to utilize the unadorned form of the panorama in order to demonstrate it. He insists, moreover, that the answer to this particularly American dilemma is equally obvious. It is ever apparent in the American republic as the proof that intimate contact between black and white can only strengthen the country's fiber. Can one encourage republican institutions while maintaining the practices of American racialism? The answer is yes. The very presence of the mulatto allows for the production of an image of American democracy that privileges race while disallowing both slavery and white supremacy. In making this argument, I work to demonstrate that the mulatto was not a rhetorical device in Brown's fiction but instead a character whose presence was wholly palpable within antebellum America, not to mention the racially ambiguous nations of the Caribbean, particularly Haiti and Cuba. If there is tragedy surrounding the mulatto it stems, not from her inability to choose between black and white, but, on the contrary, from our inability to not choose. The actual mulatto, that native-born product of American desires, was sacrificed ultimately to the exigencies of an American society anxious to modernize the structures of racial ideology, to produce a securely established racial difference.

And yet this character was not simply disestablished in Brown. The very fact that the mulatto continues in Black American literature—even as a figure, even as a fugitive—makes her impossibility difficult to establish. As we will see in chapter 3, the messiness of the mulatto figure always threatens to overtake the project of a self-contained, self-defined Black American literature and community. Thus, the impetus within Frank Webb's 1857 novel, *The Garies and Their Friends*, is always to clean, to produce clear boundaries between the black and the white, the slave and the free, the northern and the southern. Moreover, the very fact of Webb's obsession with cleaning brings us back to my argument that proper black bodies can only be produced within proper black households, households that must be cleaned literally and figuratively of the unsettling stench of white intrusion. In the process mulatto characters are either killed off or reinterpellated as black, while early Black American fiction is cleanly delineated from the abolitionist literature with which it is so obviously in dialogue.

This process is repeated, though in a somewhat different register, in the "lost" novel of Harriet Wilson. Unlike *The Garies*, this much more finely rendered work is caught between the will to establish unity between the black body and the black household and the contradictory understanding that blackness is always a contested category, one that is so unstable that the most horrific acts of violence must be enacted in order to ensure its stability and presence. Frado, the protagonist of *Our Nig*, is like Wheatley in that she is brought into the home of the Bellmonts to clean, to help establish whiteness as that which unifies the household, and yet her very presence disallows this cleanliness. Neither she nor the household in which she finds herself can ever be assured of racial purity. Thus, even the attempts that Wilson makes to save her novel from the dustbin of interracialist fiction, her direct appeals to a putatively black audience, are rather ineffectual, tragic. Instead her work, even as it demonstrates the marks of genius, continues to be unfinished insofar as it attempts to announce itself as a peculiar piece of Black American literature.

Running in a parallel vein to this argument is my continued discussion of the relation of early Black American fiction to the variety of aesthetic enterprises loosely grouped under the rubric of sentimentalism. Specifically, I work to remind my readers of the fact that there was not only one rhetoric of sentimentalism available to nineteenth-century Americans. Instead, reading both Engels and Leopold von Sacher-Masoch, I offer a model of sentimentalism that suggests it as necessarily a location of violence and degradation. That is, the critique that Wilson makes of the sentimental mode is that in its fetishization of domesticity it forces a number of normative identitarian logics, racial difference chief among them. Consequently, I read the many scenes of physical abuse embedded within *Our Nig* not as somehow incongruous within the project of sentimentalism but instead as absolutely definitive of a process in which ambiguity is squelched in the making of the well-ordered home.

Finally, I end this study with a discussion of Martin Delany's *Blake, or the Huts of America.* Therein, I reiterate my contention that, in the process of producing a Black American literature, one has necessarily to access a "black" body that could never and can never be counted on to behave properly, to act black. The work of the earliest ostensibly black authors turned, then, upon the necessity of narrativizing—and domesticating—this relationship of community to body, creating in the process an absolute conflation of the black text and the black self. The mulatto reappears in this work as well, but this time she is a much less troubled and troubling subject. Instead Delany, unlike all of his predecessors, was able finally to establish securely that ever-elusive ontological and epistemological unity much desired by writers like Walker and Webb. In the process, he deploys violent imagery in much the same manner as Wilson, but in doing so, he *is* able to distinguish the black from the white. That is to say, he harnesses the essentially Sadian technique of utilizing violence to establish a seamless narrative unity, a black universe, while also continuing the socially conservative project that we find in Leopold von Sacher-Masoch's *Venus in Furs.* Thus, the realities, including dynamic processes of racialization, that are put on display in Wilson do not preclude the enactment of Delany's (black) fantastic, but instead help constitute it.

In the brief epilogue that follows this text, I shift focus to discuss the resonance of the ideological processes I narrate within the context of twentieth-century America, suggesting that this conflation of black bodies and households becomes so well established as to seem not only original but also originary. Through a brief discussion of the exemplary figure of W. E. B. Du Bois, I trace the manner in which the logics of black corporeality, particularly the logic by which the black household produces the black body, operate in currently established precincts of American cultural life. I will argue, moreover, that these same logics continue to dictate the strategies by and through which Black American literature and the literature of the Black American have been established in the mainstream of American cultural and intellectual life. In making all of my arguments, however, I want to be careful to note that the establishment of a peculiar black body and a clean, peculiar black household was never an easy or certain matter. Indeed, my harshest criticisms are reserved for those who would continue to produce historical and cultural narratives of Black American tradition that posit a sort of reverse racial positivism. Africa and slavery establish a black corporeality that we assume has only now come to be challenged. Here I reverse that logic to demonstrate that antebellum (black) intellectuals, the authors of the Black American literary tradition, were never so certain about the particularities of the black form as we seem to be. It is my frank hope that these efforts to create a window onto the operation of racialist ideology in American culture, especially as articulated by those authors most caught up in the quandary of announcing a Black American specificity, will help to complicate further the easy connections among black bodies, black households, and black culture such that we all might begin at least to imagine life beyond the veil.

One • ENGENDERING RACE

> O heaven! I am full!!! I can hardly move my pen!!!! and as I expect some will try to put me to death, to strike terror into others, and to obliterate from their minds the notion of freedom, so as to keep my brethren the more secure in wretchedness, where they will be permitted to stay but a short time (whether tyrants believe it or not)—I shall give the world a development of facts, which are already witnessed in the courts of heaven.
>
> —*David Walker*

David Walker's *Appeal to the Coloured Citizens of the World, but in particular, and very expressly, to those of the United States of America* (1829), is a work that doggedly maintains a significant position among the handful of texts thought to announce the beginnings of a distinct community of Black American literature. Walker's *Appeal*, Henry Highland Garnet's *Address to the Slaves of the United States of America*, and Martin Delany's *Condition, Elevation, Emigration and Destiny of the Coloured Citizens of the United States, Politically Considered*, vie with Phyllis Wheatley's *Poems of Phillis Wheatley, A Native African and a Slave*, Gustavus Vassa's *Interesting Narrative of the Life of Olaudah Equiano*, and William Wells Brown's *Clotel, or the President's Daughter* for the place of honor in the lexicon of Black American founding documents. And yet there is surprisingly little that even attempts textual analysis of Walker's *Appeal.* Instead, much of what has been written about it approaches hagiography. The text has become less of an object unto itself, *Ding an sich*, and instead a sort of holy relic, evidence of a revolutionary black presence in early national America.

It is not so much that we have absolutely ignored the fact that Walker's *Appeal* was consciously modeled on the U.S. Constitution. Nor have students of the work failed to note that Walker argues fiercely against many of the racist conclusions drawn by Thomas Jefferson in his *Notes on the State of Virginia.* Consistently, however, these considerations, among others, are neglected in favor of a practice that emphasizes Walker's biography. His prominence within the Boston free black community, his ingenious scheme for getting the *Appeal* into the hands of enslaved persons through the interposition of black sailors, and his mysterious death are invariably the touchstones in narratives of both Walker's life and his *Appeal.*[1]

I am not suggesting, however, that the critical practices surrounding Walker, and the other authors I have cited, somehow do damage to the texts that they produced. On the contrary, as I argued in the introduction, this tendency to blur boundaries between the body of the author and the body of his work actually demonstrates sensitivity to the idioms out of which and through which these works announce a black self and a black community. Walker insists that we immediately confront the dichotomy existing between the body and the word. The very act of putting pen to paper forces the death of the author. He is full, a creature of heaven who ceases to exist as an entity separate from the text, even as he writes this same text into being. And yet his body remains somehow cobbled to the *Appeal* such that it can never be dismissed in any of our discussions.

What Walker achieved in his short literary career was the articulation of a grammar of black ontology in which "body" and "text" operate as the two parts of a dialectic out of which identity and community are formed. Walker's literary practice centers around demonstrations of the black's body within text. Indeed, the very fact of the representation of that body works to reenforce the specificity of (black) corporeality.

> They think because they hold us in their infernal chains of slavery, that we wish to be white, or of their color—but they are dreadfully deceived—we wish to be just as it pleased our Creator to have made us, and no avaricious and unmerciful wretches, have any business to make slaves of, or hold us in slavery. How would they like for us to make slaves of, and hold them in cruel slavery, and murder them as they do us?—But is Mr. Jefferson's assertions [sic.] true? viz. "that it is unfortunate for us that our Creator has been pleased to make us *black*." We will not take his say so, for the fact. The world will have an opportunity to see whether it is unfortunate for us, that our Creator *has made us* darker than the *whites*.[2]

Walker struggles in this passage to establish the black body as an essentially static phenomenon. The black subject is reduced to his color, color that is an immutable substance given by God and not, as many early American scientists suggested, the simple result of environment or disease.[3] In doing so, however, he produces a strategic misreading of Jefferson's confused thinking on racial difference.

Walker takes Jefferson's insult to be that he demeans a clearly defined, always evident racial community, the *blacks*. Jefferson's understanding of race waffled considerably, however, during his career and even within the pages of his *Notes*. He is well known for his observations of racial difference in which he muses about whether the Negro's color "resides in the reticular membrane between skin and scarf-skin, or in the scarf-skin itself; whether it proceeds from the colour of the blood, the colour of the bile, or from that of some other secretion."[4] Jefferson's materialism, his insistence on finding racial difference within the body, is strangely at odds with itself. As antebellum scientists cut into the bodies of their black and white subjects, they still could not locate race. Scarf-skin or membrane, bile or some other secretion, each is nominated as a possible site for race, even as none can be adequately put to the service of marking racial difference. In this way, Jefferson stood at the cusp of a new era in the development of racial theory. On the one hand, he announced a revolutionary moment in the development of American science, one driven by a desire to find racial justification for the enslavement of Africans. His ambiguities, as a modern philosopher, would eventually be answered by scientific theories and practices, particularly polygenesis and craniology, that were predicated on establishing and defending incontrovertible physical evidence of racial difference. On the other hand, Jefferson was closely associated with a school of racial thought that had been articulated most fully by Samuel Stanhope Smith, whose *Essay on the Causes of the Variety of Complexion and Figure in the Human Species* (1787) debunked the notion of race altogether by insisting on a strict adherence to Christian doctrine that held all humanity to be "of one blood," the direct descendants of Adam and Eve.[5]

The black for Jefferson existed at times as a fully formed, clearly defined entity and at times as a strange extension of himself, a creature without boundaries or any proper genealogy.

> [T]he black, after hard labour through the day, will be induced by the slightest amusements to sit up till midnight, or later, knowing he must be out with the first dawn of the morning. They are at least as brave, and more adventuresome. But this may perhaps proceed from a want of fore thought, which prevents their seeing a danger till it be present. When present, they do not go through it with more coolness or steadiness than the whites. They are more ardent after their female: but love seems with them to be more an eager desire, than a tender delicate mixture of sentiment and sensation. Their griefs are transient. Those numberless afflictions, which render it doubtful whether heaven has given life to us in mercy or in wrath, are less felt, and sooner forgotten with them. In general, their existence appears to participate more of sensation than reflection. To this must be ascribed their disposition to sleep when abstracted from their diversions, and unemployed in labour. An animal whose body is at

> rest, and who does not reflect, must be disposed to sleep of course. (Jefferson [1788] 1954, 138)

The fact of Jefferson's hard-boiled racism aside, what I find most intriguing about this articulation of American racialism is that the amorphousness of the black is so consistently and insistently reiterated. There is no center, no soul within blackness that might lead black subjects to operate independently. Fear, love, desire, pain, and remorse are all states of being that exist outside of blackness, forming and reforming a necessarily amorphous black (proto)subjectivity. My point here is supported by the fact that this discussion comes almost incidentally in Jefferson's *Notes*, in a chapter on Virginia's laws in which blacks are discussed alongside roads, livestock, ironworks, and the state treasury. It is also worth noting that Jefferson's ambiguity allowed him to be taken up alternately, at least until the 1850s, as both the champion and the foil of competing camps of racial theorists who studied the subject of "The black," and Jefferson's discussion thereof, to support notions of racelessness and racial distinctiveness respectively (Stanton 1960, 54–57).

The conceptual difficulty that drives the rhetoric of David Walker's *Appeal* is that he must produce a decidedly Black American literature that does not reproduce the ambiguity, the tension between notions of racial distinctiveness and racial boundarylessness, through which an amorphous "blackness" had been articulated. There had to be a clearly definable black body if there was to be a definable black community. The black text must always bear, therefore, the trace of the author's hand, the imprimatur of his blackness. It is not surprising, therefore, that the name "David Walker" becomes itself a marker of a transparent black corporeality in which racial difference is constant, immutable and rigidly bifurcated. This effect is largely established through Walker's unrelenting willingness to represent himself as a martyr, a subject whose death seals the specter of a once vibrant and now indelible black body within the text through which it is represented. More important, Walker refuses altogether the assumption that the "fact of blackness" is a matter that ultimately can be resolved textually. On the contrary, literature must always demonstrate the stable or, perhaps, ancient nature of black subjectivity.

> Mr. Jefferson's very severe remarks on us have been so extensively argued upon by men whose attainments in literature, I shall never be able to reach, that I would not have meddled with it, were it not to solicit each of my brethren, who has the spirit of a man, to buy a copy of Mr. Jefferson's "Notes on Virginia," and put it in the hand of his son. For let no one of us suppose that the refutations which have been written by our white friends are enough—they are *whites*—we are *blacks*. We, and the world wish to see the charges of Mr. Jefferson refuted by the blacks *themselves*, according to their chance; for we must remember that what the whites have written respecting this subject, is other men's labours, and did not emanate from the blacks. (Walker [1829] 1965, 14–15)

Again literature is given only a utilitarian value. It is the simple vehicle by which evidence of blackness is demonstrated. Racial difference is no longer the amorphous, never quite defined (non)entity that it often is within Jefferson's work, but instead has become so obvious that its weight disrupts the very flow of the text, sending Walker into a fit of italicizations and parenthetical remarks in order to graphically represent difference within an ever homogenizing textual field. The practice of hagiography that typifies the literature surrounding David Walker should be understood, therefore, as the ratification of a set of critical practices suggested by Walker himself that work to produce "black literature" not so much as a site at which corporeality is rendered transparent as a location at which the often clumsy mechanics of this discursive sleight of hand are aestheticized.

As Walker's most obvious and direct literary heir, Maria Stewart demonstrated in 1831, barely a year after Walker's death, just how well this lesson had been learned. With the publication of her short political pamphlet, as well as the religious meditations that followed a year later, Stewart continued the notion of a black literature intimately bound up with a knowable black body. Tellingly, she created a number of paeans to Walker's memory that celebrate his role as martyr and that explicitly suggest the Walker-inspired metonymic relationship of body to text:

> God hath raised you up a Walker and a Garrison. Though Walker sleeps, yet he lives, and his name shall be had in everlasting remembrance.[6]
>
> Many will suffer for pleading the cause of oppressed Africa, and I shall glory in being one of her martyrs; for I am firmly persuaded, that the God in whom I trust is able to protect me from the rage and malice of mine enemies, and from them that will rise up against me; and if there is no other way for me to escape, he is able to take me to himself, as he did the most noble, fearless, and undaunted David Walker. (Stewart [1831] 1988, 5)

Yet it would be incorrect to paint Stewart as simply Walker's first literary disciple. Instead, Stewart presses, in her work, toward the logical crises that are inevitable within the schema that Walker produces. If physical difference is that which defines the individual, and the goal of literature is to produce more and more realistic depictions of that difference, then it follows that the nominal producer of a racialized, or nationalized, literature might be properly challenged for not adequately representing that difference in his, and especially her, person. Stewart's particular difficulty was that, as she adhered to the idioms established by Walker, constantly reiterating the fact of her own black body, she ran directly into prejudices against female publicity. She produced a subject that was doubly unfit for publicity because of the fact of its blackness *and* its femininity.

> What if I am a woman; is not the God of ancient times the God of these modern days? Did he not raise up Deborah, to be a mother, and a judge in Israel? Did not queen Esther save the lives of the Jews? And Mary Magdalene

> first declare the resurrection of Christ from the dead? Come, said the woman of Samaria, and see a man that hath told me all things that ever I did, is not this the Christ? St. Paul declared that it was a shame for a woman to speak in public, yet our great High Priest and Advocate did not condemn the woman for a more notorious offense than this; neither will he condemn this worthless worm. (Stewart [1831] 1988, 75)

In one fell swoop Stewart demonstrates that the refusal of the distinction between body and text can be put to the service of bringing not only a black but also a female voice to public recognition. Her references suggest that women are not only appropriate to the task of creating a public community but also indispensable to it. Yet herein lies the difficulty. Stewart asks, "What if I am a woman?" suggesting that corporeal difference does not matter in the production of public presence, thus throwing into confusion the very logic of black subjectivity that she, in part, celebrates.[7]

It is important to note that early Black American authors wrote in a context in which the mass political subject was specifically imagined as disembodied while in reality he was most often white, male, and propertied. To produce a black presence within public life one had to challenge directly the notion that the fantasy of a disembodied and disinterested citizenry could sustain the republican project. Many of the gains within Jeffersonian, and especially Jacksonian, America involved advancing beyond this position by, among other things, extending the franchise to ever-increasing numbers of men. Yet, in doing so, there was never a clear disavowal of the idea that one could exist apart from one's body and one's interests. Instead, as more and more bodies achieved disinterested status, the female body continued to be defined specifically as a private entity precisely because of its all too apparent *em*bodiment. Indeed, in the racial theories that would develop throughout the antebellum period, the logics of race and gender began to collapse in upon one another because female difference (brain size, for example) seemed to correspond so neatly to black difference. As Robyn Wiegman has written, "the struggle to write one's way out of the inferiority conferred on blackness must be understood as a scene of multiple inscriptions: not only was the African(-American) the antithesis to Western human universalism, but the corporeal particularity of the feminine must be overwritten in the struggle for citizenship as well."[8] I take Wiegman's claims to go beyond a simple enumeration of the layers of insult visited upon "nonsubjects" within the practice of modern philosophy. Indeed, she specifically argues that the struggle to produce a public black subjectivity was always a process that was not just ancillary to but also "inseparable . . . from the distinctions of gender" (Wiegman 1995, 69).

I will be careful, then, not to offer readings of early national and antebellum Black American literature that suggest that the female body had been rejected in the struggle to insert the black (male) body into public life, in much the manner that some might argue that Jefferson rejects black bodies in his production of America. Instead, I argue that early black authors were caught up in an ideological problematic in which their articulation of a public body, a public blackness, opened the door to the very philosophical and theoretical difficulties confronted by Jefferson. If the black body was also a female body, then how could one ensure its allegiance to the black nation? Moreover, once the original differentiation of the public body was allowed, what was to stop this process from repeating itself ad infinitum? The black body becomes the black female body becomes the black female enslaved body and so on, thus further complicating an ideology of race in which the black body, the fact of blackness, is absolutely necessary in the articulation of a black presence in public life. The aesthetic practices of much within antebellum Black American literature turned, then, upon the development of what I call conjugal union, the development of more and more sophisticated mediations of this awkward give and take between the tendency to celebrate the black body, to put it on display, and the tendency of this same body toward infidelity, toward the incorporation of a set of "runaway values" that not only exceeded the label "black" but also at times challenged the very notion.

"According to the Law of Nature"

I will argue throughout this work that the household is the primary field in which the divide between body and text, body and public subjectivity is negotiated. Following the example offered by Nancy Armstrong in her *Desire and Domestic Fiction*, I would reiterate the claim that the (bourgeois) household acted as a unified public subject, subsuming and representing the competing interests out of which it had been fashioned. The domestic sphere is best understood, therefore, as the location of both a particularized set of social relations and a primary nodal point for the negotiation of competing tendencies in the process of interpellating modern subjects. The body is not denied within the domestic sphere. Instead, bodies are put to the service of constructing subjectivity, presence, face. Again, the body and the house are one and the same. We should not assume, therefore, that the domestic is simply the "artificial" construct that represents relations between "real" bodies. On the contrary, we must always remember that the bodies that we encounter in depictions of the domestic have been worked upon already, established as entities that can be seen and heard because they have been normalized within properly constituted households. Just as there can be no coherent domestic sphere prior to the accumulation of bodies, there can be no coherent (black) body prior to the interposition of the domestic sphere. Armstrong writes, "domestic fiction unfolded the operations of human desire as if they were independent of political history. And this helped to create the illusion that desire was entirely subjective and therefore essentially different from the politically encodable forms of behavior to which desire gave rise."[9] Armstrong goes on to argue that the female is the quintessential modern subject precisely because the "fact" of her body produces her as the vehicle of natural, primal desires that nevertheless can be put to the service of bourgeois individualism and the social forms that it takes. Armstrong misses the fact that what I will call the process of domesticity need not be restricted to the production of (white) bourgeois households and modes of political discourse. Instead, within domesticity bodies are produced as classed, gendered, and *raced* entities. Black families produce black bodies that become black individuals, individuals who if properly interpellated will speak a natural, transparent, black discourse.

The newspapers of the newly formed black communities of the antebellum Northeast were literally brimming with concern over (black) domesticity and the awkward give and take between that domesticity and the bodies that it negotiates. In particular, there were constant admonitions to their readers to adopt conservative habits in the face of claims about black barbarism and bestiality. An April 18, 1840, article in *The Colored American* entitled "Speak to that Young Man" is notable in its exemplary expression of concern on the part of antebellum black journalists with questions of domesticity and the threats to it. The piece details the life of a promising young scholar who secretly began "to contract some evil habits." These were ignored by his family and friends until finally and inevitably disaster struck:

> But now bad habits, which he had secretly favored in his early youth, began to develop themselves in hideous forms. Instead of entering into virtuous marriage, and enjoying all the dear delights of domestic life, his feet were often seen going towards *her house* which is the way to hell, whose steps take hold on death. His drinking cabals were frequent, and his midnight revels were not few nor far between. And so rapid were his downward strides, that in less than two years he fled from his native village, a poor, disgraced, disgraceful, broken-down libertine.—The habits which ruined him, he began to form while pursuing his academical studies.[10]

The obvious claim that one can make about this passage is that it represents the tension inherent in the production of (bourgeois) individuals from the elemental desires encompassed by the body. The bad habits that he favored come to us from out of the protagonist's youth, suggesting their basic and unrestrained nature. His drinking, reveling, and sexual practice all stand in contradistinction to the virtuous marriage and academic studies that would have suited him as a subject and citizen of modern (Black) America.

At the same time, however, the passage returns us to the very problematic around which the text/body dichotomy has been constructed. If this young man has an identity as a black that is somehow prior to his social identity and, therefore, unbreachable, then that blackness must necessarily be represented through the discourses of the body, sexuality being primary among these. To put it bluntly, that which is most "black," his natural desire, is also that which is most antithetical to the production of the black community. The tension is relieved in this passage through the logic of generational conflict by which the text has been framed. It is true that the messiness of this young man's desires complicates the production of black identity and community. It is also true, however, that he is imagined precisely as a *young* man, one whose actions do not necessarily disrupt the development of some ancient blackness. In producing this character's profligacy, the author, F. J., also (re)produces the notion of a black identity that exists prior to its protagonists.

My argument is easier to understand when one takes into account the fact that by 1830 the northern free black population, the population that was to produce the bulk of antebellum Black American literature, had just become large enough (125,000) and cohesive enough to support literary pursuits consistently, especially the publication of newspapers. Instead of being scattered throughout New England, the Northeast, and the Mid-Atlantic states, most northern Black Americans had migrated by that time to just a handful of population centers, especially New York City and Philadelphia, the uncontested pinnacles of black publishing.[11] The anxiety reflected in the call to "speak to that young man" is not so terribly different from the anxiety that many Black American intellectuals must have felt upon attempting to articulate what the nature and parameters of their young community actually were.

Even more to the point is the fact that the free black population had yet to replicate widely the bourgeois residential patterns with which the label "domestic" had become associated. As enslaved persons, northern blacks most often lived within nominally white households, usually in a situation in which only one or two black persons were present.[12] Add to this the fact that by 1850 one-third of black households in Boston included boarders and that this percentage increased to 40 percent by 1860, it becomes clear that there were severe disruptions in the ideological calculus that I have tried to explicate.[13] Black domesticity was a fragile process at best. As a consequence, one had to look to a prior historical moment in order to find the roots of the black community, to find a pure black body. In doing so, however, one was immediately confronted with competing modes of domesticity in which the blackness of the black body could never be certain, precisely because this body was too significant in the process of producing (white) subjectivity.

The implications of this problematic are demonstrated in the constant gesture to the dilemma of a desiring body, one that is always to be read as "black," but that nevertheless continues as asocial, or perhaps better put, pre-social. The desire itself becomes an indiscrete phenomenon, one that *should* produce domesticity but that very often prompts the subject to run instead.

And where is he—not by her side
  Whose every want he loved to tend
Not o'er these vallies wandering wide
  Where sweetly lost, he oft would wend!
That form he loved, he marks no more,
  Those scenes admired, no more shall see;
Those scenes are lovely as before
  And she is fair, but where is he?[14]

I will not belabor the points that I have raised already about the infidelity of the desiring black body to the project of black community formation. I will also leave off consideration of the fact that the missing bodies of my last two examples have been marked as male, while in the poem above the socialized body is female. I do, however, want to guard against producing an altogether functionalist reading of the works that I examine by suggesting that the missing male body represents not simply a particularly knotty ideological impasse within the production of Black American community and literature but also an attempt to supersede this problematic. That the character runs from the domestic sphere represents a tragedy in the production of a peculiar black domesticity. At the same time, however, it acknowledges a will to escape these processes of domestication and subjectification altogether. The runaway demonstrates desire that is disembodied precisely because it exists apart from normative modes of (black) domesticity. His is at once the real body that cannot be corralled *and* the disavowal of a peculiarly American corporeal existence altogether, evidence of an identity that does not turn upon consideration of established communal norms at all.

Henry Bibb's 1850 narrative is an example of just this phenomenon. Like so many other antebellum black intellectuals Bibb sought not only to demonstrate the reality of racial degradation in his work but also to suggest that the subject formed within slavery might indeed escape or transcend this degradation by establishing a domestic life that would stand in contradistinction to the South's own domestic institutions, including paradoxically the nominal marriages that were formed by enslaved persons themselves. Bibb, an escaped slave and one of the nation's leading emigrationists, was obsessed with the difficulty posed by the fugitive's (individualistic) desire to gain *his* freedom and his corollary responsibility to fellow slaves, particularly his own family. *Narrative of the Life and Adventures of Henry Bibb* is first and foremost an unsuccessful attempt to construct an aesthetic solution to this dilemma. From the outset Bibb makes clear his belief that marriage and the maintenance of family ties often (mis)direct the would-be fugitive's attention away from the matter at hand, escape. Indeed, Bibb believes that his own marriage worked to pacify and confuse him:

> The circumstances of my courtship and marriage, I consider to be among the most remarkable events in my life while a slave. To think that after I had determined to carry out the great idea which is so universally and practically acknowledged among all the civilized nations of the earth, that I would be free or die, I suffered myself to be turned aside by the fascinating charms of a female who gradually won my attention from an object so high as that of liberty; and an object which I held paramount to all others.[15]

The remainder of the narrative is taken up with Bibb's account of his various attempts to resolve the tension inherent in the "married" slave's desire for liberty. This tension, I would argue, is precisely the disjuncture the slave perceives between the effects of his actual stituation and the possibilities that he imagines exist within a "proper" domesticity, the enterprise of the black household. Bibb will again and again reference the near impossibility of slaves ever maintaining the sanctity of the marriage vows. "Licentious white men, can and do enter at night or day the lodging places of slaves; break up the bonds of affection in families; destroy all their domestic and social union for life; and the laws of the country afford them no protection" (Bibb [1850] 1969, 38).

The only option, therefore, was escape, yet the mechanics of running were significantly more difficult for families than for individual slaves. Bibb escapes with his wife and child, only to be returned to slavery and eventually separated from them. In the process, however, the trio creates a tableau of conjugal union that is both inspiring and tragic, representing at once the beauty and nobility of the ideal after which they seek and the inevitability of failure. After they have thrown themselves into the Red River swamps of Louisiana, pursued by slave catchers and menaced by the animals of the forest, the small family crosses a fallen tree onto an island, where they fall asleep. Suddenly, in the dead of night, they are attacked by a pack of ferocious wolves. Bibb gallantly defends his wife and child with a bowie knife that he has stolen from his former master, throwing himself into the pack as if it were the slave catchers themselves against whom he fought.

> I thought if I must die, I would die striving to protect my little family from destruction, die striving to escape from slavery. My wife took a club in one hand, and her child in the other, while I rushed forth with my bowie knife in hand, to fight off the savage wolves. I made one desperate charge at them, and at the same time making a loud yell at the top of my voice, that caused them to retreat and scatter, which was equivalent to a victory on our part. Our prayers were answered, and our lives spared through the night. (Bibb [1850] 1969, 127)

The beauty of this scene is apparent. The slave family successfully defends itself against pure animal violence, a violence that is oddly soothing in its simple and straightforward nature, a violence that is not motivated by greed or licentiousness but by pure need and instinct. More to the point, it represents a brief moment in Bibb's text in which he is able to align properly the domestic and the corporeal. The family becomes indistinguishable from the bodies that it encompasses. It is a discrete unit, motivated by a pure, natural (black) desire for survival. (See figure 1.1.) The power of this drawing resides in the fact that it so elegantly demonstrates the fantasy of an absolute unity between the black's body and his conjugal arrangements. Their run into the swamp does not destabilize their union, but instead enhances it. The wolves, moreover, operate themselves as a stabilizing foe. Their attack on the family is one and the same with their attack on individual bodies, opening up for Bibb a previously unimagined arena in which the tortured give and take between individual desire and domestic commitment ceases to exist.

The tragedy here is that this ideal is always fleeting. The moment the family steps outside of the magical boundaries imposed by the island they are captured

FIGURE 1.1 The Hunted Slave by Ansdell A. R. A. Published by Brooks and Son, High Street Oxford, September 4, 1865. Moorland Spingarn Research Center, Howard University. Used with permission.

by the dogs, (domestic) animals whose violence is not at all simplistic and straightforward, but caught up in a series of complex understandings of the black, the slave, the fugitive, and the family. Bibb does escape once again, eventually returning to Kentucky in a last brash attempt to free his wife and child. When he arrives he finds that his wife is living as the concubine of her master. This is the breaking point for Bibb. He can now justifiably relinquish his responsibilities to her and their child. He is, in a word, free.

> After all the sacrifices, sufferings, and risks which I had run, striving to rescue her from the grasp of slavery; every prospect and hope was cut off. She has ever since been regarded as theoretically and practically dead to me as a wife for she was living in a state of adultery, according to the law of God and man. Poor unfortunate woman, I bring no charge of guilt against her, for I know not all the circumstances connected with the case. It is consistent with slavery, however, to suppose that she became reconciled to it. . . . It is also reasonable to suppose that there might have been some kind of attachment formed by living together in this way for years; and it is quite probable that they have other children according to the law of nature, which would have a tendency to unite them stronger together. In view of all the facts and circumstances connected with this matter, I deem further comments and explanations unnecessary on my part. (Bibb [1850] 1969, 189–190)

Not only does this passage support Angela Davis's thesis that the female slave, because of her centrality to family life, was—and is—often imagined as collaborator, it also brings us directly back to the tension that exists between individual desire and domestic responsibility.[16] It demonstrates that, at least as Bibb has represented the matter, his wife's prior desires (her will to survive for one) supersede her responsibilities to him and their small family. She has become reconciled to her situation. She has formed attachments to her captors. She has eschewed the struggle for the uncertain freedom of the Northeast and made a sort of peace with slavery. In doing so she demonstrates that desire is produced within the domestic sphere, even if this sphere has been highly distorted by the realities of the American slave state. Her body, specifically her reproductive capability, is worked on in the course of her concubinage such that she is drawn closer to her master "according to the law of nature."

More important still is Bibb's contention that this fact and this fact alone ends the conversation. He admits that he does not know all the circumstances of the case, but adultery is adultery, coerced or not. Bibb feels, therefore, no compunction to comment further. His "inability" to understand the motivations of his wife is, in and of itself, a demonstration of the fact that he has escaped slavery, so much so that he finds it impossible to act or even think like a slave. It is almost as if all the difficult questions surrounding the complexity of black corporeal existence vanish with Bibb's wife into the suffocating miasma of the slave South. Bibb, a man who is so fair that is he is constantly "mistaken" for white, has been concerned from the outset with establishing both his family and his body within a logic that renders the two indistinguishable. It is no simple coincidence, therefore, that the narrative comes to a quick close after this episode. The tension between the family and the fugitive, slavery and freedom, seemingly has been resolved. Bibb finally and mercifully severs that which reeks of slavery—his wife—and in the process creates himself as a free man. Thus, a narrative that begins with a near white man in constant struggle to save his doomed slave family ends with a black man in an all too unremarkable marital bliss.

It is important to note again that the difficulties that Bibb faces in his work were not at all uncommon in the writing of antebellum black intellectuals. There was no escaping the specter of blacks whose own love of liberty made them unfaithful to their slave roots. Even as free blacks attempted to construct themselves as respectable and independent, the runaway youth and the unfaithful (female) spouse constantly reemerged in their literature, reminding Black American intellectuals of the tentative and unstable nature of their young communities.

Witness the short story, "Dissolving the Union" in the November 24, 1860, edition of *The Weekly Anglo-African.* The piece operates as a thinly veiled meditation on the difficulties—and dangers—of (black) acculturation into (white) culture. It is narrated by Giles, a poor white, who warns of the evil inherent in advancing blacks beyond their traditional roles in society. He tells the story of a "progressive" master who decides to educate his mulatto slave/son as a preacher. The master lacks the capital to accomplish his goal, however. As a consequence, he decides to sell the boy's grandmother. When faced with his own guilt about the affair he seeks the counsel of his minister, who advises him that:

> you can't put his grandmother to better use than to sell her to educate her grandson for the ministry. . . . How many grandmothers do you think have been sold to educate the first men in the South—our members of Congress, and lawyers, and doctors. Now is it not doing better with the money to educate them to preach the Gospel—than to serve the world?[17]

Clearly the logic of a private body that supports a public subjectivity drives the narrative. Grandmothers are sealed into their racial particularity through the act of selling them, the act of turning them into simple commodities instead of proper members of families and households. In the process, a sort of interpellative magic is enacted in which the young slave leaves his body, as it were, and goes on to become a fully actualized member, a subject, of an established white community. "He eat with the white folks, and drank with white folks, and arter he got to be a great man, he married a rich white gal, and bought a stock of mules and niggers, and sot up for a gentlemen" (Jolliffe 1860, 1). Again, the youth's publicity is directly and explicitly established in contradistinction to the undeniably embodied nature of mules and niggers. Once the black loses his body, his blackness, he gains his self. He is free to become white, as it were, to eat drink, *and* sleep with other subjects and citizens.

This concern with the profound ambivalence and uncertainty of family life in relation to individual desire—particularly as that desire was actualized in and through the market—was, as I have argued repeatedly, a constantly recurring element within early Black American writing. Articles with titles such as "On Family Government," "A Husband's Complaint," "Miseries of an Engaged Man," "Courtship," "Chances of Marriage," Miseries of an Engaged Woman," "Duties of Wives," and "Duties of Husbands" constantly appeared throughout the era. More often than not their focus was on the great difficulties that young men and women had to overcome in order to marry. Once married, the couple (especially the female partner) had to guard against the erosion of the happiness and security that acted as the glue for the domestic bond. The great danger was that through their own vanity and childishness, their desire, young people might miss the opportunity to marry and, therefore, spend the remainder of their lives as angry, parsimonious old maids, on the one hand, or lonely and withered bachelor "gentlemen," on the other.

Nowhere is this fear better illustrated than in two time lines included in *Freedom's Journal* on November 2 and 9, 1827, respectively. Entitled "The Old Maid's Diary" and "A Bachelor's Thermometer," they detail the events in the lives of two foolish individuals who end up—because of their own vanity—as bitter, old, unhappy, and *unmarried* cranks.[18]

Years

15. Anxious for coming out and, the attention of the men.
16. Begins to have some idea of the tender passion.
17. Talks of love in a cottage, and disinterested affection.
18. Fancies herself in love with some handsome man, who has flattered her.
19. Is a little more difficult in consequence of being noticed.
20. Commences fashionable, and dashes.
21. Still more confidence in her own attractions, and expects a brilliant establishment.
22. Refuses a good offer, because he is not a man of enough fashion.
23. Flirts with every young man she meets.
24. Wonders that she is not married.
25. Begins to think a large fortune not so indispensable.
27. Prefers the company of rational men to flirting.
28. Wishes to be married in a quiet way with a comfortable income.
29. Almost despairs of entering the married state.
30. Rather fearful of being called an old maid.
31. An additional love of dress.
32. Professes to dislike balls, finding it difficult to get good partners.
33. Wonders how men can leave the society of sensible men to flirt with chits.
34. Affects good homour in her conversation with men.
35. Jealous of the praises of women.
36. Quarrels with her friend, who is lately married.
37. Thinks herself slighted in society.
38. Likes talking of her acquaintance who are [sic.] married unfortunately, and finds consolation in their misfortune.
39. Ill nature increases.
40. Very meddling and officious.—N.B. a growing penchant.
41. If rich, as dernier resort makes love to a young man with fortune.
42. Not succeeding, rails against the sex.
43. Partiality for cards, and scandal commences.
44. Severe against the manners of the age.
45. Strong predilection for a Methodist parson.
46. Enraged at his desertion.
47. Becomes despairing, and takes snuff.
48. Turns all her sensibility to cats and dogs.
49. Adopts a dependent relation to attend on dogs.
50. Becomes disgusted with the world, and vents all her ill-humour on the relation.

FIGURE 1.2 The Old Maid's Diary

The calculus of corporeality, desire, and domesticity is breathtakingly straightforward. The old maid refuses a single offer of marriage and ends up as an ill-humoured, difficult spinster. Her refusal, moreover, turns upon appeasing a set of desires that flout the conventions of domesticity. Her prospective husband is not fashionable enough. His attractions do not reach her body. More shockingly still, she even eventually "shows the best part of her sex." In

Years

16. Incipient palpitations towards the young ladies.
17. Blushing and confusion in conversing with them.
18. Confidence in conversing with them much increased.
19. Angry if treated by them as a boy.
20. Very conscious of his own charms and manliness.
21. A looking glass indispensable in his room, to admire himself.
22. Insufferable puppyism.
23. Thinks no woman good enough for him.
24. Caught unawares by the snares of Cupid.
25. The connexion broken off, from self-conceit on his part.
26. Conducts himself with much puperiority [sic.] towards her.
27. Pays his addresses to another lady, not without hope of mortifying the first.
28. Mortified and frantic at being refused.
29. Rails against the fair sex in general.
30. Morose and out of humour in all conversations on matrimony.
31. Contemplates martimony more under the influence of interest than formerly.
32. Considers personal beauty in a wife not so indispensable as formerly.
33. Still retains a high opinion of his attractions as a husband.
34. Consequently has no idea but he may still marry a chicken.
35. Falls deeply and violently in love with one of seventeen.
36. *Au denier desespoir* another refusal.
37. Indulges in every kind of dissipation.
38. Shows the best part of the sex.
39. Suffers much remorse and mortification so doing.
40. A fresh budding of matrimonial ideas, but no spring shoots.
41. A nice young widow perplexes him.
42. Ventures to address her with mixed sensations of love and interest.
43. Interest prevails, which causes much cautious reflection.
44. The widow jilts him, being as cautious as himself.
45. Becomes every day more averse to the fair sex.
46. Gouty and nervous symptoms begin to appear.
47. Fears what may become of him when old and infirm.
48. Thinks living alone quite irksome.
49. Resolves to have a prudent young woman as house keeper and companion.
50. A nervous affection about him, and frequont [sic.] stocks of the gont [sic.].
51. Much pleased with his new housekeeper as a nurse.
52. Begins to feel some attachment to her.
53. His pride revolts at the idea of marrying her.
54. Is in great distress how to act.
55. Completely under her influence and very miserable.
56. [sic.] many painful thoughts about parting with her.
57. She refuseses [sic.] to live any longer with him *solo.*
58. Gouty, nervous, and billious to excess.
59. Feels very ill, sends for her to his bedside and intends espousing her.
60. Grows rapidly worse, has his will made in her favour, and makes his exit.

FIGURE 1.3 The Bachelor's Thermometer

the end, her pleasures become only the pleasures of the body, with the affections of dogs and cats filling in for the varied and sedate pleasures of marriage. Likewise, our bachelor enters the romantic arena blushing and palpitating, but eventually begins to understand that physical beauty is not the most significant aspect of successful domestic union. Again, however, the lesson is learned too late. As a consequence, he is forced back into his body, becoming gouty and billious, the object of the sympathetic affections of his nurse.

It would be easy enough for my readers to argue that there is nothing peculiar within Black American cultural life about this abiding emphasis on corporeality and domesticity, the body and the house. After all, even though there is abundant evidence to support the claims that I make in this regard,[19] one still might argue that familial ties were absolutely important to the very survival of *all* Americans, black and otherwise. The fate of individuals in relation to marriage was, moreover, a constant obsession of a wide range of persons throughout the nineteenth century. I would like to bring back into consideration, however, the fact that what we are exploring here is the manner in which corporeality and domesticity are both represented within text, within literature, and how they operate ideologically in the production of that same literature. While it is true that Black American intellectuals were reworking materials and themes that were rather common in antebellum life, they also were writing their community into existence or, rather, they were bringing a community of writing into existence, producing a familial narrative of the national union, a domestic fiction. The examples that I have just used in the preceding paragraphs were all taken from *Freedom's Journal*, the *first* newspaper published by Black Americans. The editors were exceptionally self-conscious, then, about how they should represent the black community to itself and to the rest of the American community. "We wish to plead our own cause. Too long have others spoken for us. Too long has the publick been deceived by misrepresentations, in things which concern us dearly."[20]

Still, I want to resist the temptation to regard early Black American literature as some empty vehicle in which reality is directly represented. Instead, I must point out again that the production of a specifically black literature involves the schematization of corporeality—and domesticity—as processes that are necessarily prior to and separate from the literature itself. The constant reproduction of the body/house dichotomy works to aestheticize a paradox that is even more basic to the production of "black literature." The (black) body must proceed the (black) word and the (black) community, even though the "desires" of that community and the exigencies of that literature always take precedence over the body's "natural" desires.

This argument is further supported by the methods utilized by some of the Black American's detractors in their efforts to castigate and trivialize her attempts to prove her humanity and civility. *The Black Republican and Office Holders Journal*, a one-time spoof of *The Black Republican*, featured several items that are particularly interesting in the way they reveal the intersection of body, domesticity, and the black struggle for self-definition. The first piece, "Married," lampoons the widespread practice of prominently listing weddings within Black American newspapers.

> On de fifty-lebenth ob lase month by Rev. Deacon Snow, Mr. Saul Jumbo to Miss Olive Phillips. No cards played at the wedding.
>
> On seventh month . . . after the order of friends, Adonijah Sourphiz to Abagail Pasterboard, both of Purchase Quarter.[21]

Even more to the point are two short items included under the heading "Particular Notice":

> The Free Love Society meets on Thursday evening next on important business. Several colored sisters from the South will be present. H. G. Branbread, Pres.
>
> Freedmenhaus and Lee, two eminent Communists from Germany, will instruct emancipated negroes in the rights of property. Terms low, but no credit given. Apply at Free Love Hall.[22]

Not only do the authors of these passages lampoon the desire of Black Americans to create and maintain families, they also suggest that the black community will never reach the point of familial—and national—purity precisely because of the fact of blackness, their penchant for card playing, and free love. Even if they could somehow escape all this, they still would be incapable of establishing revolutionary social practice themselves. Instead, they are always dependent on outsiders, running directly into the arms of (white) German communists and sex radicals as they struggle to produce their community. Still, I believe that the most significant and interesting aspect of this odd document is not so much the fact that it represents the fantasies of white racists but that it demonstrates so clearly the great challenge the production of a black literature posed to the competing notions of American racialism. The editors of the *Black Republican and Office Holders Journal* understood quite clearly that their Black American contemporaries were in a pitched battle to gain control over the discourses of corporeality that worked to establish one's ability to participate in public life. Their work within the paper, then, is to refuse this rescripting of the corporeality/publicity calculus. The over-the-top dialect and the primitive drawing that accompanies it point to a black body that is so complete, so natural, so there that it necessarily destabilizes the rational modes of print culture. The racists turned themselves, then, to the very modes of (graphically) representing the body that their victims had established already.

I would like to weave together the threads of the arguments that I have initiated in this chapter through a brief reading of the *Narrative of the Life of Frederick Douglass*. In doing so, I will argue that Douglass's work is *more* successful as a narrative than Henry Bibb's because Bibb is *less* successful at establishing authorial control over the bodies that are represented within his text. At the same time, however, it is the manner of this success, Douglass's remarkable abilities as a narrative formalist, that mark his narrative as a thing apart from the early Black American novels that his work is often presumed to have announced.

The struggle to create a black presence from within the extremely fair skin that Bibb wore, the struggle to extricate this enslaved body from slavery, the struggle to maintain a slave marriage and to rescue a slave child, is much more coarsely narrated within his literature than are similar matters within Douglass's. There is never a moment in Bibb's work in which the elegance of his prose eclipses the awkwardness of the bodies being narrated, whereas Douglass's claim on American literature is based largely on the precision with which he marks the divide between body and subjectivity, slavery and literacy, such that the evidence of a transcendent humanity is ever present, even when Douglass describes his deepest moments of degradation. "I was broken in body, soul, and spirit. My natural elasticity was crushed, my intellect languished, the disposition to read departed, the cheerful spark that lingered about my eye died; the dark night of slavery closed in upon me; and behold a man transformed into a brute!"[23]

This passage appears in a narrative in which there is surprisingly little about the methods that Douglass used to escape, little about the realities of the physical abuse he most likely suffered, and almost nothing about his relationship with the free black woman who helped him escape and who would eventually become his wife. This is not to argue that questions of the body do not perplex Douglass. Instead, I suggest that Douglass's narrative is never overwhelmed by these questions. His work is much tighter, perhaps more rigid, than Bibb's.[24] In this manner, Douglass's narrative is less novelistic than Bibb's in that it achieves a singularity of voice that was often absent in early Black American literature, particularly, as we will see, within the work of antebellum novelists.

What I am attempting to establish is a critical distinction between novels and narratives that does not turn upon a logic of development in which the narrative gives way to the more mature form of the novel as the Black American community develops throughout the nineteenth century. On the contrary, what I am suggesting is that in Douglass's *Narrative* the emphasis is on the production of a discrete formal language that might suit the black as a modern (public) subject. His style disallows the play between languages, the polyglossia, that Bakhtin nominates, as the defining feature of the modern novel. As we will see in chapter 2, Douglass's major attempt at fiction, *The Heroic Slave*, was a marked aesthetic failure in that Douglass was not able to produce the complexity of language, form, characterization, and plot demanded by the novel.

In making this argument I would point to Douglass's use of the female in the maintenance of a formal rigidity in which the body is rendered distinct from both text and subject. In reading Frederick Douglass's narrative, then, one must not simply continue to reproduce a seamless connection between the female and the natural, the female and the body. Instead, we must work to uncover how and why this connection produces an ancient blackness. As a number of critics have noted, Douglass presses the "fact" of a messy, desirous, unfaithful body onto the figure of the female in order to establish for himself a disembodied public subjectivity.[25]

> Before he commenced whipping Aunt Hester, he took her into the kitchen, and stripped her from neck to waist, leaving her neck, shoulders, and back entirely naked. He then told her to cross her hands, calling her at the same time a d—d b—h. After crossing her hands, he tied them with a strong rope, and led her to a stool under a large hook in the joist, put in for the purpose. He made her get upon the stool, and tied her hands to the hook. She now stood fair for his infernal purpose. Her arms were stretched up at their full length, so that she stood upon the ends of her toes. . . . [A]fter rolling up his sleeves, he commenced to lay on the heavy cowskin, and soon the warm, red blood (amid heart-rending shrieks from her, and horrid oaths from him) came dripping to the floor. I was so terrified and horror-stricken at the sight, that I hid myself in a closet and dared not venture out till long after the bloody transaction was over. I expected it would be my turn next. (Douglass [1845] 1984, 23)

Here we see evidence of a process by which Douglass gains his "self" through the "corporealization," some might even say the bestialization, of his Aunt Hester. He is able to transcend his body because he forces Aunt Hester to inhabit hers so fully. Yet in making this claim we tend to leave unanswered the question of why it is necessary that "the body" be represented as female.

I already have pointed to Nancy Armstrong's argument that the female is the quintessential modern subject precisely because she is imagined as existing outside of political discourse. She is a subject whose desire and individuality are not separate from the body but embedded within it. Female desires are always natural and disinterested, even as they become indistinguishable from bourgeois desires. From this one might argue that as the female is invoked in Douglass's narrative, she carries with her a purportedly pre-social set of desires that can never be fully reduced or squelched by the exigencies of slave society. Aunt Hester's whipping at the hands of her master is precipitated by the fact that she is driven by desire to leave the plantation to visit her lover, even after having been warned repeatedly not to do so. The fact that she is stripped to the waist only works to demonstrate the deep connection between these deeply felt desires and her own black body. This body becomes, in fact, such a palpable reality, a thing that comes before representation, that it tends to warp the language in which it is rendered, forcing the master to reach toward the profane, "d—d b—h," in order to find adequate means of representation.

Douglass does not, however, simply dispense with Aunt Hester's body. He does not simply "other" her. Instead, Aunt Hester's body becomes a sort of prosthetic by which Douglass is able to bring definition to a desire that exists outside of plantation domesticity, a pure desire that predates its representation even in Douglass's text, a desire that might be properly labeled "black." Aunt Hester becomes, in the process, a sort of garment, one that renders Douglass visible within public space, that gives him publicity. To put it bluntly, in representing Aunt Hester's body Douglass might have been able to construct himself as a *dis*embodied subject, but in wearing that body, as it were, Douglass constructs himself as a black subject. As Gayle Rubin has argued, the female body and the *figure* of the female body act in a variety of cultures as the vehicles by which men express their imagined linkages to one another, their kinship.[26] As a consequence, the woman's body becomes the site of abstraction, of fiction. In Douglass's work this means that the whipping of Aunt Hester does not just express the (fictional) relationship between black and white men but also operates as one of the sites at which racial difference is established.

The central formal feature that distinguishes Douglass from the early novelists is the fact that not only the female body but indeed all bodies that are not Douglass's continue faithfully in their roles as prosthetics. Aunt Hester does survive her whipping, but only as a being whose own debased subjectivity has been fully integrated with Douglass's. As the whip is applied to her back she becomes a figure of bestialization *and* the transcendence of bestialization, but she does not become a fully developed character. There are none in Douglass's narrative. Character exists outside of individual bodies and, as a consequence, is not problematized by the presence of competing desires and competing realities. The work of this chapter, then, has been not only to demonstrate the ideological problematics around which Black American literature has been constructed but also to suggest several formal strategies for addressing them, strategies that are precisely *not* novelistic because of the very fact of their formality. In the following chapters we will examine how the first Black American novelists—William Wells Brown, Frank Webb, Harriet Wilson, and Martin Delany—established the Black American novelistic tradition as a set of procedures by which to both embrace and reject, domesticate and run from these same forms.

Two • AMERICAN PANORAMA

> [A] re-evaluation is necessary of the American writers of the middle of the nineteenth century. For the first time in the history of modern literature they were grappling with problems that could not be seen clearly in the American democracy. They could not write with the consistency and sustained force of European writers for whom the problems were narrower.
>
> —*C. L. R. James*

> The great aim of the true friends of the slave should be to lay bare the institution, so that the gaze of the world may be upon it, and cause the wise, the prudent, and the pious to withdraw their support from it, and leave it to its own fate.
>
> —*William Wells Brown*

"Excess" is the factor that one must immediately confront in any reading of William Wells Brown's 1853 novel, *Clotel, or the President's Daughter.* It is a work that seemingly refuses to contain itself, to establish a voice that might properly be understood as Black *or* American. Instead of seamlessly weaving together its materials and themes into one grand whole, a world unto itself, Brown seems almost to revel in revealing how awkwardly hobbled together this conglomeration of advertisements, gossip, sensational tales from the abolitionist press, and reworked images from his own previously published slave narrative actually are. This is not to mention Lydia Maria Child's 1847 short story "The Quadroons," and the fantastic story of the escape of Ellen and William Craft from slavery, both of which are abundantly apparent in the narrative of *Clotel*.[1] This fact, the reality that Brown never establishes the authorial control that is so very apparent in the novels of twentieth-century (Black) America, continues as almost an embarrassment within some quarters of Black American and American literary and cultural criticism. The *first* Black American novelist must be, so the positivistic logic of literary development would have it, the *worst* Black American novelist. Thus, typically the most generous thing that one hears about *Clotel* is that it represents a transition between the narrative and the more mature form of the novel, an idea that, however patronizing, is still the standard reading of the text.[2]

What I would suggest as an alternative and, I hope, more enlightening mode of inquiry is actually to take Brown's detractors at their word. I want to acknowledge and mark *Clotel* as a bad Black American novel. I would even go so far as to suggest that *Clotel* is not best understood as the seminal text of the Black American novelistic tradition, but instead a self-consciously racialist (though anti–white supremacist) meditation on the tragedy and promise of American republicanism, tragedy and promise that, as I will argue below, are immediately apparent in the distinctly American, distinctly hybrid body of the mulatto. I take Brown's tendency to underemphasize a specifically Black American nobility, then, not as evidence of artistic or intellectual inability, but instead as an indication of his desire to move beyond the quandary of American (white supremacist) racialism.[3] Specifically, I will argue that Brown's aesthetic enterprise was one in which he self-consciously worked to elide the "fact of blackness," the fact of an alien, African corporeality not quite suited to the physical and ideological realities of the American enterprise, the fact that was constantly reiterated in the abolitionist culture with which Brown was in dialogue.

This is not to suggest that Brown attempted to produce an image of America outside of human form. On the contrary, Brown's interest in frankly racialist conceptions of the connection between body and character were as much in evidence in his work as that of any of his contemporaries. For Brown, however, the body need not be a stumbling block in the production of a native American republicanism. Instead, the body of the mulatto, the body that always clearly indicated American origin, was taken by Brown as *the* answer to the particularly knotty questions surrounding race, slavery, and the "physiognomy" of the American nation.

In making this argument I will point to the fact that the massive corpus of (liberal racialist) abolitionist writing, painting, and performance that largely defined Brown's ideological and aesthetic universe was marked by what at this distance seems an unquenchable desire for graphic representation of slavery and the Negro, and in particular the slave's body. The images of enslaved Africans that regularly peered out at American audiences from the pages of liberal and nominally abolitionist journals like *Harper's* always represented a lush black body, one that could at the very best be recognized as exotic, peculiar, or perhaps even noble and at the very worst as positively bestial. Figure 2.1 was taken from

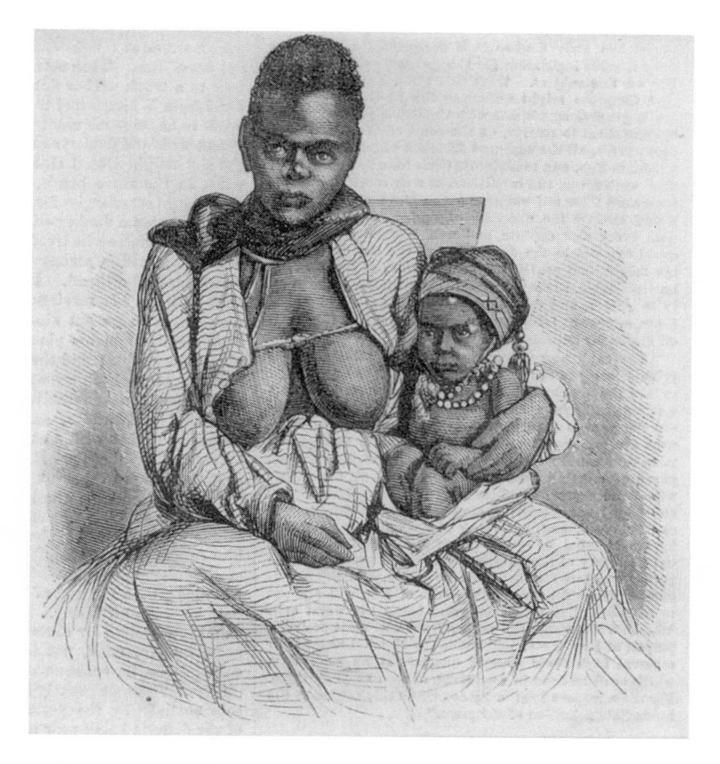

FIGURE 2.1 The Only Baby Among the Africans. *Harper's Weekly*, June 2, 1860. Moorland Spingarn Research Center, Howard University. Used with permission.

a series of daguerreotypes of Africans freed from the slaving ship *Wildfire*. This image demonstrates a fascination with the breasts of African women that has only recently come to the attention of scholars of American slavery and the slave trade. As can be seen in Figure 2.2, there is much to be done on the manner in which representations of the slave trade worked to establish an inevitable and irreversible logic of racial difference even as they pressed for the cessation of new importations from Africa. I would counterpoise this with Brown's demonstration of the (newly American) mulatto body, especially his own mulatto body. Indeed, much of the credit for Brown's relative financial success as a writer can be attributed to the fact that he allowed himself—that is to say, he allowed his body—to be seen in intimate relation to his texts. *Clotel*, Brown's narratives, his travel and historical writings were all written to reveal the body of the author to the reader. All eighteen works that Brown published—and republished—in his lifetime, with their ubiquitous portraits of Brown demonstrating his black white form, and their constant repetition of scenes from

FIGURE 2.2 The Slave Deck of the Bark *Wildfire* Brought into Key West on April 30, 1860. *Harper's Weekly*, June 2, 1860. Moorland Spingarn Research Center, Howard University. Used with permission.

Brown's life, refused the distinction between the body of Brown and his body of work (see figure 2.3). The fact that he often sold his books and pamphlets at "lectures" that lasted for hours and included readings of his play *The Escape*, performances of abolitionist songs, and sharp debate with dissenters in the audience, reveals again the intimate relation of Brown's flesh to his text.

FIGURE 2.3 William Wells Brown. Frontispiece for the *Narrative of William Wells Brown, A Fugitive Slave* (1848).

Thus, I want again to make it clear that I have not set out to demonstrate the manner in which the mulatto is used as a simple figure in Brown's literature, one who exists as evidence of some reality located outside itself. On the contrary, even when the ambiguous body of the mulatto is put on display, it nonetheless enacts a logic by which real racialized bodies always stand prior to their representations. The mulatto's body operates not as the refutation of racial distinctiveness but as its proof. She was the true hybrid, the third subject whose presence refracted the purity of her antecedents, the black and the white.[4] This is precisely where Brown refuses the twisted logic of American racialism. For Brown it is not the case that a black is a black is a black whether the individual so marked is the grandson of an African chief or the daughter of an American president. On the contrary, Brown had readily available to him a counter logic of race in which the mulatto was understood as a *clearly* defined racial character.

In his all but forgotten essay of 1855, *St. Domingo: Its Revolutions and Its Patriots*, Brown, following closely John Beard's *The Life of Toussaint L'Ouverture, the Negro Patriot of Haiti* (1853), argues that the mulatto does *not* exist as only some sort of half presence in the production of Haitian New World society. On the contrary, Brown specifically stresses the centrality of the mulatto population in both the revolution in Haiti and the transnational struggle for democracy of which it was a part. Mulattos, Brown informs us, are related to whites by the "tenderest ties of nature" that work to make them feel their degradation "even more keenly than the bond slaves." Many, having been educated in France, became intimately aware of the "principles of freedom that were being advocated in Europe and the United States."[5] Thus, this group with its colored skin and white "nature" was destined to rescue the republican project from its French and American hijackers.

> The habits of the mulattoes, their intelligence, energy, and boldness, naturally pointed them out as the leaders of the slaves. They fraternized with them; they became popular from the very tinge of their skin, for which they had recently blushed when in company with whites. The mulattoes secretly fomented the germs of insurrection at the nightly meetings of the slaves. They also kept up a clandestine correspondence with the friends of the blacks at Paris. (Brown 1855, 8–9)

Brown understood the mulatto to be precisely American, her lightly tinged skin representing not only the admixture of races but also, and most importantly, the fact of an American nativity. Yes, she is intelligent, but hers is an intelligence borne in a body suited to the environment in which she finds herself, no small feat in fever-ridden colonial Santo Domingo. Quick and bold, her skin holds just enough tinge to allow for successful fraternization with the blacks, but not so much as to get in the way of that all-important intercontinental correspondence. In viewing the body of the mulatto, one might truly see America, or rather the promise of America, decked out in human form.

I will reiterate, then, a simple point, but one that is key to understanding the remainder of my argument. The mulatto was not deployed so often, or so obviously, in Brown's work only to demonstrate the tragic state of American racial and sexual relations or to offer graphic evidence of a common humanity. She was also understood as a living representative of a potentially revolutionary conception of American republicanism, one that, though frankly racialist, might deliver America from slavery and the institutions of white supremacy. As I read her (omni)presence within *Clotel*, I will treat her not simply as a figure that

Brown manipulates to advance an abolitionist agenda but also as an evocation of a self-consciously racialist answer to the catastrophe of American republicanism: the mulatto as representative (wo)man.

In attempting to offer an image that runs counter to the notions of tragedy and degradation with which the mulatto figure has been associated, I am specifically concerned to address a number of questions regarding the "necessarily" split nature of black subjectivity in which the black exists both as an entity unto itself *and* as a reflection of white fantasy and neurosis. As Stuart Hall asks in his recent consideration of the "afterlife" of Fanon, particularly the Fanon of *Black Skin, White Masks,* "Can the split—black skin/white masks—which threatens to destroy the black subject from within, be healed? Is the subject not *inevitably* a site of splitting? And if so, what is the status of the 'universal, unified subject' . . . ?"[6] It is one of the major contentions of this work that the authors whom I examine are indeed attempting to establish a unified subjectivity, a subjectivity that in most cases is self-consciously understood as black. At the same time, however, they must always grapple with the fact that blackness in America has been worked upon, such that the black author must extricate "black purity" from the often grotesque images of blackness that suffused American culture.

In the case of William Wells Brown and his novel, *Clotel*, however, I want to defer this claim and consider instead the idea that in *Clotel* Brown proceeds down a treacherous, if no more noble, path of racial aestheticism. The mulatto exists for Brown not only as an historical actor but also in many ways *the* historical actor, a whole and self-possessed being who was, in fact, the only New World character *not* always turned in upon itself, not subject to the racial neuroses so apparent in antebellum America. Can the split—black skin/white masks—that threatens to destroy the black subject from within be healed? Brown attempts to answer this question by pointing to what he takes as the *obvious* example of the mulatto, the character who allows us to reconceptualize the original split between black and white, between the black and the representation of the black, as an organic melding, the production of a true American.

Panoramic Views

> *William Wells Brown, the subject of this narrative, was born a slave in Lexington, Kentucky, not far from the residence of the late Hon. Henry Clay. His mother was the slave of Doctor John Young. His father was a slaveholder, and besides being a near relation of his master, was connected with the Wicklief family, one of the oldest, wealthiest, and most aristocratic of Kentucky planters.*[7]

The fact of the new American, the racialized subject who marks the possibility of a postslavery, post–white supremacist culture, was not a matter that Brown represented as rare within American life. On the contrary, the mulatto is always apparent in any of the discussions that Brown initiates. It should come as no surprise, then, that Brown's own mulatto status is the first thing represented within his narrative, the same narrative that was bound together with *Clotel*. From the start he is understood as particularly American, kin to the most aristocratic of Kentucky planters and drawn from the same soil as Clay. The difficulty that Brown confronts, then, is one of perception. The mulatto in America, no matter how cultured or "white," might always be returned to a black default status. Brown's work as an artist, therefore, was not to bring the mulatto into being, but instead to properly represent the mulatto's inevitability within the project of American republicanism. Thus, he is always concerned to juxtapose the mulatto, no matter how stunning or accomplished, with examples of the mundane and the banal.

It seems inevitable, given the aesthetic logic I have just outlined, that Brown, in his confrontations and collaborations with the realities of American racialism, should turn to the aesthetic strategies deployed in the particularly nineteenth-century form of the panorama. Ubiquitous in the urban culture of Britain and America, this early form of mass entertainment worked, as with all forms of spectacle, to reveal an already apparent order. It was the "show" that displayed nineteenth-century Americans—and Britains—to themselves.[8] Steeped in the aesthetics of realism, the panorama worked by establishing a metonymic relation among multiple sites of signification, inviting us to understand each site as one and the same with the nation itself. Just as much of the painting within nineteenth-century America was obsessively concerned with realistic detail, with compiling evidence of a verifiable (American) essence, the panorama, like the world fairs in its future, showed again and again the signs that were to be read in direct relation to nationality.

Each of Brown's works is heavily marked by extratextual elements that purport to demonstrate the veracity of Brown's claims and the images that he uses to make those claims. *Clotel* was itself very often read as reportage, and the fact that Brown drew heavily from works that his audiences were certain to have read, seen, or heard suggests a specific interest in grounding the novel in a reality that was not only prior to its representation but also might be accessed readily. Moreover, the belief that Jefferson fathered several slave children, and even the more chiseled idea that his beautiful and extremely accomplished daughter was not only enslaved but also sold "down south," was widely disseminated within abolitionist circles and beyond. What Brown wants, then, is that America be seen properly, that its horrors be exposed at the same time that the promise of a postslavery, post–white supremacist republicanism be recognized, a promise that for Brown *and* his various audiences had necessarily to come in human form.

I am indebted here to the recent work of Peter Brooks who, reading Freud, Lacan, and Melanie Klein, suggests that the deepest split that one must endure, the split between self and body, is necessarily referenced in the act of writing where the immaterial "word" is conveyed through the "materiality of the letter." Thus, Brooks argues, narrative literature is obsessed with the recovery of the body for the project of signification, the body as "the place on which messages are written."[9] I nominate Clotel's body as just such a site of signification. At the same time, I do not care to recreate the Cartesian split between self and body, man and woman, black and white so very apparent in much modern narrative. Instead, I suggest that Clotel does such a monstrously bad job at black heroism because her body specifically refuses the logic of infinitely expanding binarisms that would have allowed for the production of a knowable "blackness." Clotel's mixed-race body is understood by Brown as the very site at which the splits (racial, sexual, psychological, and ideological) that plague America can be healed—domesticated, if you will—thus producing in one not so dark body that which is properly and inevitably American. As Clotel is sold, betrayed, humiliated, and eventually killed what is being enacted is less a paean to the long-suffering slave than an encomium for a stifled democracy.

Brown, ever mindful of the necessity of driving home a point, mounted an actual panorama in 1850 (three years before the publication of *Clotel*) for the viewing pleasure of the liberal Britains who where then shielding him from the ravages of the recently passed Fugitive Slave Act. Though the actual images displayed in the panorama are no longer available to us, we do have Brown's guide, *A Description of William Wells Brown's Original Panoramic Views of the Scenes in the Life of an American Slave, From his Birth in Slavery to His Death or His Escape to His First Home of Freedom on British Soil.* "During the summer of 1847 I visited an exhibition of a panorama of the River Mississippi," Brown explains. "I was somewhat amazed at the very mild manner in which the 'Peculiar Institution' of the Southern States was there represented, and it occurred to me that a painting, with as fair a representation of American Slavery as could be given upon canvass, would do much to disseminate truth upon this subject."[10] Thus Brown gives a precisely rendered statement of his aesthetic. His intention is to show America just as it is. Writing as a Garrisonian abolitionist, Brown insisted that the demonstration of the American slavocracy's depravity was enough, in and of itself, to wreck the country's "domestic institution." He is eager, then, for a "fair representation," one in which nothing is lost in the exchange between America and its graphic simulacrum.

> The large building before us is the Capitol of the United States; and the concourse of people on the right of it, are holding a meeting to sympathize with the French Revolution of 1848.
>
> You will also observe, on the left of the Capitol, a gang of Slaves. . . .
>
> Although it is very common to see Slaves chained and driven past the Capitol, yet the managers of this meeting are very reasonably disconcerted at having a gang of Slaves driven so near them, at the very time that they are making speeches and passing resolutions in favour of Republicanism in France. (Brown n.d., 8)

The obvious work that Brown does here is to show how ugly the view of America has become. The slaves are not simply driven by a sign of American republicanism, but by that which is indistinguishable from it, the U.S. Capitol.

Moreover, in the coffle that Brown presents one finds not only the mother separated from her child, or the slave who is viciously whipped, but also "slaves as white as their masters, and a great deal better-looking," suggesting again the sacrifice of decidedly native and vibrant (mulatto) *Americans* to the work of animals" (Brown n.d., 7–8).

I will not belabor this point for long, but I would like to observe that the story, or, rather, the view of two mulatto girls who find themselves in the slave coffle, contains many of the major elements of *Clotel* itself. A white man "marries" a black slave woman. The two, along with their beautiful and accomplished daughters, live a privileged, comfortable life until death takes both the parents and the girls are sold, presumably as New Orleans sex workers. This view, which was among the most fully narrated in Brown's panorama, worked specifically to press European audiences toward an awareness of the white cannibalism that was then taking place as part of the practice of American slavery and in the name of the American republic. The girls do indeed possess *all* the markers of a cultured American identity. They are beautiful and talented, and of course "perfectly white," yet nonetheless their only value lies in their abilities at sexual gratification. Brown suggests, then, that in devouring them America also devours any opportunity for a truly republican (American) enterprise.

Before we leave this matter I will visit one more site in Brown's panoramic view of the American scene, View Thirteenth, "Tanning A White Boy." Among the last of the fifteen views that Brown presents, this image worked specifically on the extremely widespread fear in antebellum America that, contrary to the rhetoric of the slaveholders and their apologists, the institution of slavery blurred the racial distinctiveness that it purportedly protected.

> The view now before us presents the case of two men in the act of tanning a white boy, that he may more readily be retained in slavery. It is not the uncommon occurrence for a white boy of poor parents to be reduced to a state of chattel slavery, in a Slave State. The writer was personally acquainted with a white boy in St. Louis, Missouri, who was taken to New Orleans and sold into slavery. (Brown n.d., 22)

The evidence here is irrefutable. While one could make a credible argument that even the white/black body of the mulatto might be properly marked so as to effectively guard against the incursion of black on white, it is not possible to cancel the "fact" of this white boy's white body without also undoing the logics of not only slavery but also the entire enterprise of racial distinction. By tanning the white boy and remanding him into slavery, by reembodying him as black, the whites themselves belie the notion of a great gap existing between them, the blacks and even the "Men Monkeys" so evident within white racialist fantasies. Ongoing efforts to explore the interior of Africa and the interior of Western fantasies of "Black Africans" resulted in the production of many images in which the difference between the African and the human was confused, thus anthropomorphizing the ape while dehumanizing the black (see figure 2.4).

FIGURE 2.4 New Man-Monkeys. *Harper's Weekly*, November 12, 1859. Moorland Spingarn Research Center, Howard University. Used with permission.

Speaking of the *Troglodyte Kooloo-Kamba* featured at the far left of this drawing, the unnamed commentator writes, "M. Du Chaillu considers this troglodyte a nearer approach to humanity than any other member of the quadrumana family. It lives mostly in trees; and in order to catch branches it has very long and wonderfully—stout fingers—in general appearance not unlike those of a very large negro hand." Brown's insistence that his audiences recognize the importance of the mulatto to the possibility of an American republicanism should be understood, therefore, as an essentially conservative conception of racial difference, one in which the white, the black, *and* the mulatto were always understood as distinct, if not mutually exclusive.[11]

The critique that I believe one might properly make of my explication of Brown's discursive and aesthetic strategies is to suggest that in (re)centering the mulatto in Brown's various narratives I do not properly address the fact that Brown speaks of and in relation to the mass of (black) enslaved persons. I would counter this by reiterating the fact that Brown *does* recognize some significant difference between the humanity of the black and that of the mulatto. Where the mulatto is almost always seen as an individual, a self-possessed being with a specific and often sensational story of how she came to be enslaved, blacks exist for Brown most often as one great conglomeration, almost a force of nature. In speaking of the blacks in Haiti, Brown describes them as a "storm that had swept over the whole plain of the north, from east to west and from the mountains to the sea" (Brown 1855, 10).

Even the great Toussaint L'Ouverture was for Brown the very antithesis of the clearly defined individual, a man with a story separate from the great march of history. Instead, like Jeremiah he represents the will and the genius of the people. He "rises up" from the community of which he is the exemplar.[12] He is the grandson of an African chief and with his "iron frame" and "unaffected features" he would be "selected, in any company of men, as one who was born for a leader" (Brown 1855, 12). He possesses, moreover, "superior knowledge of the character of his race," so much so that he gains, before he is betrayed, the highest position in the French army. Thus, Brown uses Toussaint as a warning that "[t]he exasperated genius of Africa would rise from the depths of the ocean, and show its threatening form," *not* as the example of a modern subjectivity (Toussaint's readings of Raynal notwithstanding) capable of demonstrating—and embodying—the tortured philosophical and ideological quandaries of (American) republicanism (Brown 1855, 38). The problem for Brown was that the black's body always referenced a separate non-American past, always got in the way of full interpellation as an American native. The mulatto, however, was fully prepared, culturally *and* biologically, for the great march toward the American tomorrow.

Frederick Douglass, Madison Washington, or the President's Daughter

I have spent considerable energy explaining why I will *not* argue the merits of *Clotel* as the seminal text of the Black American novelistic tradition, skipping, for example, a rehearsal of the argument that Brown's use of a mulatto protagonist is a factor of black color consciousness and represents, therefore, a tragic beginning in Black American literature. On the contrary, I have suggested from the start that much of the artistry within *Clotel* stems from the fact that it is improperly black, that it is not primarily concerned with the development of a Black American literary tradition or presence. Brown's confrontation is not directly with the assumption of black inferiority, the idea of the black as bestialized, incapable of reaching the heights of thought and sentiment. Instead, Brown's focus is the somewhat more discrete question of how one might save the republic in spite of the fact of racial difference.

In bringing these claims more sharply into focus, I will address directly the strategies that Brown deploys in the production of what he undoubtedly understood as one of the first *American* heroines, Clotel. In doing so, I will again turn to Frederick Douglass as an exemplary figure in the production of contempary notions of black subjectivity. Specifically, I will argue that Douglass, like Brown, must produce his literature from within the thickly textured field of American racialist discourse, but unlike Brown, he concedes from the start the particularly American conceit of two races sharing one national genealogy.

While Brown's project is precisely to make visible a *readily available* alternative racialist discourse that allowed a distinct identity for the mulatto, Douglass enacts, as Robert Stepto and Henry Louis Gates have argued, a binaristic logic by which he does bind together slavery and literacy, body and text, black and white, but always in a manner that stresses struggle and mutual (mis)recognition.[13] Douglass confronts not only, then, those practices that would bestialize the Negro but also those that would never allow him to gain an identity distinct from that of the white. Douglass's heroic struggle with the slave breaker, Covey, is properly understood, therefore, as marking the young slave as not only a man but also a thing apart, an independent, self-contained conscious being.

I argued in the previous chapter that in his 1845 narrative, Douglass displaces the reality of (racial) degradation onto his Aunt Hester as a means by which to reserve for himself a noble (black) manhood suiting him, and his fellows, for citizenship in the American republic.[14] The fact of the gendered nature of this displacement has been taken to represent the reality that the slave whipping (with its often titillating revelation of female flesh) had become a stock in trade of abolitionist cultural production, as well as the "fact" that Douglass, though himself a suffragist, was inclined toward the same patriarchal norms so apparent among the authors of the American Renaissance. What I will argue here is that the gendered relations so apparent in this scene reference the very alternative racial logic that I have been at pains to demonstrate. Master Auld delivers his whipping to Aunt Hester because she spurns his attentions and disobeys his orders by visiting her slave lover on another plantation. We see enacted, then, a classic example of triangulation in which black and white men express homoerotic, (ab)normative desire through their contestation with the female body. The panic in this instance revolves, however, not simply around the poles of gender and sexuality but race as well.[15] As Master Auld whips Aunt Hester he does draw this slave closer to his white body. Yet he also denies any sense of mutuality between himself and either his "lover" or his "rival." Douglass, on the other hand, viewing the entire performance from the safety of his closet, is able to destroy both for himself and his audiences (who presumably look on from just over his shoulder) the specter of racial mixing that the spectacle evokes, not to mention the racial mixing so apparent in his own genealogy.

The female figure becomes in this schema not simply the character who might topple the project of black manhood but also the character who represents the possibility, and the palpability, of a racialist discourse that privileges racial mixing. Though I cannot take up the matter fully in this study, I would like to point to the example of Harriet Jacobs and her *Incidents in the Life of a Slave Girl*, a text that draws a rich portrait of the limited and treacherous possibilities open to a mulatto character who takes a white lover and then uses that relationship to free herself and her children from slavery. Indeed, what continues to amaze generations of readers is the fact that Jacobs, though enslaved and presumably "black," not only pushes so forcefully against the limits of her civic and racial status but also does so by manipulating domestic, even American, social and ideological realities that recognize *racial* difference within the enslaved population.[16] "In complexion my parents were a light shade of brownish yellow, and were termed mulattoes. They lived together in a comfortable home; and though we were all slaves, I was so fondly shielded that I never dreamed I was a piece of merchandise."[17]

I ask that we juxtapose the strategies of characterization demonstrated by Clotel, Harriet Jacobs, and even Aunt Hester with those deployed by Douglass in his production of a noble black masculinity. I mean to focus here not only on Douglass's privileging of male bodies, particularly his own male body, in the production of his literature, but also his will to curtail awareness of black ambiguity, an ambiguity referenced by Phillis Wheatley, David Walker, Thomas Jefferson, and the host of mulatto characters who come to us out of American fiction. Douglass, like many of his contemporaries, looked to produce a graphically available (anthropomorphic) answer to the quandary of American republicanism. He did so by taking what I will argue throughout this study was the modern, and essentially postbellum, position of assuming a racial difference rigid enough to squelch the thorny question of amalgamation, but not so rigid as to bring us back to the subject of black (in)humanity.

We arrive, then, at the point on our panoramic tour at which we can see fairly represented and without even the hint of artifice, the Black Man. He is the character whom Douglass celebrates in his aesthetically unsuccessful novella, *The Heroic Slave*. Published in 1853, the same year as Brown's *Clotel*, the work details the career of Madison Washington, a "real" slave who in 1841 led a successful revolt aboard the slave ship *Creole* as it was headed down the Atlantic coastline toward the New Orleans markets. The victorious Washington was able to force the crew to sail to Jamaica, where the entire party disembarked as free people. The story is narrated by a Mr. Listwell, a white northerner, who happens upon the distraught Madison while traveling in the South. The wretched slave secreted himself in a grove a short distance from his plantation where presumably unobserved he could speak his misery: "I am a *slave*,—born a slave, an abject slave,—even before I made part of this breathing world, the scourge was platted for my back; the fetters were forged for my limbs. How mean a thing am I."[18]

The striking aspect of the slave's rhetoric is precisely that it is crafted so well. It is remarkable, upon consideration, that this slave, this abject slave, has such a developed command of English oratory. His is not the language of the minstrel stage, nor even the pleasantly "African" tones then emanating from the pens of American abolitionists. The heretofore indifferent Listwell is so moved, in fact, by the pathos of Madison's speech that he is immediately converted to the abolitionist cause. There is no whipping, no rape, no physical abuse or deprivation whatsoever. Instead, Listwell is moved solely because he sees that Madison is not some degraded creature, but his equal, a man of great feeling and faith.

There is more work to be done, however, in the production of the image that Douglass hopes to disseminate. He must somehow reconcile the fact of Madison's transcendent humanity with the even more palpable fact of his black body. Douglass must refuse the lie that black physiognomy always references black bestiality and substitute for it a logic by which the black body itself can be taken as *proof* of black humanity.

> His whole appearance betokened Herculean strength; yet there was nothing savage or forbidding in his aspect. A child might play in his arms, or dance on his shoulders. A giant's strength, but not a giant's heart was in him. His broad mouth and nose spoke only of good nature and kindness. But his voice, that unfailing index of the soul, though full and melodious, had that in it which could terrify as well as charm. He was just the man you would choose when hardships were to be endured, or danger to be encountered,—intelligent and brave. He had the head to conceive, and the hand to execute. (Douglass [1853] 1984, 303)

I hope at this juncture that it is readily apparent to my readers that the strategies used here parallel those used by Brown in his description of Toussaint L'Ouverture. The humanity of the black is revealed precisely by paying attention to his remarkable body. He is given to us as an example of the great hulking Africanity that was so apparent in the country's racist fantasies, yet this black body is somehow so pure, classic, Herculean that it speaks to the reality of an ancient black humanity, one infinitely suited—at least in Douglass's aesthetic—to manage the difficulties of American republicanism.

This explains why Douglass takes such pains to maintain the sanctity of Madison's body. Just as in the narrative, the one significant scene of white barbarism is displaced onto another black character, an old slave man whom Washington encounters during an attempt to break free. The unfortunate old man takes a whipping that by all rights should have gone to the black hero. His crime is that he tries to buy provisions with a dollar that the fugitive Madison had given him, thereby arousing suspicion among the townspeople. When they come back to the grove where the two slaves encountered one another, they find no fugitive, the clever slave having hidden himself away to await the old man's return. The whites then punish their informant, giving him thirty-nine lashes for "misrepresentation" as Washington looks on from his hiding place, avoiding the whipping and the taint of vulnerability it would have conferred.[19]

Brown refuses, however, to accept the simplicity with which Douglass narrates the move from enslaved person to free*man*. He suggests, in fact, that the sort of frontal assault on the American racial economy that we see in Douglass's characterization of Madison Washington is always doomed to failure. Brown even goes so far as to lampoon Douglass's vaunted confrontation with Mr. Covey, in which he literally wrestles his humanity from the slave-breaker. Like

Douglass, Brown presents us with a scene in which a powerful (black) male slave, Randall, attempts to assert his masculinity and subjectivity through a direct physical confrontation with his overseer, Mr. Cook. In the course of the struggle the overseer calls out, just as Mr. Covey had, to three separate individuals for assistance, all of whom refuse. Again the slave wins the battle, presumably forcing recognition and respect from his master. But Brown refuses to leave the matter there. Instead, he shows us all too clearly that the power of the slave state can never be assumed to rest solely in the hands of a single white person. Randall's defeating Cook is altogether different from escaping slavery.

A week after the battle was finished the overseer returns to the fields with three armed white men. They confront Randall and order him to the barn. When he refuses, another battle ensues in which Randall at first bests the men, only to find that there are indeed limits to his heroism.

> [One] drew out his pistol, and fired at him, and brought him to the ground. . . . The others rushed upon him with their clubs, and beat him over the head and face, until they succeeded in tying him. . . . Cook gave him over one hundred lashes with a heavy cowhide, had him washed with salt and water, and left him tied during the day. The next day he was untied, and taken to a blacksmith's shop, and had a ball and chain attached to his leg. He was compelled to labor in the field, and perform the same amount of work that the other hands did. (Brown 1848, 30)

Randall's fatal mistake was his assumption that he could beat the white men at their own game. The naive, unself-consciously straightforward black subject is always doomed to failure, his best intentions often turning in upon themselves. More important still is the fact that Brown clearly refuses to accept Douglass's conception of an insurmountable black body, one that might maintain a noble black subjectivity even in the face of the worst degradation. As I will discuss at length below, Brown refuses to privilege either the black or the male body. Instead, he is terrifically fascinated with the possibilities inherent in producing the mulatto's body as the very essence of the American republic.

> *Young ladies have you tongues? Beware how you conduct them. The tongue is a little thing to be sure, but a little axe will cut down a great tree. And a little tongue, in the mouth of a slanderous woman, is "sharper than a serpent's tooth."*[20]

The use of a woman as protagonist in *Clotel* must have represented for Brown's audience a rather bold, even bombastic, move. The (mulatto) woman, particularly the young (mulatto) woman, may have been recognized, on the one hand, as a paragon of virtue, but she was also seen as a dangerous, potentially treacherous, and undoubtedly chaotic force within (Black) American life and culture. More to the point, she was seen as a primary vehicle of scandal, that discursive axe that could and did unsettle the most sacrosanct assumptions about community and character.

> No music sounds so melodious to the ears of the *scandal monger* as the story of a friend's errors; she is eager to be the first to obtain the delightful tidings, in order to have the honor of propagating it first . . . she considers not but herself may be the next object for the envenomed charges of scandal to fall upon; me thinks if she would place herself for a few moments in the situation of the person scandalized, consider all their grief and shame, at the blight cast upon their fair fame, by her tongue she would recoil in horror.[21]

Female scandal was, then, a powerful phenomenon in antebellum (Black) America, so much so that it always came loaded with the most poignant associations: grief, shame, blight, and horror, not to mention delight.

By recognizing the connection between woman and scandal we can see that Brown's decision to create a female protagonist was designed both as a break with established norms—indeed, as a spectacle of impropriety—and as a reconnection to a powerful tradition of female discursive practice in which submerged truths are brought to the surface.[22] Still, I would suggest that we misread somewhat the epigram with which I began this portion of the chapter. Though I read Clotel as an essentially scandalous creature, I do not mean to imply, as the quote above does, that hers is a scandal borne on the tongue. On the contrary, Clotel speaks rather infrequently in the course of the narrative, oftentimes inhibiting her speech in order to avoid detection as a runaway. The scandal of Clotel is not the scandal of her tongue, but the scandal of her body, a body that certainly tells a story about illicit interracial sexual activity, but also a story about the hypocrisy of America, a country with a set of racist ideological structures so twisted that they allow the enslavement—and reenslavement—of Thomas Jefferson's daughter. In the face of all this, Clotel takes the great leap that not only makes apparent the mendacity of American whites but also pushes the novel's narrative strategies to their limits. She puts on the clothing of a man, assumes the persona of a white planter, and then escapes from slavery with the assistance of her body servant (the allusion is almost too rich for comment) and fellow runaway, William.[23]

Again, Brown brings us directly back to the entire logic of scopic availability with which we have been so concerned. Clotel has been thoroughly displayed to the reader by the point at which she changes her dress. On the auction block, at the quadroon ball, in the soft glances of a lover and the hot gaze of a jealous mistress, Clotel's entire person is delivered up for our inspection. The curl of her hair, the tint of her eyes, the quality of her dress, and the manner of her carriage are presented in what seems an almost obsessive manner. Whites, blacks, slaves, and freemen all seem incapable of not looking at Clotel.

> There she stood, with a complexion as white as most of those who were waiting with a wish to become her purchasers; her features as finely defined as any of her sex of pure Anglo-Saxon; her long black wavy hair done up in the neatest manner; her form tall and graceful, and her whole appearance indicating one superior to her position. (Brown [1853] 1969, 66)

This is America. White, fine, neat, and graceful, this daughter of an American president is captured within the gaze of the crowd in a horrific frame that nonetheless eloquently reveals the truth inscribed on her body, the fact of an American nobility. Importantly, however, the moment of desire is always the moment of violence. The moment that she is most enveloped by her lover's gaze is the very moment at which he purchases her, turning her out as it were, producing a slave mistress where an unspoiled child once stood.

I do not mean to suggest, however, that it is the gaze itself that Brown critiques. On the contrary, I have committed myself already to the idea that Brown's novel is best understood through the lens of the panorama so that the gaze is not only expected but also invited. Brown's concern is that the participants in the spectacles that he narrates do not trust their own eyes. Their senses of perception have been so retarded by the exigencies of the slavocracy that they cease to see Clotel at all, instead substituting grotesque images of themselves. As Clotel descends from the auction block, as she is betrayed by her lover, separated from her child, and sold, she must come herself to understand the reality of misperception in which she is trapped. The harsh truth she must eventually accept is that in an America so marred by slavery and white supremacy very few can see well, very few can acknowledge truth, even when it confronts them directly. To survive, then, Clotel necessarily had to join in the spectacle of misrepresentation, of dissimulation, from which she had, up to this point, remained aloof. She must enact an appropriately American logic of corporeality in order to live, even if this means taking up a logic that she recognizes as false.

I would point here to the fact that Brown, unlike Douglass, works so assiduously to reveal his own artifice and cunning. In his first narrative, Brown describes his time as the assistant to a slave trader, Mr. Walker. While thus employed he was responsible for preparing the slaves for market, a process in which the slaves were oiled, shaved, blackened, and carefully coached in the intricacies of black dissimulation.

> I was ordered to have the old men's whiskers shaved off, and the grey hairs plucked out where they were not too numerous, in which case he had a preparation of blackings to color it, and with a blacking brush we would put it on. . . . These slaves were also taught how old they were by Mr. Walker, and after going through the blacking process they looked ten or fifteen years younger; and I am sure that some of those who purchased slaves of Mr. Walker were dreadfully cheated, especially in the ages of the slaves which they bought. (Brown 1848, 43)

Of course, Brown is commenting on how he was forced himself to dissimulate in order to survive slavery. He is also describing, however, a process by which black dissimulation is commodified. The lie is always more profitable than the truth. It is not the case, therefore, that one can be so certain about the blackness of the black, even and especially the black slave. While Brown does accept the notion of racial difference, he does not go so far as to suggest that this difference cannot be worked upon by the architects of slavery and abolition alike. All that blacking and oil work to further separate the slave's purchasers—and the slaves themselves—from the reality of their bodies even as it continues the notion that demonstrable racial difference is the inevitable outcome of American modes of corporeality. More to the point, it brings us directly back to Brown's recognition that the "blackness" of the black body was already a hopelessly overdetermined matter. One might easily make the argument, in fact, that blackness becomes for Brown even more untenable, even more obviously constructed and unstable at precisely the moment when it is most apparent.

This image of slaves' being prepared for market does not drop from Brown's corpus with the publication of his narrative. Instead, it reappears within both *Clotel* and *My Southern Home.* In these latter instances, however, Brown's character is reconfigured as Pompey, the seemingly amoral servant of the white slaver. Again, his job is to *re*produce slaves for the markets, all the while claiming that he maintains his own authenticity. "Pomp, as he was usually called by the trader, was of real Negro blood, and would often say, when alluding to himself, 'Dis nigger am no counterfeit, he is de ginuine artikle. Dis chile is none of your haf-and-haf, dere is no bogus about him."[24] This evocation of black authenticity falls from the lips of a character whom we already recognize as a reconstruction of Brown's already heavily constructed image of himself. The effect is magnificent. Pomp's speech, rendered in the presumably authentic vernacular of the black slave, strikes a discordant note in comparison to Brown's own highly crafted prose. His black skin, skin that we can imagine has been "prepared" for the performance, bears no trace of miscegenation. He is the "ginuine artikle, none of your haf-and-haf." And yet his words and the details of his "life" are given to us by the mulatto Brown. Moreover, they are words and details that were altogether available to Brown's readers as images from the minstrel stage Pompey, a "Black American type" whom white Americans were certain they knew and understood, is observed in this illustrated fable (see figure 2.5) by a white gentleman who is taken not only by Pompey's body, that shock of glistening wool, those shapely feet, that mouth, "A negro's substitute for pockets," but also with Pompey's speech, evidence itself of a sharp, if clouded and always concealed, mind bent on trading in the bodies of pigs in order to buy freedom. When the white gentleman takes Pompey at his word, however, and offers him the dollar with which to purchase his first pig, the fable brings us quickly back to the black's embodied stasis with Pompey reappearing sometime later, "All drunk and reeling." Thus, Brown lays the groundwork for a reconsideration of the authenticity of his characters—and himself—at the very moment at which he raises the standard of truth and reality.[25]

This brings us again to the simple fact that Brown reiterates throughout the course of his career. The black figure, the figure so very apparent in the stories that America tells itself about itself, cannot be distinguished from the representational strategies that had come to define blackness. The great gift that

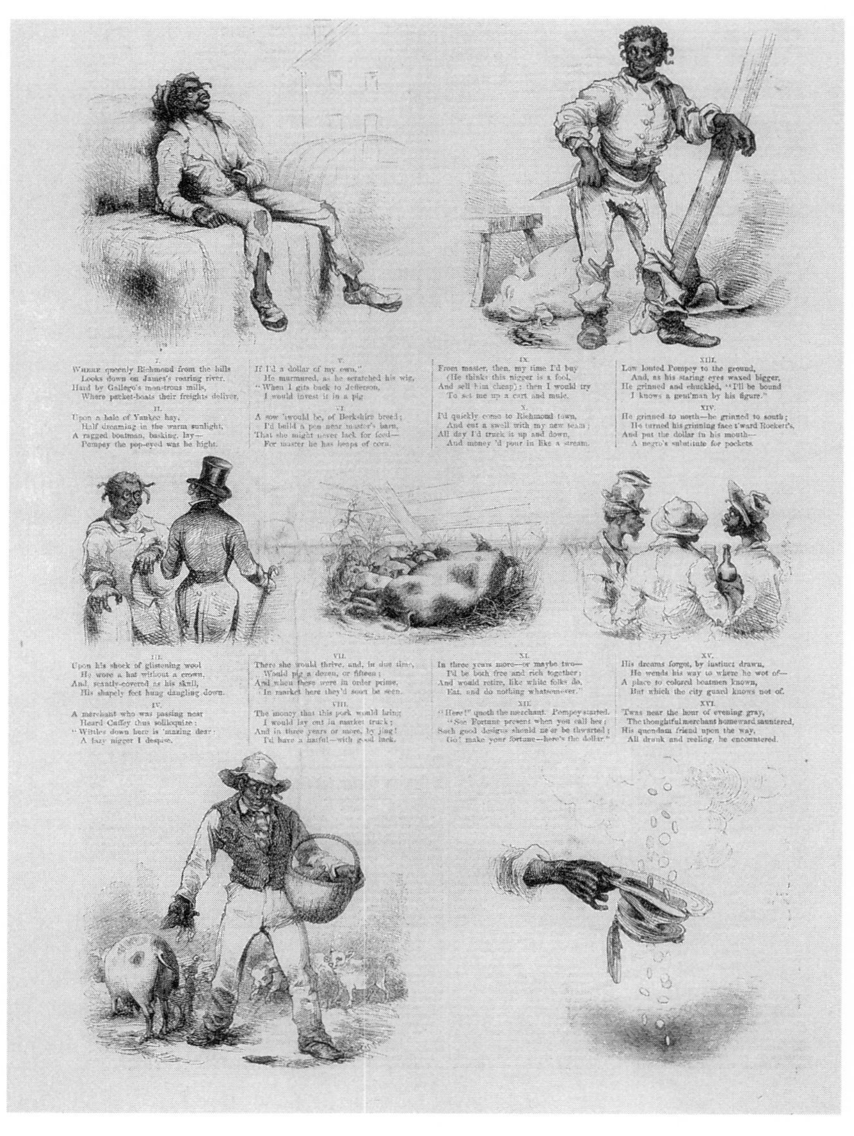
I.
WHERE queenly Richmond from the hills
Looks down on James's roaring river,
Hard by Gallego's mon-trous mills,
Where packet-boats their freights deliver,

II.
Upon a bale of Yankee hay,
Half dreaming in the warm sunlight,
A ragged boatman, basking, lay—
Pompey the pop-eyed was he hight.

III.
Upon his shock of glistening wool
He wore a hat without a crown,
And, scantly-covered as his skull,
His shapely feet hung dangling down.

IV.
A merchant who was passing near
Heard Cuffey thus soliloquize:
"Wittles down here is 'mazing dear:
A lazy nigger I despise.

V.
If I'd a dollar of my own,"
He murmured, as he scratched his wig,
"When I gits back to Jefferson,
I would invest it in a pig

VI.
A sow 'twould be, of Berkshire breed;
I'd build a pen near master's barn,
That she might never lack for food—
For master he has heaps of corn.

VII.
There she would thrive, and, in due time,
Would pig a dozen, or fifteen;
And when these were in order prime,
In market here they'd soon be seen.

VIII.
The money that this pork would bring
I would lay out in market truck;
And in three years or more, by jing!
I'd have a hatful—with good luck.

IX.
From master, then, my time I'd buy
(He thinks this nigger is a fool,
And sell him cheap); then I would try
To set me up a cart and mule.

X.
I'd quickly come to Richmond town,
And cut a swell with my new team;
All day I'd truck it up and down,
And money 'd pour in like a stream.

XI.
In three years more—or maybe two—
I'd be both free and rich together;
And would retire, like white folks do,
Eat, and do nothing whatsomever."

XII.
"Here!" quoth the merchant. Pompey started.
"See Fortune present when you call her;
Such good designs should ne'er be thwarted;
Go! make your fortune—here's the dollar."

XIII.
Low louted Pompey to the ground,
And, as his staring eyes waxed bigger,
He grinned and chuckled, "I'll be bound
I knows a gent'man by his figure."

XIV.
He grinned to north—he grinned to south;
He turned his grinning face t'ward Rockett's,
And put the dollar in his mouth—
A negro's substitute for pockets.

XV.
His dreams forgot, by instinct drawn,
He wends his way to where he wot of—
A place to colored boatmen known,
But which the city guard knows not of.

XVI.
'Twas near the hour of evening gray,
The thoughtful merchant homeward sauntered,
His quondam friend upon the way,
All drunk and reeling, he encountered.

FIGURE 2.5 Pompey's Philosophy—[Imitated From the French.] *Harper's Weekly*, April 3, 1858. Moorland Spingarn Research Center, Howard University. Used with permission.

Clotel brings, then, is that even as she is marked as black, her body continues nonetheless to carry within it the evidence of another (racial) reality, the reality of a self that cannot be circumscribed by the strictures of slavery and white supremacy. When Clotel puts on a white man's clothes she does not become a white man. On the contrary, she continues as her own mulatto female self.[26] What changes is not her body but her modes of narrating the reality of that body. Indeed, Clotel's great strength is her ability to hide herself behind the very lies by which she had been defined.

> *"The man was bundled up in a capacious overcoat; his face was bandaged with a white handkerchief, and its expression entirely hid by a pair of enormous spectacles.*
>
> *"There was something so mysterious and unusual about the young man as he sat restless in the corner, that curiosity led me to observe him more closely.*
>
> *"He appeared anxious to avoid notice, and before the steamer had fairly left the wharf, requested, in a low, womanly voice, to be shown his berth, as he was an invalid, and must retire early: his name he gave as Mr. Johnson. His servant was called, and he was put quietly to bed. I paced the deck until Tybee light grew dim in the distance, and then I went to my berth.*
>
> *"I awoke in the morning with the sun shining in my face; we were then just passing St. Helena. It was a mild beautiful morning, and most of the passengers were on deck, enjoying the freshness of the air, and stimulating their appetites for breakfast. Mr. Johnson soon made his appearance, arrayed as on the night before, and took his seat quietly upon the guard of the boat.*
>
> *"From the better opportunity afforded by daylight, I found that he was a slight build, apparently handsome young man, with black hair and eyes, and of a darkness of complexion that betokened Spanish extraction. Any notice from others seemed painful to him; so to satisfy my curiosity, I questioned his servant, who was standing near, and gained the following information.*
>
> *"His master was an invalid—he had suffered for a long time under the complication of diseases, that had baffled the skill of the best physicians in Mississippi; he was now suffering principally with the 'rheumatism,' and he was scarcely able to walk or help himself in any way. He came from Vicksburgh, and was now on his way to Philadelphia, at which place resided his uncle, a celebrated physician, and through whose means he hoped to be restored to perfect health.*
>
> *"This information, communicated in a bold, off-hand manner, enlisted my sympathies for the sufferer, although it occurred to me that he walked rather too gingerly for a person afflicted with so many ailments."* (Brown [1853] 1969, 175–76)

I have been concerned thus far almost exclusively with revising the narrative of *Clotel* that marks it as America's first black novel, suggesting instead that Brown specifically produced the work as a "view" of America, a complicated critique of the manner in which slavery continued to erode the foundations of U.S. republicanism. I have argued also that Brown turns to the body of the mulatto, the body of the most obviously native actor on the American stage, in his efforts to reveal both American depravity and American promise. Thus, I have insisted upon taking seriously Brown's "excessive" aesthetic practices. The overflowing nature of his texts, the absolute willingness, as with the passage above, to consume and reframe massive amounts of racist effluvia demonstrates that Brown could not establish a black corporeality that somehow existed prior to its representation, representation produced often by those who purported to despise black bodies.

What I would like to turn to now, in this final portion of the chapter, is the extreme critique that Brown makes of what I will call "the state of whiteness" in the American republic. Brown borrowed the passage above, with its titillating view of the fleeing slaves, almost verbatim from a report in the Newark, New Jersey, *Daily Mercury* of January 19, 1849, in which the writer claimed to have been an unknowing witness of the steamboat portion of William and Ellen Craft's *actual* escape. The effect, particularly for a British audience predisposed to recognize slavery's enfeebling properties, is to demonstrate not only the mechanics of the couple's escape but also, and importantly, the mechanics of the obvious (white) racial degradation that makes their escape possible.

This view is given us by a self-professed "believer in physiognomy" who recognizes, as does Brown, a direct relation between body and character. Thus, when a strapping Negro enters the scene accompanied by a man who is described variously as mysterious, unusual, restless, womanly, slight, handsome, dark, and Spanish, we see enacted again the tendency to equate physiognomy with both individual and racial character. The black is established while the mulatto is emerging, literally covered over by the trappings of an enfeebled white masculinity. The likeness of Ellen Craft in the dress of a male planter was used as the frontispiece for William Craft's *Running a Thousand Miles For Freedom, or the Escape of William and Ellen Craft From Slavery* (1860). It was also reproduced by the couple and sold to the European crowds who came to hear their story (see figure 2.6). Still, this does not explain how the subterfuge that freed the Crafts from slavery and acted as the key to Brown's aesthetic practice actually worked. Specifically, it does not speak to the almost inevitable nature of the white man's enfeeblement, a view of which Brown is eager to establish. The profligate, aristocratic South had given itself over to their brutish, if lushly embodied, slaves, so much so that the marks of their degradations were literally written on their bodies. What produces Mr. Johnson's masculinity are the very signs of his weakness, that handkerchief, those spectacles, all the markers of disease and invalidity. This is what says to his observers "white." Indeed, our narrator is so eager to accept the fact of his brother's feeble body that he seeks out the black interlocutor, making him, in the process, both (the white's) body and mind.

I will stop short of making the argument that what we see here is a species of homosexual panic, though the homoerotic nature of Jim's relation to both his master and the white observer are indisputable. Still, the specter of profligacy hovers in the foreground of this spectacle. Again, it is this very notion of the white, and especially the white southerner, as always already suspect, that allows the couple to enact their escape. One should remember Brown's "Tanning a

FIGURE 2.6 Ellen Craft

White Boy" image and the specter of a debased southern whiteness that it conjured, as well as his contention that the degraded nature of the South and of the entire nation was obvious within the presumably superior bodies of aristocratic planters. Note, however, that Brown is just as meticulous about maintaining the sanctity of the mulatto female body as Douglass is about the sanctity of the black male body. We should remember how elegantly defined Clotel was when we first encountered her mulatto figure on the auction block. Moreover, even as Clotel hides behind a debilitated white masculinity she does not become enfeebled herself. Instead, her body, as with the mulatto bodies of revolutionary Santo Domingo, continues to be vibrant, her walk "rather too gingerly for a person afflicted with so many ailments."

Then why does she die? Why does a character with these impressive attributes throw herself into the waters of the Potomac, in full view of the White House, instead of surviving to (re)establish her family and advance the cause of a postslavery America? There are two obvious answers to this question. The first would point to the way in which the pristine nature of Clotel's body is maintained precisely by destroying that body. In running, Clotel extricates herself from the clutches of a lecherous white masculinity. If she stops, if she reintroduces herself into American social life, she will be caught, if not by the planters then by a black community (with its own developing notions of corporeal existence) that is itself dirty, impure. Secondarily, I would reiterate my contention that though Brown does utilize a mulatto character to great effect in his narrative, he nevertheless is concerned with demonstrating not only the promise of the mulatto but also the tragedy of America, a tragedy carried about in the (dead) body of the president's daughter, a tragedy that is necessary if a black conjugal union is to be achieved. This claim places Brown in direct dialogue with any number of American artists and intellectuals who understood the mulatto's dead body as the site of calamity. I propose, in fact, that we view Thomas Satterwhite Noble's 1867 drawing *Margaret Garner* in just this light. Every gesture in this drawing speaks directly to the question of who will control both the black's body and the logic of her embodiment (see figure 2.7). The work draws upon the fantastic story of Margaret Garner, who in 1856 escaped with her husband and four children from Kentucky into Ohio. When finally cornered by her former master in Cincinnati, she stabbed one of the children, purportedly her favorite, to death. The drawing works to establish just the poetics of American racialist discourse that I have been at pains to demonstrate. Black and white individuals, ferocious in their commitments to normative American modes of corporeality, confront each other over the already dead bodies of two figures, the most prominent of whom exists in both light and dark, black and white, its body giving evidence of no absolute allegiance to either. Following the logic of this essay, this scene marks the point at which the promise of America is finished, dead at the feet of constantly warring and inevitably homicidal racial combatants.

Brown himself establishes just this sense of (American) tragedy in his treatment of Clotel's sister, Althesa, who won the heart of a good and faithful white lover, Henry Morton, a man who lifted Althesa from slavery, educated her, "legally" married her, and then placed her in a fine New Orleans mansion. Again, the couple, just as their antecedents in Brown's panoramic views, produced two beautiful daughters, both of whom were unaware that their mother was once a slave. And yet Althesa and Morton are never able to extricate themselves from the reality of the world in which they live. They cannot remain

FIGURE 2.7 Margaret Garner (1867). Thomas Satterwhite Noble. From the collection of Dr. and Mrs. Mark Noble Mueller.

hermetically sealed within their marriage, oblivious to the strictures of the slave state. The fall from grace, from ignorance to understanding, from innocence to guilt, had inevitably to come. That the couple dies from yellow fever and that their daughters are remanded into slavery suggests, as I have argued already, that Brown is at pains to represent the tragic loss of the possibility embodied within the much maligned mulatto population of the antebellum United States.

Brown does seemingly offer an out to this distressing state of affairs through the character of Clotel's daughter, Isabella. The girl, just as beautiful and perhaps more accomplished than Clotel herself, follows in her mother's footsteps by exchanging clothing with her black lover in order to facilitate his escape, thereby forcing her removal to the New Orleans markets, where she is purchased and wed by a chivalrous, loving Frenchman, Mr. Devenant. Her husband then takes her to France and installs her as his wife, bringing the narrative a full three hundred and sixty degrees to the same moment of racial and social crisis precipitated by the interracial "marriages" of her mother and aunt. Devenant's death, however, does not force Mary back into slavery. On the contrary, she remains in France under the charge of her husband's father until a chance encounter brings her back into the arms of her original lover, George. The 1853 version of the novel then comes to a quick close with a final celebration of the great advances made by Black Americans since the "death" of Clotel. Thus, Brown's novel comes to an awkward and screeching halt, with

Brown leaving aside the many conceptual and ideological issues that he had brought to the fore in favor of a hackneyed rehearsal of the terrific gains that had been made by Black Americans in early national and antebellum America.

It is this awkward closure that marks the first real failure in Brown's literature. He succumbs to the drive to depict black subjectivity within the same simplistic forms that he had resisted all of his writing career, to produce a seamless unity between corporeality and domesticity. Two young lovers are given a second chance to form conjugal union. Their trial by fire rids them of the taint of degradation, while their location outside of the United States protects them from the enervating realities of the American slavocracy. Indeed, their story leads to a rather hackneyed celebration of the grand achievements of "the race." It is almost as if in a few short pages, *Clotel* becomes *The Heroic Slave.*

I propose, however, that we not readily accept this strange, forced closure. Instead, even as he "finishes" this version of *Clotel*, Brown continues to leave open many of the conceptual matters with which he was concerned. The very process by which *Clotel* was constructed points to the fact that Brown was constantly experimenting with his ideas concerning the "true" nature of race, sex, and national belonging. *Clotel* continued for years to be a work in progress of sorts. Brown published two other versions of the work: *Clotelle: A Tale of the Southern States* and *Clotelle, or, The Colored Heroine* in 1864 and 1867, respectively. In the 1867 version, which I will read briefly here, Clotel's daughter, Mary, acts as her mother's double. She takes a slightly altered version of her mother's name, Clotelle, and becomes the title character in the later work. Moreover, she reproduces many of the narrative devices that Brown deploys in the earlier novel—specifically, the exchange of clothing that precipitated her removal to New Orleans and eventually France.

In 1867, however, the nation had already largely settled the question of the mixed-race, mulatto American. The Thirteenth, Fourteenth, and Fifteenth Amendments refused altogether the notion of racial ambiguity within federal law, and presumably within most other features of American civic life. As a consequence, Brown produces in his final version a strange mélange of endings and new beginnings. Once again, Clotelle (Mary) marries Devenant. Once again, he dies, though this time we are treated beforehand to a brief description of the couple's travels throughout Europe and East India. Once again, Jerome (George) finds Clotelle after Devenant's death. Unlike the earlier version, however, the young woman reencounters her father, Mr. Linwood, who has come to Europe "crack-brained," broken and tortured by remorse. She literally restores the man to good health by alleviating his guilt and persuading him to free his slaves. In the process, she opens the door for some form of reconciliation between the newly formed community of freed people and their white southern "fathers." Even more striking is the fact that Clotelle and Jerome enter fully into the war effort, Clotelle as nurse and spy, Jerome as soldier.

This time, though, Brown refuses closure. He allows the domestication neither of Clotelle nor of her (black) lover turned husband, Jerome. On the contrary, the war, the never-ending struggle for freedom, separates them, placing Clotelle in the hospital, Jerome on the battlefield. It seems, in fact, that at the moment of reconciliation, the moment when white fathers and black lovers seemingly come together as one, Brown offers one final—and bizarre—twist: the violent and senseless death of Jerome in an attempt to retrieve the dead body of a white officer.

> Twelve men had been killed in the effort to obtain the body of the brave Payne, but to no purpose. Humanity forbade another trial, and yet it was made. . . . Four men sprang forward . . . one was Jerome Fletcher. . . . They started upon the run; and strange to tell, all of them reached the body, and had nearly borne it from the field, when two of the number were cut down. Of these, one was Jerome. His head was entirely torn off by a shell. (Brown [1867] 1969 106)

This decapitation does more than deprive Clotelle of a husband. It also signals Brown's unwillingness to offer an easy ending, one in which the severe crisis of republicanism that gave rise to the Civil War could be settled, figuratively or otherwise, through marriage. Unlike Clotelle, Jerome was unable to retrieve his white "father" in his white body, to reconnect to an already disestablished racialist ideology in which racial mixing was accepted and perhaps privileged. Moreover, by decapitating Jerome, by enacting this symbolic castration, Brown disallows the production of the black father and, therefore, refuses once again both the security of absolute closure and the promise of a new beginning, the promise of a pure black body. It is almost as if in the new American racial economy Brown is suddenly forced to recognize a stable Black American community, one in which the mulatto has indeed become simply a figure, while "mixed race" persons have been reassigned as simply and unequivocally black. Yet Brown cannot so easily reorient his conception of the possibilities of American republicanism. Instead, he leaves his novel essentially unfinished. Jerome's head has been blown off. Mr. Linwood is "crack-brained" and not ever quite present, and Clotelle becomes a spy, passing as both white and black, thereby establishing herself as the liminal, half-formed mulatto figure that Brown had resisted so assiduously, the same figure presumably decomposing at the bottom of the Potomac.

Strikingly, Brown avoids the brief recitation of the advances made by Black Americans that he had included in his 1853 work for a description of Clotelle's short stay with an old black couple, Jim and Dinah. The novel ends, then, with a *re*articulation of Brown's minstrelesque vision of black domestic life.

> The woman, like many of her sex, was an inveterate scold, and Jim had but one way to govern her tongue. 'Shet your mouf, madam, an' hold your tongue,' said Jim, after his wife had scolded and sputtered away for some minutes. 'Shet your mouf dis minit, I say: you shan't stan' dar, an' talk ter me in dat way. I bought you an' paid my money fer you, an' I ain't a gwine ter let you sase me in dat way. Shet your mouf dis minit: ef you don't I'll sell you; 'for God I will.

> Shet up, I say, or I'll sell you.' This had the desired effect, and settled Dinah for the day. (Brown [1867] 1969, 114)

I would like to suggest that this rather evocative description of black family life parallels and signifies upon the hackneyed image of the noble and "free" married couple, Isabella and George, living happily ever after in the safety of Europe. Where one might imagine that the latter couple will spend the remainder of their days in marital bliss, we know that Jim and Dinah will continue to bicker and fight. Jim scolds, "Shet your mouf" three times before Dinah will stop her "sputtering," the two achieving a truce that we are assured will last only for the day. Moreover, the vernacular in which the couple communicates is itself a marker of the fact that they may never possess the wealth, the education, the "culture" to transform themselves into representative Americans. And yet it is this vernacular, this particularly American speech, that must necessarily represent the new promise of America. The refined mulatto has been transformed into something else, an entity *not* unto herself. The best that can be hoped for, then, is that Jim and Dinah do continue their bickering, at least insofar as it establishes a postbellum discourse of American republicanism. Dinah's inveterate scolding, much like the sharp tongues of generations of nags and scandal mongers, provides for Brown a particularly fruitful location for the production of meaning and culture.

I began this chapter by noting the excessive nature of William Wells Brown's literary practice, suggesting that it should not be understood as evidence of Brown's inability, but instead as proof of the complex and contradictory nature of the practice of American republicanism. I subsequently worked to establish the fact that Brown addresses these matters through the presentation of the mulatto, that distinct and therefore particularly American character whose presence is so inevitable within American life that it is best demonstrated through the obvious aesthetic strategies of the panorama. Still, these efforts were not enough to establish absolute boundaries around either Brown's individual works or his aesthetic enterprise taken as a whole. Instead, Brown's literature remains open, excessive, subject to revision.

I would ask now, as we proceed to the next chapter, that the reader continue to understand *Clotel* as an open text. Even though, as I have suggested, the view of the real mulatto character, Clotel, gave way to the figurative mulatto character, Clotelle, this does not mean that the story comes to an end. Instead, I would direct you to the possibilities just beyond our grasp. I ask that we imagine that Clotel survives her leap into the Potomac, that she climbs from the water and into the "extensive forests and woodlands of the celebrated Arlington Place," and that she continues as a runaway, a third figure who will appear constantly within the fictions on display in this study. Our journey turns, then, toward the comfortable environs of the antebellum North, where Black America was coming to write itself into existence, even as it was constantly confronted with the black/white faces of American fugitives.

Three • CLEAN HOUSE, PECULIAR PEOPLE

> The book which now appears before the public may be of interest in relation to a question which the late agitation of the subject of slavery has raised in many thoughtful minds; viz.—Are the race at present held as slaves capable of freedom, self-government, and progress?
>
> —*Harriet Beecher Stowe*

The Race

Even though I have struggled in this study to demonstrate that (black) bodies both constitute and are constituted by domesticity, by households, I do not want to suggest a simple symbiosis between body and house. Instead, I maintain an emphasis on ambiguity and indeterminacy, arguing that corporeal existence is always and inevitably awkward and unstable, even as it is figured as transparent and natural. Thus, by collapsing notions of domesticity and corporeality into one another, by insisting that they are essentially one and the same, I do not mean to resuscitate the very conceptual rigidity that I have attempted to combat. Domesticity should not be understood, then, as a static phenomenon, the achievement of a sort of guarded peace between individual desire and communal interest. Instead, domesticity is better understood as an irregular process of regulation, of law, in which the constant flight and return of desiring bodies is negotiated. Moreover, a domesticity produced through unstable bodies must necessarily reproduce the very ambiguity by which these bodies, "its" bodies, are defined. The household, the home, must suffer the same gaping orifices—

physical, ideological, and otherwise—as the "open" and "vulnerable" bodies that produce it and that it produces. The fact of this domestic instability ensures the dynamic nature of the body/household dialectic in that it guarantees the production of irregular bodies, deformed bodies, grotesque bodies, bodies that may threaten the cohesion of the very households from which they have been produced even as they help to reestablish the domestic boundaries that they traverse.

The "domestic sphere" exists, then, as a fiction at least so far as it is taken to be sociologically demonstrable, the locus of a stable set of "real" economic and social relations that exist apart from the public, particularly the market.[1] One might argue, in fact, that since the idea of the domestic is intimately tied to bourgeois articulations of an essential difference between public and private, that the marketplace, an important, if not the important, location for the production of the bourgeois, always encroaches upon domestic life. As the bourgeois patriarch leaves his home to produce wealth in an open marketplace he is always sullied. Promiscuous money dirties his hands, strangers of "alien" classes and races press upon his person, fallen women threaten his morality and health. The whole stinking miasma of the marketplace sticks to him as he returns to his presumably self-contained household, necessitating the ubiquitous scrapers, sewers, mats, and back entrances so apparent in and about the homes of bourgeois Americans.

His "cleanliness" must be understood, therefore, as a discursive strategy, one designed to affect a bourgeois individualism distinct from the sullied public market.[2] Cleaning becomes, as a consequence, a primary technology in the production of self and other. I am clean while the other is dirty. The rub is that the very act of cleaning must necessarily bring one into contact with the same discomfiting and destabilizing dirt that threatens the production of the bourgeois. As Peter Stallybrass and Allon White have argued, the bourgeois household and the bourgeois individual are produced and reproduced through the machinations of armies of outsiders who ferret out and expel foul, dangerous waste.[3] These same "extra-domestic household members" also ensure the cleanliness of that which enters both the home and the bodies that it contains Yet they seem never to rid themselves completely of the dirt that they manage. They provide an always frightening and sometimes intriguing bridge to the dirty world that exists outside household boundaries. Indeed, the very fact that they are paid for their services brings us back to the difficulties of the sullied and sullying marketplace that the household is designed to resist. This is precisely where the fiction of the domestic sphere is produced. Somehow the conceptual difficulty of the dirty servant must be addressed. Somehow a stable, exclusive family structure must be maintained, even as this maintenance necessitates the presence of destabilizing outsiders. When we turn to Freud's notion of the family romance, then, it is important to remember, as Stallybrass and White have demonstrated, that Freud's theory is itself a fiction established to guard against the breakdown between (bourgeois) domesticity and (dirty) public life. His family, his household, even if in crisis, is always composed simply and exclusively of a father, mother, and their children. The cook who feeds them, the nurse who suckles them, the nanny who bathes them, the teacher who educates them, and the maid who manages their dirt, shit, semen, urine, and blood are nowhere in evidence.

This is the ideological structure out of which Frank Webb's 1857 novel *The Garies and Their Friends* was produced. The novel opens with a description of the refined, well-educated, and good-tempered Clarence Garie, the white father of the ill-fated interracial family. His wife, Emily, a woman whose light brown complexion suggested "the faintest hint of carmine," had been bought some ten years earlier in the Savannah slave market. Thereafter, Mr. Garie treated her as his protégé, arranging for her education and lavishing her with attention until finally the two become one, producing first one child, then another, Clarence and Emily, neither of whom has any idea that he or she is black, much less a slave. Nevertheless, it is the issue of the children and what will become of them if Mr. Garie suddenly dies that prompts the family to leave the idyllic surroundings of their Georgia plantation for the relatively more free environment of Philadelphia. There the Garies hope that their presence will be tolerated, if not exactly accepted.

Immediately we see how overdetermined Webb's work is by the ideological complexities inherent in the production of families and individuals. In the logic of the novel, Garie's sin is not exclusively that he marries a black woman, though this is by no means a work that celebrates amalgamation. Instead, Garie's sin is that he has been so lax in policing the distinction between the market and the household. He buys his "wife" and owns his children and no amount of grace, good intention, or fine feeling can absolve him of this. On the contrary, as his well-meaning, aristocratic uncle warns him before he leaves for Philadelphia, the very fact that Garie treats his family well and not as his concubine and bastards furthers the dissolution of boundaries between black and white and, most important, between public and private, market and home.

> [Y]ou can't expect to live there as you do here; the prejudice against persons of colour is much stronger in some of the Northern cities than it is amongst us Southerners. You can't live with Emily there as you do here; you will be in everybody's mouth. You won't be able to sustain your old connections with your Northern friends—you'll find that they will cut you dead.[4]

The elderly gentleman pinpoints the difficulties inherent in the Garies's attempt to bring their southern, alien, unclean notions of family out of the confines of their plantation home and into the publicity of the modern North. Their narratives of self and community are raw, unworked, lacking the clear distinction between master and servant so necessary to the production of the bourgeois and the domestic.

The whole family is composed, in fact, of runaways. They attempt to escape the ideological structures out of which notions of normative individuality are constructed. They endeavor to establish a grotesque household that can produce only grotesque bodies. They strive to cross the rigid boundary between North and South without cleaning up first, shaking off the dust from their long physical and ideological journey. The tragedy of the Garie family is that all of its members, save young Emily, are divided against themselves. It is not just that they are produced out of multiple and competing desires, but that they adopt no clear logic in the negotiation of the same. Garie loves a black woman and imagines himself a natural democrat, yet he clings tenaciously to the slave culture that produced him. His "wife," moreover, plays dangerously close to the line separating the servant from the family member, creating herself more on the model of the Haitian *menagere*, the black woman who was combination household manager and live-in lover/companion for white planters and merchants in prerevolutionary Santo Domingo, than the fully established bourgeois matron.[5] Young Clarence, on the other hand, passes for white after the death of his parents. He is never, as a consequence, able to establish either a stable black or a stable white identity. He pines away not only for his white lover, Birdie, a fact to which we will return below, but also for a racial economy that would allow for indeterminacy, a racial economy that was perhaps southern but most decidedly not American.

Standing in contradistinction to the Garies are the Ellises, "a highly respectable and industrious coloured family," consisting of a tender mother, a hard-working father, and their three children: the beautiful and accomplished oldest daughter, Esther, the shrewish and extremely fastidious middle child, Caddy; and a rambunctious young son, Charlie. It is the Ellis family that in every particular acts as the mirror of the Garies's various identities. Where the Garies are masters the Ellises are servants. (Caddy Ellis takes particular pains to prepare the Garies's Philadelphia mansion for its new occupants.) Where the Garies are rich the Ellises are relatively poor. Where the Garies seem to be always at leisure the Ellises are working constantly. Most important, where the Ellises are a "mixed" family the Ellises are "purely" black, secure in their understanding of where they stand in Philadelphia's racial economy.

It would seem that the narrative should proceed along a rather obvious and well-worn path. The bad mixed-race family will be destroyed while the good black family will be strengthened, possibly acquiring some of the resources and social standing of the "bad" family in the process. Yet Webb's narrative is quite a bit more complex than this. It is true that by the end of the novel both Mr. and Mrs. Garie are dead. It is true that through a number of improbable narrative turns Charlie and Emily (now reconfigured as black) recover much of the fortune stolen from the Garies by the novel's villain, Mr. Stevens. It is also true, however, that the once virile Mr. Ellis becomes an invalid, a grotesque body, his mind wandering into and out of moments of recognition and lucidity, the fatal fall that reduces him to this state a result of the same race riot that consumes the Garies. Thus, we are left in a situation in which both of the fathers with whom the novel began are excised from the text, leaving their families to re-form themselves with whatever resources still remaining at their disposal.

In attempting to understand why Webb complicates his narrative by producing Mr. Ellis as "undead," it is important to consider just how decidedly hostile he is to the "unclean" tendencies that produce the "southernness" of the slave South. Significantly, Mr. and Mrs. Ellis, though always free, immigrate from the South as adults. Mrs. Ellis was a childhood friend of Mrs. Garie while Mr. Ellis helped to rear a young slave boy who will reappear later in the novel as the accomplished Mr. Winston. It is difficult, therefore, not to reach the conclusion that by debilitating Mr. Ellis, Webb demonstrates a fear of "southern principles" that is so great that anyone associated with them must be tamed, if not destroyed. Indeed, Mr. Ellis is himself figured as a (southern) runaway. In his attempt to warn his fellow immigrants, the Garies, of the approaching mob he is spotted by a group of men who chase him onto a roof and attempt to throw him over the side. When he resists, clinging to the side of the building, they chop off several of his fingers, at which point he falls to the street below. The half-conscious, half-dead state in which Webb leaves him suggests the author's ambiguity in relation to a character who apparently has none of the uncleanliness of the Garies, but who is southern nonetheless. He must have imbibed, therefore, many of the old patterns, the old pre-bourgeois mores, of the southern plantocracy. Mr. Ellis is described as gray and bent even before he is attacked and positively old and dottering afterward. This is even though Webb has done him the incredible service of making him a carpenter and joiner, a powerful position in a novel obsessed with households and the construction of households. But, as I have argued repeatedly, Ellis has too much of the stench of the unreconstructed southerner about him. His household runs the risk of producing the same grotesque ideological lapses as does the Garies's. Can it be any wonder, then, that after the riot is over Mr. Ellis is not only disabled but also his home has been burned to the ground?

I will even go so far as to claim that what Webb is engaged in is a sort of domestic eugenics, one in which the goal is to produce properly socialized modern individuals who maintain proper racial and domestic distinctions. Mr. Ellis committed a grave error by allowing his son, Charlie, to be placed into service in the home of Mrs. Thomas, his wife's girlhood mistress. Mr. Walters, the nominal hero of the novel, whose virility—and modernity—are unmatched and who subsequently becomes a surrogate father for Charlie, immediately announces the novel's critique of such mixing:

> If you can't get on without the boy's earning something, why don't you do as white women and men do? Do you ever find them sending their boys out as servants? No; they rather give them a stock of matches, blacking, newspapers, or apples, and start them out to sell them. What is the result? The boy that learns to sell the matches soon learns to sell other things; he learns to make

> bargains; he becomes a small trader, then a merchant, then a millionaire. Did you ever hear of any one who made a fortune at service? (Webb [1857] 1997, 62–63)

The critique stems not only from purely pecuniary considerations but also from the horror that the loosening of boundaries between the household and the market enacts in the psychologies on display in the text. The servant is kept in a sort of limbo in which he sells not only his labor but also his person. Charlie is horrified at the livery that Mrs. Thomas expects him to wear, understanding all too clearly that the suit works to produce him as the woman's ornament. Moreover, the other servants in the household, Aunt Rachel and Mr. Robberts, are figured as grotesque creatures. Aunt Rachel is hysterical and violent while Robberts is sycophantic and buffoonish. Both, moreover, exist in bodies deformed by long service in the Thomas household, Aunt Rachel with her supersensitive corns and Mr. Robberts with his rheumatism and delicate shins. Mr. Ellis's mistake, then, is that he has allowed Charlie to leave his properly constituted household for an irregular, excessive, grotesque home with a history of producing grotesque bodies.[6]

Charlie does escape the Thomas home after taking advantage of the vulnerable bodies of his assailants. Mrs. Thomas's wig is knocked from her head. Mr. Robberts's shins come in for their share of abuse, and Aunt Rachel's corns are given no mercy. Still, the specter of some intangible southern "messiness" lingers about the household constructed by Mr. Ellis. Charlie, always a rambunctious and boyish youth, is sent to deliver his sister's dinner to her as she prepares the Garies's new home for their arrival. On the way he stops to play marbles with a group of boys, at which point he inadvertently exchanges the pail with his sister's dinner for that of another boy. When Caddy opens the container and finds only the remnants of someone else's meal she goes into a rage and begins to beat Charlie so viciously that he falls down a flight of stairs. In the process, he is terribly injured and must be removed to the Warmouth estate of a Mrs. Bird, a rich white woman who had been impressed some time before by Charlie's recitations at the local black public school. Again, Mr. Ellis's household is broken up and supplemented by a liberal interracialism that the novel repeatedly rejects. Yet Charlie, unlike Clarence Garie who leaves behind his family only to fall hopelessly in love with his Birdie, remains unceasingly loyal to his own (black) community and (black) household. He insists upon returning to Philadelphia the moment he receives a painfully written note from his older sister, Esther, detailing the horrors his family and community have suffered.

> My Dear Little Brother,—We are all in deep distress in consequence of the misfortunes brought upon us by the mob. Our home has been destroyed; and worse than all, our poor father was caught, and so severely beaten by the rioters that for some days his life was entirely despaired of. Thank God! he is now improving, and we have every reasonable hope of his ultimate recovery.

> Mother, Caddy, and I, as you may well suppose, are almost prostrated by this accumulation of misfortunes, and but for the kindness of Mr. Walters, with whom we are living, I do not know what would have become of us. Dear Mr. and Mrs. Garie—[Here followed a passage that was so scored and crossed as to be illegible. After a short endeavour to decipher it, he continued:] We would like to see you very much, and mother grows every day more anxious for your return. I forgot to add, in connection with the mob, that Mr. Walters' house was also attacked, but unsuccessfully, the rioters having met a signal repulse. Mother and Caddy send a world of love to you. . . . Give our united kind regards to Mrs. Bird, and thank her in our behalf for her great kindness to you.—Ever yours, Esther. (Webb. [1857] 1997, 263–264)

Here we see the novel in an act of self-reflection. The entirety of the dual logics of domesticity and corporeality has been reduced into this brief note. Mr. Ellis is all but disembodied as his home is reduced to a smoldering heap of ashes, while Mr. Walters's house remains erect (all allusions intended), a haven from the roaring crowd. The Garies, moreover, are not only removed from the narrative but also rendered literally illegible. They have been scored over and scratched out, marked as things apart, wretched and impermissible mistakes in the literature that Webb is attempting to construct.

This is, in fact, the place in the novel at which Webb most explicitly announces his project as the production of a specifically Black American literature. Webb not only summarily dismisses the unclean (southern) interracialism of the Garies but also clues the reader into the fact that his work should be read as a thing apart from the abolitionist literature with which it is clearly in dialogue. Mrs. Bird comes to us, of course, from Harriet Beecher Stowe's *Uncle Tom's Cabin*, where she assists the runaways, Eliza and Harry, in their journey toward freedom. In the process, she gives Harry the clothing of her own dead son, just as Charlie's Mrs. Bird gives him the clothing and "things" of her own long deceased "Charlie." As Gillian Brown has argued, however, this act was not an invitation for the runaways to join their respective Bird households. Instead, it is at once an act of recognition and differentiation in which the black is hailed as human and "equal" while simultaneously restricted from certain (white) modes of domestic intercourse.[7] While Harry and Charlie may receive the clothing of their respective doppelgängers, they are nonetheless never hailed as members of these white families, grotesque replacements within already barren households. Clarence attempts just this type of domestic sleight of hand, becoming the "white" child of Miss Ada and eventually the "white" lover of Birdie, but his deformed, overly desirous, disloyal body cannot forever continue the charade.

The fact that Stowe introduces Webb's novel as itself emblematic of the particularity, the blackness, of Philadelphia's black community should come, therefore, as no surprise. "In this city they form a large class—have increased in numbers, wealth, and standing—they constitute a peculiar society of their own, presenting many social peculiarities worthy of interest and attention"

(Webb [1857] 1997, v). The key concept here is peculiarity, a cultural and racial ontology that is somehow equivalent to whiteness, but not exactly equal. Again, the effort in the novel is to define a modern racial identity that is distinct and peculiar, that does not bleed into whiteness thereby producing monsters like Clarence. Thus, Webb's phobic response to the "fact of southernness," particularly in relation to Mr. Ellis, is indicative of a desire for the clear, clean differentiation that Zygmunt Bauman argues is *the* distinguishing characteristic of modern thought.[8] Mr. Ellis, precisely because of the fact of his southernness, can be presumed incapable of maintaining a clean household. Charlie is always being shipped from one white elite home to another while Ellis's daughter, Caddy, is prone to such an excess of domestic feeling that she almost kills her brother. Indeed, Caddy's hysteria, her absolute fear that nothing can ever be clean enough, speaks to a dirtiness within the Ellis home, a basic ideological instability that her constant cleaning resists. I would argue, in fact, that Caddy demonstrates the same obsessiveness of other "southern" maids, among them Aunt Rachel and Stowe's Dinah, that comes from the incredibly difficult task of "cleaning" households that have been deeply, indelibly stained.

I will go further and suggest that what Webb recoils at is the "yellowness" of the South, the mixing of races and racial ideologies, a mixing that had not established an intermediate group but which made that possibility palpable. Garie's detractors accuse him of having been bewitched by a "yaller wench," a fact that made him incapable of behaving "like other men who happen to have half-white children" and "breed them up for the market and sell them" (Webb [1857] 1997, 59). Mr. Winston, a man who though once a slave could easily pass physically and socially as white, is told in no uncertain terms that, "Either you must live exclusively amongst coloured people, or go to the whites and remain with them" (Webb [1857] 1997, 41). Young Clarence Garie, meanwhile, dies an agonizing death in which fiery spots appear on his cheeks, spots that correspond to the black spots that had broken out on his body in the dream of his lover, Birdie. It is no accident that these symptoms are exactly those of yellow fever.[9] Indeed, as we will see throughout this study, yellow fever was a constantly recurring motif in the earliest fiction produced by African Americans, a motif that mimetically represents the national phobia surrounding interracialism.

The point that I am driving toward is that with *The Garies* Webb is attempting to aestheticize a process of racial modernization in which notions of racelessness and indeterminacy become untenable. The fumbling, protoscientific "racial" theories of early national America were being abandoned for a racial ideology that allowed the black to enter the public sphere precisely by rejecting the notion of disembodiment that so overdetermined public discourse. The black could enter, but only as a black, as an individual whose body was not peripheral to his subjectivity but constitutive of it. Moreover, that body became a factor not of biology but of ideology, of domesticity, such that even a nominally "white" body like Emily Garie's could be reconstructed as "black" within properly black homes. The argument that I am making flies directly in the face of the common sense of American racialism. The idea that the production and reproduction of the American slave state necessitated the development of forms of racial distinctiveness with which we are now familiar stems from a lingering exceptionalism in American and African-American studies that disallows the idea that racial indeterminacy was a significant and defining aspect of American culture, so much so that technologies as blunt and imprecise as Jim Crow were developed to contain it.

The truth is that Webb must have been extremely aware, as indeed the rest of the country was, of not only the fact that alternate racial economies existed in almost every other country in this hemisphere but that these alternate economies were constantly encroaching upon "U.S. territory." I have mentioned already the *menagere* and her importance, financial, racial, domestic, and otherwise, to the life of Santo Domingo. She was only one figure, however, in a pantheon of (foreign) racial interlopers who seemed bent on sullying American ideals—and bodies. We should remember that the revolution in Santo Domingo was proceeded by years of unrest among the slaves in the colony, precipitating the emigration of more than 10,000 persons, many of them persons of color, who brought with them not only property, human and otherwise, but also "revolutionary" notions of race and domesticity. The residents of Hispaniola were not so particular about avoiding the touch of the tar brush. Nor did they balk at the notion of persons of African descent holding other persons of African descent in bondage. In 1792, French-speaking immigrants petitioned the Pennsylvania legislature for exemption from the newly enacted abolition laws. They were refused. The point, however, was that even though these new additions to the community were suspiciously regarded as perhaps "black" themselves, they nevertheless were far from democratic. Race mixing did not necessitate racial egalitarianism.[10]

The presence of these alien amalgamationists was even more strongly felt within the antebellum south. After 1792, many southern states forbade or seriously curtailed the immigration of slaves from (revolutionary) Santo Domingo.[11] This did nothing, however, to stop refugees from entering Louisiana, which was notorious not only for its large number of mixed-race persons but also for the liberal manumission policies of both the French and the Spanish, policies that actually encouraged white fathers to free their slave children (Berlin 1974, 109). The result was that by 1788, free Negroes composed more than one-third of the population of New Orleans (Berlin 1974, 112). When the United States purchased the Louisiana Territory in 1803, not only then did the numbers of free Negroes in the United States drastically increase but also a set of "foreign" racial ideologies became part of the national dialogue. This fact, along with the great success of the Louisiana free Negro population whose numbers increased fourfold between 1803 and 1810, drove many racially conservative Americans to distraction (Berlin 1974, 116).

It is surprising, therefore, that Webb offers such a simplistic and conservative reading of the revolution in Santo Domingo, one designed I argue to posit a particularly American politics of racial identity. Through the character of Mr. Walters, the most two-dimensional of the protagonists, Webb is able to spirit away many of the complexities surrounding race in both countries. Mr. Walters, a black real estate speculator who amasses a considerable fortune through sheer hard work and intellect, stands at the pinnacle of respectable and cultured life in black Philadelphia, his taste and accomplishments rivaling those of any white man in the Americas. To his credit he holds particular affection for both the Garies and the Ellises, harboring Mrs. Ellis, Esther, and Caddy in his home during the riot and attempting to warn the Garies, using Mr. Ellis as an unsuccessful messenger, of the advancing mob. After the riot is over and some level of normality returns to their lives, he invites the remnants of both families, with the one exception of Clarence Garie, to remain under his roof. Eventually he marries Esther, installing himself as the new (good) husband and father, stepping in where both Mr. Garie and Mr. Ellis failed.

What makes Mr. Walters superior to the other men, particularly Mr. Ellis, is the fact of his singularity. While he is not white he is certainly not a slave or a servant, he has not even a trace of that nasty southern funkiness about him. Moreover, he has no family other than the instantly produced one that comes to him after the riot. The reader is not forced to consider, therefore, the possibility that Walters's body, and thus his character, might have been polluted by a (dirty) home or (grotesque) domesticity. At the same time, even as he is aggressive within the public sphere, particularly within the market, his blackness and the constant inconvenience that it causes, forces him to remain distant from his (white) business peers. Unlike the novel's villain, Mr. Stevens, he maintains his (black) self as a thing apart from the marketplace. From the first he is described as a creature who maintains a delicate balance between the black and the white, the inside and the out, such that there is always a (black) core that remains inviolate. "Mr. Walters was . . . of jet-black complexion, and smooth glossy skin. His aquiline nose, thin lips, and broad chin, were the very reverse of African in their shape, and gave his face a very singular appearance" (Webb [1857] 1997, 121–122). Walters is both "The black" and its inverse. Embedded within the skin of the Negro are the nose, the lips, the chin, but not the mind of the European. He is the symbol of the African's creation of a space for himself in western culture, a peculiar space that, however hemmed in by whiteness, remains purely black. Indeed, it is through the characterization of Walters that Webb is able to wrench his narrative out of and away from the competing and conflicting racial ideologies represented by the revolutionary figures of Santo Domingo while nonetheless appropriating the patina of virility and modernity with which they were associated.

During Mr. Garie's first visit with Walters he is transfixed by a portrait of Toussaint L'Ouverture in the uniform of a general. The piece stands among all the many markers of Walters's cultivated taste: the richly papered walls, the paintings of American and European masters, the rich vases and well-executed bronzes, and those "charming little bijoux which the French only are capable of conceiving" (Webb [1857] 1997, 121). In the midst of Euro-American refinement we find the black hero, as cultivated as his surroundings, yet nevertheless separate and ready for struggle. Thus, Toussaint stands as the hero who produced the revolution in Santo Domingo as a black event, a great triumph of pure Africanity. Moreover, Walters, as the reflection of Toussaint, is pressed to the service of guarding against the boundary crossings, the shuttling between black and white, household and market, that are the great obsessions of the novel. Walters argues vehemently against sending Clarence Garie away after the death of his parents, claiming that by passing, by producing himself as a (black) white man, Clarence can only bring himself to ruin:

> with all I have endured, and yet endure from day to day, I esteem myself happy in comparison with that man, who, mingling in the society of whites, is at the same time aware that he has African blood in his veins, and is liable at any moment to be ignominiously hurled from his position by the discovery of his origin. (Webb [1857] 1997, 276)

Again, we see an explicit disavowal of indeterminacy, this one mediated through a character heavily associated with the decidedly "black" revolution in Santo Domingo. Still, as C. L. R. James has suggested, narratives that would place Toussaint exclusively at the center of a black liberation struggle do damage to the truth of both Toussaint's life and the revolution with which his name is associated. James argues that the relationship of Toussaint to European, and in particular French culture, was anything but detached. At no point during the revolution in Santo Domingo did Toussaint relinquish his faith in the principles of the French Revolution. Even as he languished in a French prison during the final days of the insurgency he continued to think of himself as a citizen and patriot, loyal to France and the ideals of liberty, equality, and brotherhood. Until nearly the moment of his death he continued to plead with Bonaparte to recognize him as his loyal servant.

> [A]s to fidelity and probity, I am strong in my conscience, and I dare to say with truth that among all the servants of the State none is more honest than I. I was one of your soldiers and the first servant of the Republic in San Domingo. I am today wretched, ruined, dishonoured, a victim of my own services. Let your sensibility be touched at my position, you are too great in feeling and too just not to pronounce on my destiny. . . . (p. 264)

The tragic aspect of Toussaint L'Ouverture's life and career was that even as he was feared and hated by the French and the Creoles alike, he continued to be—like the fictional Walters—one of the first men of the West. Though nearly illiterate, he maintained an impressive correspondence with a variety of the best educated and most finely cultured figures in both Europe and the New World. He sent his two sons to be educated in France with the specific intent that they should learn to emulate the fine manners of French-born citizens. Moreover, his exceptional generosity toward the family that once enslaved him and whites in general is legendary.

Toussaint was a man of crisis. Had the blacks of Santo Domingo not risen it is likely that he would have lived out his life as an anonymous individual perhaps steadily climbing out of slavery and into the ranks of free black merchant and military society. Instead, he became caught up in a set of international crises: the revolution, the counterrevolution, the quixotic campaigns of Bonaparte, and the remarkable success of the slaves in Santo Domingo. He came into the (American) public consciousness as a prominent figure on the international stage, but one who was precisely embodied as a black, a man, an ex-slave, a revolutionary, and a general. No sense of indeterminacy is brooked in his representation.

I will develop further the notion that (national) crises produce particularized modes of corporeal existence in the second half of this chapter. I would like to end this section, however, by lingering for a moment on James's own discussion of yellow fever as it affected the combatants in the Santo Domingo revolution.

> It seems that this sickness is that which is called Yellow fever or Siamese disease; that this sickness reigns every year in the Antilles at the time of the passage of the sun in this hemisphere. . . . This sickness is heralded in some people by symptoms which are either slight pains or pains in the bowels or shivering. In others, the sickness affects them suddenly and kills within two days or three; but of those attacked not one fifth have escaped death. (Quoted in James 1963, 331)

Again, we see this dirty, engulfing yellow fever figured as the very sign of the boundary crossings that so offended the sensibilities of bourgeois Americans. Not only did it affect a dissolution of the body, it also broke down longstanding social distinctions, attacking "equally those who are in comfortable positions and who care for themselves well, and those whose means do not permit them to take precautions necessary to their health" (quoted in James 1963, 332). The implication in James work is that even as the combatants fought against each other they had necessarily to struggle against the dreaded yellow fever. The success of the revolution can be attributed, at least in part, then, to the havoc that the fever wreaked on unseasoned European soldiers. The battles in Santo Domingo took place precisely within bodies, so much so that at the end of the revolution racially indeterminate Santo Domingo gave way to black Haiti.

I make this point only to reiterate my earlier claim that what Webb is attempting is the aestheticization of a process of racial modernization in which racial stability, a stable blackness, is produced at the expense of a racial ambiguity and indeterminacy. This process was understood by Webb, moreover, as specifically "American," as deeply resistant to the influence of foreign interlopers. By reiterating "black" distinctiveness Webb celebrates American distinctiveness, suggesting an American public sphere that was not bounded by an insurmountable whiteness, by racism, but by a racialist ideology that at once privileged racial equality and racial difference. In the next section I will suggest that it is through public crisis, the riot, that the domestic institutions necessary for the enactment of this new racial order were both established and secured.

The Riot

Body and household operate as constitutive elements in a dynamic process of identity formation. Moreover, the relation between the two is heterodox, promiscuous, always inviting impurity, uncleanliness. Thus, the work of Frank Webb, like the work of maids, is to clean, to produce domesticity and order in an environment constantly threatened by disorder. In making this argument I have attempted to broaden consideration of the domestic, untethering it from narratives in which the "family" becomes a hermetically sealed unit threatened by the very members, the maids, who help reproduce it. I have not, however, suggested that what we see in *The Garies* is a critique of the family romance. Instead, I believe that Webb has attempted to produce a rather remarkable rearticulation of this narrative form in a distinctly black vernacular. He is faced at the outset, however, with the problem of how to establish the fiction of (black) bourgeois stability necessary to the production of a recognizable domesticity. Slaves, servants, runaways, and amalgamationists people the romance that Webb is attempting to synthesize. And yes, he does kill them off, cripple them, and simply drop them from the text with alacrity. Still, there is something messy about his narrative, something necessitating a great, unmerciful cleansing, if the work is to be read as representative, peculiar.

I have intimated already the productive nature of the riot, suggesting that it works to reproduce (black) households in the bourgeois forms that Webb privileges. Moreover, many of the images that Webb uses to describe the event are precisely images of cleaning, easily leading one to the conclusion that the riot represents in itself a necessary act of purification. After the newly formed black family has gathered in the home/fortress of Mr. Walters, Esther Ellis undergoes a remarkable transition, becoming ardent in her desire to defend her new home, so much so that she runs the risk of slipping outside of the logic of (black) respectability and becoming monstrous herself.

> As we came through the streets to-day, and I saw so many inoffensive creatures, who, like ourselves, have never done these white wretches the least injury,—to see them and us driven from our homes by a mob of wretches, who can accuse us of nothing but being darker than themselves,—it takes all the woman out of my bosom, and makes me feel like a—" here Esther paused, and bit her lip to prevent the utterance of a fierce expression that hovered on the tip of her tongue. (Webb [1857] 1997, 205)

Esther is in danger. Like the Garies, who will shortly meet their bloody fate, she is on the verge of becoming unspeakable, illegible. She is almost a—. And yet we see unleashed in her a fury so powerful and so pure that it attracts all to her. Mr. Walters first recognizes his own desire for Esther during this scene.

Thus, the protestations of her family and friends are swept aside and Esther is allowed to stay with the men to load their guns during battle.

It is not this action, however, that earns the reverential respect that will stick with her throughout the text. In a novel with such a rigid and clearly defined logic of gender hierarchy Esther could only sully herself with such manly behavior. Instead, it is when Esther reverts back to her original state, a role defined by an all-encompassing domesticity, that she gains her own presence. When a small fire is made in the war room no one takes much notice of it until one of the cinders flies from the hearth and onto the pile of cartridges laying near at hand. "Esther alone, of the whole party, retained her presence of mind; springing forward, she grasped the blazing fragment and dashed it back again into the grate. All this passed in a few seconds, and in the end Esther was so overcome with excitement and terror, that she fainted outright" (Webb [1857] 1997, 209). Perhaps it is too much to say that Esther's act of heroism is little more than the typically domestic practice of "taking out the ashes." Still, the logic of cleanliness is altogether apparent here. Esther saves the nascent black family of which she is a part, as well as her own femininity, her own legibility within domestic ideology, by reestablishing her role as literal guardian and caretaker of the hearth.

That the reader recognizes this fact is so important to the continuation of Webb's narrative strategies that he does not allow this already heavily didactic scene to carry the entire burden of representation. Only a few pages before Esther's heroic actions Walters meets Caddy and Kinch on the stairs, carrying up a huge pot of boiling water. "Is it possible Caddy," asked Mr. Walters, "that your propensity to dabble in soap and water has overcome you even at this critical time? You certainly can't be going to scrub?" (Webb [1857] 1997, 207). Caddy assures Walters that she has no such plans and then continues about her business. At a key point in the battle, however, Caddy does indeed make her mark as an extraordinary household manager and domestic warrior. As the white mob seems certain to overtake the house, their axes already chopping at the front door, Caddy and Kinch open an upstairs window and poor a noxious combination of boiling hot water and cayenne pepper onto the heads of the assailants below, thus saving the entire household. " 'We gave 'em a settler, didn't we, Mr. Walters?" asked Caddy, as he entered the room. 'It takes us; we fight with hot water. This, said she, holding up a dipper, is my gun. I guess we made 'em squeal" (Webb [1857] 1997, 214). Finally Caddy, a character whose "will to clean" has up to now bordered on the perverse, has been reintegrated into a proper domestic enterprise. She literally cleans away the white interlopers from the black household, using domesticity as a powerful—and appropriately female—mode of defense.

Still, even this process, this cleansing, is full of ambiguity, a dirtiness that is never quite resolved in the text. The riot brings to a head not only the virulent, ugly racism of white Americans but also, and importantly, the pressing questions of class and class loyalty that must necessarily perplex any person reading the novel. The representation in *The Garies* of the white working classes is, in fact, almost entirely negative. Not only is the riot described as a largely, though not exclusively, proletarian affair, but it is also these same white workers who constantly plague the lives of the protagonists. White servants insult Charlie. White workers refuse to take him as an apprentice. And white hooligans not only attack his family but also burn down his home. Moreover, this cleansing riot, this riot purported to be by and of the working classes, has its own history. It was clearly modeled on a number of violent "race" riots that took place in the antebellum Northeast, particularly the Philadelphia riot of 1834, a riot that Eric Lott maintains worked to produce a blackness distinct from the whiteness of the "white" working classes, disestablishing in particular the dirty notion of the "black" Irishman.[13] As a consequence, the riot comes to us as an already well-established character, one with a past and a contradictory present.

Webb's present (1857) was one yet marred by the ugliest practices of American slavery. So it is not just a passing observation I make when I point out the fact that the riot, and the resistance to it, are not the actions of either slaves or slavers. It is not a whipping, a fight between master and slave, a run toward freedom, nor is it the simple act of reading or writing. Indeed, incredulous responses to demonstrations of Black American literacy are all but disallowed in the text. This conflagration, though it continues the themes of violent attack so omnipresent within slave and abolitionist literature, is figured as an act that is specifically not defined by enslavement, but by the notions of freedom, individuality, race, and community that were congealing in the antebellum Northeast. This (northern) violence is figured, then, as a thing apart, the demonstration not of helplessness, nor inability, but of presence and definition. The race riot is not possible without the race. The point would not have been lost on Webb's readers, all of whom were being asked to imagine not just an end to slavery but also the beginning of a Black American community and a Black American literature. Stowe points to just this fact when she asks, "Are the race at present held as slaves capable of freedom, self-government, and progress?" Can these blacks exist as anything other than slaves, can they clean up, rid themselves of the fetor from their none too distant pasts? I have asked that we reconsider the riot as a figure of cleaning, an event that finally rids the community of that sticky southernness with which it has been plagued, helping to produce it as cleanly and distinctly black. I ask now that we consider its utility in the production of a literature defined by its peculiarity, a literature that is not southern, not abolitionist, and not exactly American.

What I am suggesting is that the riot works to announce a peculiar Black American literature by bringing into play not only the antiproletarian rhetorics to which I have alluded already but also the very antiabolitionist, antislave rhetoric against which the work reacts. The phrase, "I am no abolitionist" is repeated constantly in the text. Moreover, the novel allows a fair amount of hostility to the very bourgeois communities out of which it is most often imagined that abolitionism developed. Webb suggests repeatedly that northern charity and philanthropy were but the shadows of a bald capitalism precisely attuned to the rhythms of white supremacy. The white upper classes of Philadelphia and environs are sometimes figured, as with Mrs. Bird, as wellsprings of old-fashioned domestic values that remain so pristine as to override the overwhelming (white) aversion to blacks. At the same time, Webb regularly demonstrates not simply the hypocrisy of white bourgeois characters but also the means by which codes of bourgeois domesticity enable this same hypocrisy. When Mrs. Stevens, the wife of the villain whom we will take up shortly, finds that young Clarence and Emily Garie are enrolled in the same school as her own children, she sabotages the family by expertly manipulating the discursive tools of polite society, a society that announces itself precisely through rhetorics of philanthropy and charity. First she intercepts Mrs. Kinney as she is on her way to a meeting of "a female missionary society for evangelizing the Patagonians" (Webb [1857] 1997, 154). After persuading that lady to let her use her name, she visits Mrs. Roth, a lady who "swore by Mrs. Kinney," and thus armed, confronts Mrs. Jordan, the proprietor of the small school in question.

> [I]f this matter was known to me alone, I should remove my daughter and say nothing more about it; but, unfortunately for you, I find that, by some means or other, both Mrs. Kinney and Mrs. Roth have become informed of the circumstance, and are determined to take their children away. I thought I would act a friend's part by you, and try to prevail on you to dismiss these two coloured children at once. I so far relied upon your right judgment as to assure them that you would not hesitate for a moment to comply with their wishes; and I candidly tell you, that it was only by my so doing that they were prevented from keeping their children at home to-day. (Webb [1857] 1997, 158)

It only takes a moment or two before the spinster teacher tallies her expenses and assets and sends the children packing, thereby doing her part to maintain stability in a community in which she is only marginally and tentatively a member. Honor, respect, friendship and propriety have been maintained, even as the teacher cringes at the vulgarity of her actions. Mrs. Stevens, however, might raise her head even higher in society. Again, she has acted the part of the good neighbor, giving to the young teacher the very fruits of her domestic labors: her children and her gossip. In the process she has masterfully utilized the very tools of the philanthropist and the civic activist in another successful foray against the steady efforts to establish black presence in civil society.

Webb regularly treats the reader to such scenes, allowing no ambiguity whatsoever in his articulation of bourgeois—and abolitionist—complacency in the demoralization of the free black community. After Charlie's return from Warmouth he becomes obsessed with the idea of reestablishing familial normality by taking a job and picking up where his father failed. He is met at every turn, however, by prejudice against his race that interestingly enough has taken hold precisely among the liberal whites from whom he might have expected support. Tellingly, Charlie who, unlike his father, has become an expert drawer and penman, is rebuked by whites as he attempts to enter as a fully defined agent within the field of representation. Where his father built Charlie writes. As Charlie mails his first letter to a respective employer, Webb wastes no time alerting the reader to what a powerful and propitious act this is:

> How many more had stopped that day to add their contributions to the mass which Charlie's letter now joined? Merchants on the brink of ruin had deposited missives whose answer would make or break them; others had dropped upon the swelling heap tidings which would make poor men rich—rich men richer; maidens came with delicately written notes, perfumed and gilt-edged, eloquent with love—and cast them amidst invoices and bills of lading. Letters of condolence and notes of congratulation jostled with each other as they slid down the brass throat; widowed mothers' tender epistles to wandering sons; the letters of fond wives to absent husbands; erring daughters' last appeals to outraged parents; offers of marriage; invitations to funerals; hope and despair; joy and sorrow; misfortune and success—had glided in one almost unbroken stream down that ever-distended and insatiable brass throat. (Webb [1857] 1997, 288)

I doubt that it would be possible to represent any more graphically how writing, and "anonymous" communication generally, holds together the calculus of market and household that I have been at pains to demonstrate. Love notes and bills of lading, mothers's tender epistles, and business invoices are all literally bundled together in a standardized process of mass communication. The promiscuity of the various—and varying—discursive modes on display works, moreover, to produce none other than the grotesque body, the "distended and insatiable brass throat" with which we have been so much concerned.

More important still is the fact that by the time Charlie's letter finally reaches its destination, Charlie has himself been figured as grotesque. The fact of standardized communications removes the impress of the author's hand from his text. It separates the fact of the black's body from the necessity of his representation. Charlie's clear prose and standard script both recommend him to his potential employers and hide the fact of his peculiarity, returning him to a state of disembodiment from which the black is excluded already. When he presents his (black) body at the offices of Mr. Western, a drawling southerner, and Mr. Twining, a parsimonious Yankee, the latter objects to allowing the black child, no matter how skilled, to apprentice in the office. When confronted with the fact that such apprentices are numerous in the South, he responds, "Ah, but New Orleans is a different place; such a thing never occurred in Philadelphia" (Webb [1857] 1997, 291). Mr. Western then counters, "You Northern people are perfectly incompwehensible. You pay taxes to have niggers educated, and made fit for such places—and then won't let them fill them when they are pwepared to do so. I shall leave you, then, to tell them we can't take him. I doosed sowwy for it—I like his looks" (Webb [1857] 1997, 292).

Here we have what seems to be a striking reversal of the anti-southern logic that has permeated the text. Mr. Western is able to see Charlie for what he is, a particularly gifted black child who is as capable, if not more so, as any of his peers. We have not gotten away, however, from the notion of (southern) uncleanliness. Instead, I would suggest that Webb allows and respects southern difference as long as that difference is clearly marked, as long as it does not pass itself off as bourgeois normality.

Mr. Western presents a particularly fine model for the relationship among body, text, and self that Webb is attempting to establish. The fact of his southernness is so omnipresent, so pressing that it is graphically represented within the text itself. "You northern people are perfectly incompwehensible," he argues, suggesting that their representations of themselves do not correspond to the fact of the peculiarities of their ethnicity. They give the black the tools to create himself as disembodied "equal," while simultaneously vigorously policing the boundaries between "black" and "white" bodies. Western's southern peculiarity screams out at every turn, however. It is anything but incompwehensible. He can accept Charlie's presence in the office because it does nothing to detract from his own clearly defined race and ethnicity. "We need not care what others say—evewybody knows who we are and what we are?" (Webb [1857] 1997, 292).

Charlie later meets a similar fate in the office of Thomas Blatchford, a prominent Philadelphia abolitionist and bank note engraver. Upon applying at Blatchford's office, Charlie is met with the instant approval of the kind-hearted gentleman. Soon thereafter Mrs. Ellis and Mr. Walters meet with Blatchford to negotiate the terms of Charlie's employment and set a time for him to begin work. When Charlie enters the shop on what is to be his first morning of gainful employment, he is met by a hostile group of journeymen who threaten to quit if Blatchford allows him to stay. " 'We won't work with niggers!' cried one; 'No nigger apprentices!' cried another; and No niggers—no niggers!' was echoed from all parts of the room" (Webb [1857] 1997, 297). Blatchford collapses under the weight of their demands and sends Charlie on his way, explaining that he had just received several large orders for new bank notes and that a strike just then would ruin him. Again, we see a racial liberalism in which the black is tolerated, sympathized with, even championed, as long as he is not embodied, not present. Blatchford has given himself over totally to a logic of capital gain in which the will literally to produce more capital eclipses all of his vaunted claims of racial egalitarianism. Abolitionism exists in this logic only at the level of representation and fails in the presence of a single black body.

Tellingly, Charlie finally gains a position from a Mr. Burrell, Mr. Blatchford's less successful business associate, who specifically rejects abolitionism. "Now, you know, my dear, that no one would call me an Abolitionist," he says to his young wife as he relates to her the events that had taken place in Blatchford's office (Webb [1857] 1997, 300). Burrell holds, however, a set of ideals that are deeper and more genuinely felt than Blatchford's professed abolitionism. He has produced himself as a proper northern bourgeois, one who is able to manage the difficulties of maintaining a loving domestic life and an active presence in the market. His anger at Charlie's treatment is turned to action by the machinations of his young wife and infant son, who together appeal to a part of him that can never be sullied by the exigencies of the market. Moreover, when he brings the matter before the two elderly men who work for him, and had worked for his father before him, he is met with a response definitive of "proper" relations between workers and employers.

> Laws me! Colour is nothing after all; and black fingers can handle a graver as well as white ones, I expect.
>
> I thought it best to ask you, to avoid any after difficulty. You have both been in the establishment so long, that I felt that you ought to be consulted.
>
> You needn't have taken that trouble. . . . You might have known that anything done by your father's son, would be satisfactory to us. I never had anything to do with coloured people, and haven't anything against them; and as long as you are contented I am. (Webb [1857] 1997, 304)

The point is, of course, that Blatchford's establishment is run by the dictates of the market. When the workers reject Charlie they reject not only his black body but also a developing system of management in which decisions are made by a specialized set of managers and then announced to operatives who presumably respond appropriately. Burrell is certainly bourgeois, but for him this is an identity that is also produced out of (domestic) notions of loyalty and right feeling. His workers gain not only income from him but also affection and a certain intergenerational continuity that lead them to accept his direction.

Even more striking still is the fact that prior to Charlie's employment, prior to his entrance into public life, his race is announced. Colour may be nothing at all, but this does not mean that one cannot and should not notice the obvious racial distinction displayed by those black and white fingers that have taken hold of the lathe. Webb must always reject earlier racialist notions that allow for only a nebulous (public) blackness. Thus, even as he establishes this tableau of paternalism he is careful not to allow the same domestic and racial instability that the work specifically rejects. This argument is brought into focus when one considers the fact that the story of the Garies repeats in striking detail the infamous story of Ralph Quarles, a rich, southern planter who in the early 1800s bought his slave wife, Lucy Jane Langston (Horton and Horton 1997, 105). Again, interracial domestic intimacy is allied with slavery such that the black's closeness to the white is exactly that which is understood to impede public presence, to impede liberty. That this story is eclipsed by the equally available history of the 1834 Philadelphia race riot represents, I believe, an attempt on Webb's part to refashion an older, more ambiguous discourse of blackness into the stark, binaristic notions represented by the riot while calling into question the severe divisions between (white) labor and (white) capital that allow such an event to occur.

The logic becomes quite tricky here. For while Webb insists upon a clear distinction between worker and bourgeois, market and household, black and white, he is also searching for a means by which to negotiate these divisions. The notion of right feeling comes, then, to operate as a means by which various communities can interact and communicate. Mr. Burrell is not black, not labor, and not female, but he is able to access these peculiar communities through established notions of civility. This stance is preferable in Webb's schema to a polite racial liberalism, even abolitionism, because, on the one hand, it does not necessitate mixing, the pollution of the household and the body, but on the contrary privileges traditional divisions of race and class. On the other, it does allow for some level of civility between black and white, even if it is a civility based on the mutual recognition—and celebration—of racial distinction.

The rich characterization of the novel's villain, Mr. Stevens, stems from the fact that he is responsible for advancing so much of the aesthetic project that I have just described. It is Stevens who by initiating the riot helps to stabilize the awkward project of interpellation, of hailing a Black American community into existence, that Webb is attempting. Stevens is literally and figuratively a minstrel as he walks the thin line separating classes and races. He is the consummate performer such that *The Garies'* narrative is driven by the expectation that he will be found out, revealed as a fraud, returned to an original and natural state, one that reflects the grotesque households through which he has been produced: "he was rather above than below the middle height, with round shoulders, and long, thin arms, finished off by disagreeable looking hands" (Webb [1857] 1997, 124). Stevens, as we will see below, is always engaged in a process of concealing what those "disagreeable-looking" hands demonstrate, that he is a fraud, one who cannibalizes those around him, devouring them, wrapping himself in their skins in a vain attempt to reembody himself, to wear the respectability and vigor of his victims.

Stevens, or "Slippery George," is a "pettifogging" attorney, one whose speciality is aiding the most criminally active, if legally astute, members of both the gentry and the working classes. He is totally a man of the market, one who would and does gladly give up the rituals and practices of bourgeois domesticity for the sake of economic gain. As such he actualizes the profound danger posed by individual—and individualistic—desire not mediated through properly composed households. Specifically, he demonstrates how a man like Walters, a man of the market, could be led to monstrous excess without the restraint of (black) family and (black) community. "If I was black," Stevens tells his wife in a conversation about Walters, "I would sacrifice conscience and everything else to the acquisition of wealth" (Webb [1857] 1997, 127).

Black or not, Stevens does acquire wealth and he does it the old-fashioned way. He breaks up black or ostensibly black households. The riot was, we are told, not simply the result of pent-up white working-class resentment to blacks, abolitionists, and racial liberals, but instead a well-thought-through white bourgeois conspiracy—concocted by Stevens—to snatch up property in an area of the city with a high rate of black home ownership.

> You are probably aware that a large amount of property in the lower part of the city is owned by niggers; and if we can create a mob and direct it against them, they will be glad to leave that quarter, and remove further up into the city for security and protection. Once get the mob thoroughly aroused, and have the leaders under our control, we may direct its energies against any parties we desire; and we can render the district so unsafe, that property will be greatly lessened in value—the houses will rent poorly, and many proprietors will be happy to sell at very reduced prices. (Webb [1857] 1997, 166)

Thus, we have a succinctly stated, remarkably clear articulation of the practice of redlining in American cities, a practice that has been so persistent because it has such marked utility.

The production of the black area as the riot area not only forces capital upward and inward toward a narrower conglomeration of the bourgeois but also reestablishes the blackness of the black community. As the black runs from the privacy of her peculiar domestic sphere, she is more easily seen. Her body and the domestic arrangements through which it is figured become available for the visual consumption of the mob.

> Throughout the day parties of coloured people might have been seen hurrying to the upper part of the city: women with terror written on their faces, some with babes in their arms and children at their side, hastening to some temporary place of refuge, in company with men who were bending beneath the weight of household goods. (Webb [1857] 1997, 203)

Women, children, men under the weight of household goods, the entire tableau of black domesticity running, are on display in this passage. Even though the logic of antebellum race riots was to remove blacks and blackness, very often just the opposite was accomplished. These eruptions of violence tended to force blacks to establish firmer intraracial social ties, as well as construct more clearly defined ghettos.[14] The point is that the black, as a clearly defined agent who stands in contradistinction to the white, is made visible, legible within the public sphere. It is not lost on Webb, however, that this process takes place through the manipulation of minstrelesque performances enacted most successfully by Mr. Stevens.

Shortly after Stevens announces the plan to his associates he is revealed to be immersed even more deeply within the text's class and race masquerades than we had first imagined. The timely death of a penniless aunt and Stevens's subsequent inheritance of a set of letters that his mother had written to her estranged father reveal that Stevens is actually a long lost cousin of Mr. Garie, a first cousin, in fact. Stevens's southern mother had married below her station to an abusive northern husband. She had subsequently been cut off by her aristocratic southern family, the same family of which Mr. Garie was now the scion. The fact of his impure genealogy becomes an inescapable reality for the reader. Stevens is at once a dirty southerner and a dirty mechanic. Moreover, he compounds these sins by refusing to embrace these identities, instead using them to attack his own southern relations, the Garies, and to manipulate the workingmen who are his natural compatriots.

I repeat my claim that Stevens is always in performance. I will also go further to suggest that all of his actions leading up to the riot are designed to demonstrate his skill and alacrity as a minstrel, one who works with and through any number of media. We know already that he is an uncouth lawyer, skilled at manipulating written representations of order to further ends that always tend toward disorder. The contract, both written and verbal, is Mr. Stevens's primary mode, his most dastardly crimes always being trumped up as civil business transactions between peers.

When Stevens walks one afternoon into the old clothes shop belonging to Kinch's father and commands the young boy to array him in the worst apparel that he has to offer, he is only continuing in the performative vein out of which his character had been established already. "I never knew before, said he, mentally, "how far a suit of clothes goes towards giving one the appearance of a gentleman" (Webb [1857] 1997, 184). The point is obvious. Stevens engages as fully in the spectacle of transvestism when he is in the fine garments of a gentleman as he does in the shabby drag of the minstrel performer. Interestingly, many of the participants in the 1834 Philadelphia riot wore black masks and old clothes in order to represent a black figure that was not yet wholly available within antebellum America. The inauthenticity of these false representations is always, however, uncovered. The ostensibly white performers become so beguiled by their own masquerade that they allow all manner of clues as to their "real" identities.

While Stevens is trying on his costume he loses the slip of paper on which he had written down the targets of the riot that he was then planning. Moreover, in his rush to rendezvous with Whitticar, his underworld contact and operative, he decides not to change back into his own clothing, instead leaving his card with Kinch so that the boy can return them to his home. Kinch, or Snowball as Stevens calls him, does not, however, correspond to the image of him that Stevens has constructed, the image that he is attempting to access through his own drag performance. Instead Kinch, a character who will later establish himself in remarkably close proximity to the dandy figure that was a staple of minstrel performance, exists within the alternate (black) narrative that I have attempted to describe. After some small bit of bumbling he eventually gives both the list and the card to Mr. Walters, thereby alerting "the black community" not only to Stevens's treachery, not only to the impending riot, but also to its own existence within the public sphere. The addresses that the list contains operate collectively as a geography of the nascent Black American community. It demonstrates that which needs defending, that which can only be maintained through communal action.

Even more to the point, it demonstrates a (black) peculiarity that is not bourgeois, not abolitionist, nor even working class. Instead, the note, the card, and the revelations that they engender establish a "true" blackness that stands in contradistinction to both the farcical notions out of which Stevens produces his racist plot and the competing articulations of communal identity. The black exists as a thing unto itself and not simply as the adjunct of an already established whiteness. Indeed, the novel is always eager to ridicule any example of black presence that is produced through white racialist fantasies. In one of the most interesting scenes in the novel, Webb forces Stevens into the character of the monstrous black dandy that might have been so easily hoisted onto our good fellow Kinch. As he leaves the bar in which he has just met with Whitticar, he seems to have transformed himself, through the very double dealing at which he is expert, into the "racey" character that he presumably only represents.

> The coat that temporarily adorned the person of Mr. Stevens was of peculiar cut and colour—it was, in fact, rather in the rowdy style, and had, in its pristine state, bedecked the member of a notorious fire company. These gentry had for a long time been the terror of the district in which they roamed, and had rendered themselves highly obnoxious to some of the rival factions on the borders of their own territory. (Webb [1857] 1997, 186)

It is almost inevitable, then, that Stevens should run into one of these hostile gangs just at the moment when all of his dirty dealing has seemingly been done. They claim him as a "Ranger" (roamer, runner) and viciously beat him, ignoring the (false) protestations that his clothing does not reflect his character. Finally, they take him to a wheelwright's shop and cover his face completely with tar. Thus, Stevens becomes not only the bourgeois decked out in the trappings of the white working classes but also the very black beast that he has attempted to represent.[15] "Hallo! here's a darkey!" a group of young gentry exclaims as they encounter him on his way home. "Ha, ha! Here's a darkey—now for some fun!" they continue as they force him into a rain barrel (Webb [1857] 1997, 189). When finally Stevens recognizes Mr. Morton, one of his co-conspirators, he manages to get the intoxicated man to help him reach his house, trying (unsuccessfully) to wash the tar from his face along the way. After they reach their destination, Mr. Morton jokes to Mrs. Stevens that her husband has brought "a gentleman from Africa with him" (Webb [1857] 1997, 192). And of course this sentiment is remarkably close to the truth. Stevens has brought home the very frightening gentleman from Africa that so plagued the imaginations of white America, the very beast bent upon defiling the various domestic enterprises on which the country had been founded, the beast that as we will find below was both vicious and immensely dangerous to its neighbors. The beast that kills.

It has been established already that the attack on the Garies was successful, killing both Mr. and Mrs. Garie and their newborn child. What I have not established is that it was during this act of extinguishing the Garies that Stevens also extinguishes his last hold on bourgeois respectability. The Garies are never warned of the mob that is approaching their home. Moreover, they never know of their relation to the Stevens family, nor the fact that Stevens has committed himself to removing them as an impediment to a vast fortune. His plan is, of course, to use another to commit the actual act, preferring to keep himself clear and clean of the charge of murder. Yet when the presumed assailant, McCloskey, proves incapable of committing the crime, Stevens panics and pulls the trigger himself, killing Mr. Garie. Mrs. Garie, though she has run from the house with the children and hidden herself in the woodshed, dies at the same moment as her husband, silently giving birth to their stillborn child, the very emblem of the interracialism that the novel—and novelist—have attempted to counteract. McCloskey meanwhile secures the will of the dead gentleman, keeping it for years in order to extort money from Stevens and his children after him, until on his death bed he reveals his horrible secret and returns the will. Stevens, old and demented by the time of this final revelation, a character who has become like Mr. Ellis a grotesquely hyper-embodied creature, repeats the trauma of his counterpart and throws himself to the street below as the constable with the "keen gray eyes" comes to reveal him for what he is.

I have attempted to broaden the discussion of domestic ideology within American literature and culture to suggest that the domestic is implicated not simply in the production of class and political identity but in the production of racial identity as well. Specifically, I have nominated the "household" (versus the family) as a more accurate lens by which to bring into focus the complex manner in which individuals are rendered visible within the public sphere. In the process, I have rejected the notion that black presence was disallowed because of the "fact of blackness." Instead, I have argued that the black did enter the public sphere, but only as an already embodied individual. Moreover, the household operates as the primary means of this corporealization, producing properly black subjects from the motley and often racially indeterminate group of pre-modern, strange[16] figures who dotted the landscape of antebellum America and its environs. Further, I have suggested that the riot that stands at the center of *The Garies* should not be understood as distinct from the processes of domestication with which we have been concerned. Instead, even as I recognize the potential for radical destabilization within the riot, I have suggested it as part of the process of "cleansing" that was central to the production of a peculiar Black American domesticity and a peculiar Black American literature. In the next chapter, I look to the work of Harriet Wilson who, like William Wells Brown before her, is never able to domesticate fully the desirous bodies that she puts on display. On the contrary, the ambiguous, mixed-race subject so very apparent in *Clotel* makes one last effort to be both seen and heard, whether she disrupts the blackness of the Black American literary project or not.

Four • BLACK, WHITE, AND YELLER

> You can philosophize, gentle reader, upon the impropriety of such unions, and preach dozens of sermons on the evils of amalgamation. Want is a more powerful philosopher and preacher.
>
> —*Harriet Wilson*

I would like to pause for a moment in order to make explicit some of the concerns that have helped frame the rhetorical strategies and theoretical practices of this study. Specifically, I want to acknowledge the fact that my readings of corporeality and domesticity within the production of antebellum Black American fiction have been produced in response to long-established critical practices that emphasize the influence of sentimental and abolitionist fiction in the production of Black American literature. It is widely assumed, for example, that early Black American writers owe a great debt to Harriet Beecher Stowe and the army of "scribbling women," many of them abolitionists, of whom she was the exemplar. Indeed, the tendency to read the four novels produced by Black Americans prior to the Civil War as essentially derivative rescriptings of classic pieces of abolitionist fiction, including slave narratives,[1] continued more or less unabated until at least the late seventies, when Houston Baker, Barbara Christian, Barbara Smith, and Robert Stepto led a march away from stale narratives of influence and toward feminist, new critical, and poststructuralist forms of textual and cultural analysis.[2]

This prior emphasis on sentimental influence is not, however, simply an altogether outdated mode of inquiry. The self-conscious manipulation and critique of themes gathered from within sentimental and abolitionist fiction is obvious within antebellum Black American writing. Indeed, in the rush to produce a textually based, theoretically sophisticated practice of Black American literary criticism we often have missed opportunities to understand why and how the formation of a "Black American literature" has been so heavily overdetermined by the various discourses of the body, including not only race but gender and sexuality as well.[3] My work up to this point has been to offer readings of textual influence that do not take the antebellum preoccupation with black bodies and households as incidental, but as essential to the process of producing as "black" what might otherwise be regarded as sentimental, or abolitionist, or perhaps simply American. The idealist rhetorics of family, freedom, and nation are always juxtaposed with a black body that is taken to be beyond deciphering, both preceding and eclipsing its representation.

It can hardly be argued, therefore, that Black American authors found within the sentimental some natural and inevitable set of aesthetic practices ready to be reestablished within Black American literature. On the contrary, it was only with great effort that the sentimentality of Stowe and Richardson was able to establish its hegemony within "domestic" literatures, including that of Black Americans. Moreover, as I will demonstrate at length below, the hegemony of the sentimental is always contested, always on the verge of dissolution. In the case of Harriet Wilson's *Our Nig*, the author invokes the tropes of sentimentality—the young woman facing (sexual) danger, the couple separated by circumstance, the celebration of marriage and domesticity—in a manner that is marked by its tentativeness and constant deferral. I would argue, in fact, that one cannot understand how sentimentality operates in *Our Nig*, how its hegemony is established, unless one also understands the methods of its contestation. Even as the reading public saw the precipitous rise of sentimental fiction within the nineteenth century, they nonetheless had available to them a wealth of writing that did indeed take up matters of the heart and hearth, but that was nonetheless hostile to sentimentality.[4] By making this point I hope to force serious consideration of the rather profound critique of sentimentality that is abundantly apparent in *Our Nig*. In my reading of the novel, therefore, I will not continue to rely as heavily as I have on the established models of the sentimental, especially *Uncle Tom's Cabin*. Instead, I will demonstrate the use to which Wilson put alternative narratives of the domestic, particularly those that insist upon the necessity of violence—physcial violence—in the production of conjugal union.

In making this move to "alternative narratives of the domestic," I will establish more firmly my claim that the great conceptual triumph of sentimental fiction was not only, as Nancy Armstrong has cogently argued, that it helped produce an innocent and disinterested subjectivity that allowed for the transparency of bourgeois social and political hegemony but also, and importantly, that in doing so the family, the nuclear family, came to be synonymous with the domestic, a thing apart from household, or clan. The messiness of the domestic enterprise is belied, allowing for the unfettered and unspoken politics of (bourgeois) class and (white) race hegemony. Further, I will not allow the assumption that the essentially political and socially transformative nature of domestic fiction (including sentimental fiction) was a reality that has been revealed to us only recently. Instead, I make the argument that Armstrong's work is essentially derivative, if powerfully so, reproducing a critique of domesticity that was fully available to both European and American writers of the nineteenth century. Indeed, the boom in the literature of manners and morality that she documents is itself evidence of the tentative nature of the sentimental enterprise.

Both sentimentalists and their detractors were consumed, in fact, with the same twisted logic that celebrated individuality, free will, and "disinterested affection" in the production of marriages and families, a logic that nonetheless insisted that this will and individuality be squelched at the very moment the marriage contract was enacted. The individual freely chooses a deindividualizing bondage. Importantly, it has long been understood that the myth of equality within marriage is always produced through forms of textual representation: the marriage contract, the sentimental novel, and so forth. It does not take too great a conceptual leap to understand, then, how antisentimentalists (Engels, Sade, and von Sacher-Masoch to name only the most obvious) not only constantly insisted upon the inevitability of violence within the domestic enterprise but also that this violence might be properly understood to be a factor of the formal (textual) strategies by which domesticity is represented.

Frederick Engels's *Origin of the Family* (1884) produces a narrative of family, of familiarity, that places the institution squarely within the processes of social and economic development that resulted in the production of the modern West. More to the point, Engels understood that the myth of individualism undergirding the marriage contract was the same myth by and through which bourgeois class hegemony had been enacted.[5] It is incorrect, then, to assume, as many have, that the relation that Engels draws between work and family life is somehow only metaphorical. The relationship of husband to wife is not *like* the relationship of owner to worker, owner to slave. On the contrary, they are one and the same. "The first class opposition that appears in history coincides with the development of the antagonism between man and woman in monogamous marriage" (Engels [1884] 1942, 58).

Engels struggles throughout the text to establish more securely this rather pessimistic reading of the marriage relation. In doing so he places his work in solid opposition to the logic of sentimentalism and the literature of sentimentalism that dominated the literary and philosophical landscape in which he worked. He goes so far as to suggest that family relations are based, not on sentiment and affection, but on a raw and antihumanist desire to produce and horde wealth. More to the point, Engels struggles in *Origin of the Family* to produce a narrative of family that is not based in the idealist (sentimental) modes with which he was familiar. He was particularly eager to move beyond the established narratives of bourgeois patriarchy and toward an essentially materialist history of the family. It should come as no surprise, then, that he relies as heavily as he does on the work of Lewis H. Morgan, an early physical anthropologist specializing in craniology. By doing so, Engels produces his narrative of family out of a set of incontrovertible sources—the skulls of indigenous Americans, instead of the suspect texts of Christianity and Western antiquity. Thus, the most stunning critique that Engels offers is not that families are sites of both reproduction and domination, but that this fact has been obscured by the means of its previous narrativizations. He writes:

> Modern civilized systems of law increasingly acknowledge first, that for a marriage to be legal, it must be a contract freely entered into by both partners, and secondly, that also in the married state both partners must stand on a common footing of equal rights and duties. . . . This typically legalist method of argument is exactly the same as that which the radical republican bourgeois uses to put the proletarian in his place. The labor contract is to be freely entered into by both partners. But it is considered to have been freely entered into as soon as the law makes both parties equal on *paper*. (Engels [1884] 1942, 64)

I would suggest that the triumph of *Origin of the Family* is essentially one of literary critique. Engels points out in no uncertain terms the sophistry of the marriage contract, the "document" that somehow renders invisible the immense differences in access and social standing between members of a marriage. Moreover, by following Morgan, Engels attempts to establish a narrative of marriage and family that does not take part in the same process of textual obfuscation. Instead, he seeks to establish through Morgan a sort of body history, one that escapes the idealist, text-based modes by which notions of "natural" familial relations had come to be represented. Engels evinces, in fact, a profound trust in bodies. The body always tells the correct story; it always represents true facts that can be gleaned, more or less easily, by the skilled observer. The history of the body's being is buried in flesh.[6]

In reading Harriet Wilson's *Our Nig* in relation to *Origin of the Family*, I am eager to understand not only how Wilson's own understanding of bodies and embodiment stands in relation to Engels's, but also why Wilson insists upon establishing the essentially violent character of the domesticity that she narrates, the same domesticity that produces the bodies on display in the text. Why is it necessary to the proper functioning of the white household that the black body be so viciously abused? I would suggest that what Wilson accesses through the representation of punches, slaps, lashes, and insults is the recognition not only that domesticity is founded upon and within systematic and historically entrenched modes of violence but also that it is itself one of these modes. Since the domestic is *the* primary vehicle by which bodies are brought into order, by which they are established as raced and gendered entities, it is necessarily violent because the process of racing and gendering subjects is always violent. That is to say, violence against bodies not only helps to establish a clean distinction between black and white but also does so precisely by foregrounding pain, hunger, freezing, and so on, none of which can ever be articulated fully. The very moment at which one expresses the most human of conditions—pain, for example—is the moment at which one announces an unbreachable gulf between self and other. The phrase "I hurt" may indeed invoke a great many emotional responses, but it cannot relay physical discomfort from one point to the other. Wilson's novel should not be understood, therefore, as the simple documentation of the horrors of white supremacist culture and the triumph over the same. Instead, we are compelled throughout to witness a violent process of black corporealization, in which a racially ambiguous individual is presumably produced as a black through the sadistic machinations of her allegedly white mistress. It is almost as if the black cannot be seen in the absence of abuse. She cannot be actualized in a properly sentimental novel. Instead, as we will see clearly below, she only gains presence when sentimentality is warped, when the Negro becomes so scarred that she can no longer be ignored.[7]

The fact of violence is, of course, well established in Engels. Still, he does understand the bourgeois marriage relation, however begrudgingly, as an advance over the more severe forms that come to us out of antiquity. His narrative is always framed by a hopefulness, a belief in the wizardry of modernization, an unshakable faith that the bourgeois marriage relation will transform into ever more productive and equitable forms of conjugality. Even as Engels marks the site at which patriarchy became the dominant mode within domestic relations, he also celebrates its passing, prophesying the coming of a new era. Unlike Engels, the "progress" that Wilson marks is always a halting, never quite finished business. Sentimentalism and the domestic relations that it attempts to narrate are always touch-and-go affairs in *Our Nig*. I would suggest in fact that Engels, unlike Wilson, never concedes the dialectical relationship of corporeality and domesticity. Bodies are not produced by domesticity, nor are they productive of it. Instead, they both exist as separate and distinct entities with bodies (in particular Morgan's native American skulls) acting only to reveal the "truth" of a heavily sentimentalized conjugality. For Wilson, however, bodies fall right and left in the wake of the bourgeois, white supremacist discourses of the domestic with which the novel is in dialogue, even as these same discourses work to reproduce certain modes of corporeality. Still, even as (black) bodies are scarred by their proximity to modes of domesticity that privilege (white male) bourgeois hegemony, they nonetheless can gain presence, face, and voice through this same process. The scars themselves help produce subjectivities that stand outside or, perhaps better put, alongside the logics of sentimentality. I would resist the impulse, however, to label these subjectivities as simply black, or "other." Instead, with Wilson we see at least the possibility that a self can be constructed, even if the mode of that construction is violence, that stands outside of both the logic of sentimentality and the logic of white supremacy.

I turn, then, to Leopold von Sacher-Masoch's *Venus in Furs* (1870), not only because the work offers yet another anti-sentimental narrative of domesticity, nor even that it expressly establishes the essentially violent nature of the domestic, but also because it offers a remarkably clear articulation of the means by which "alternate" subjectivities might be established in proximity to, if not exactly within, the sentimental. Von Sacher-Masoch is like Engels in that he refuses to deny the body in his narratives of domesticity. Thus, his critique of the marriage contract, a contract articulated precisely through sentimentalism, was that it belied the reality of the animal nature, especially that of women. Wanda, Venus in human form, is always in fur as she whips the body of her lover/slave, Severin/Gregor, the animal skin acting as a synecdoche for the cruel nature heretofore stifled by the established patriarchy of the cold North. It follows, then, that when men subjugate themselves to the contractual (sentimental) marriage agreement, when they accept the lie of women's equality, their trustworthiness within the domestic enterprise, they necessarily open themselves to attack and intimidation. The sentimental becomes not simply, as Engels would have it, the evocation of patriarchy or the transcendence of patriarchy. On the contrary, it represents the (female) triumph over patriarchy. Von Sacher-Masoch makes exactly this point in *Venus* when, after many pages, Severin finally places his signature on the document sealing his destiny.

> "You are shaking," said Wanda calmly. "Shall I guide your hand?"
>
> She gently took hold of my hand and my name appeared at the bottom of the contract. She read the two documents once more and placed them in the drawer that stood by the ottoman.
>
> "Good. Now give me your passport and your money." I took out my pocketbook and handed it to her; she examined the contents, nodded and put it away with the rest. . . .
>
> Suddenly she kicked me away, leapt up and pulled the bellrope. Three slender young Negresses appeared, like ebony carvings, all dressed in red satin and each with a rope in her hand. . . .
>
> She signaled, and before I knew what was happening, the three Negresses had thrown me to the ground, tied my hands and feet and secured my arms behind me like a man about to be executed. I could hardly move an inch.
>
> "Give me the whip, Haydee," ordered Wanda, with chilling composure. The Negress handed her mistress the whip on bended knee. . . .
>
> "Tie him to the pillar here."
>
> The blackamoors lifted me, wound a stout rope around my body and tied me upright to one of the massive pillars that held up the canopy of the big Italian bed.[8]

There is no way the reader can be left uncertain as to von Sacher-Masoch's attitude in relation to the sentimental (marriage) contract between man and woman, a contract that supposedly recognizes absolute equality between the two. What von Sacher-Masoch knows is that the contract simply unfetters that which is dangerous in woman, in woman's body, by precluding the practice of male against female violence that is the key to proper domesticity. When man agrees to no longer intimidate woman, to no longer treat her as a subordinate, he allows her to gain the upper hand. One must be either the hammer or the anvil. No intermediate state of domestic stasis is possible. Moreover, von Sacher-Masoch clearly understands the sentimental as the vehicle by which this monstrous state of affairs is enacted. Severin looks into the bewitching eyes of his beloved as he signs away his right to manhood. And when Wanda is confronted by the last emblems of Severin's resistance, the trembling that is the only marker left of the patriarchal common sense, she "gently" guides his hand, thereby throwing away even the semblance of male agency. His name is not written. It appears.

We have seen already that Engels understands the *false* notion of individual free will within the marriage relation to be one and the same with the *false* notion of individual free will within the relation between worker and owner. Von Sacher-Masoch, for his part, extends this observation to make explicit one of the more damning implications within Engels's work. The contractual relation between husband and wife is one and the same not only with that between owner and worker but also with that between master and slave. Von Sacher-Masoch is unlike Engels, however, in that he does not understand the contract as obscuring the violence in the relation between the dominant and the subordinate. Instead, he believes that the contract destabilizes necessary hierarchies—man over woman, owner over worker, master over slave, white over black—hierarchies on which civilization has been established, hierarchies that may indeed entail violence, but that nonetheless keep the greater violence of the natural, the anarchistic, at bay. His is an essentially conservative, Arnoldian conception of culture, one that reflects immense anxiety in relation to the discourse of individuality that had taken hold in the practice of modern philosophy and literature precisely because that discourse belies the "fact" that *all* human interaction is overdetermined by biology. *Venus in Furs* is best understood, therefore, not as a piece of profligate, uncivilized proto-literature but, on the contrary, as the ratification of a set of societal norms, including not only patriarchy and bourgeois hegemony but also racialism and white supremacy, norms that take the body as a fact that can never be dismissed.

The words *slave, slaves*, and *slavish* are repeated no less than seventy-nine times in *Venus*. I have struggled, then, to reorient our understanding of the text away from its associations with pornography and toward its consideration of modernity and modernization because this allows us to make sense of the profoundly conservative racial politics being articulated by von Sacher-Masoch. The Negresses who aid Wanda in her first real thrashing of Severin/Gregor speak volumes about the newly modernized race relations of both Europe and the New World. Here we have women (women!) only one or two steps out of slavery who dare to handle roughly the male, bourgeois, and decidedly white Severin with impunity. Their presence demonstrates the farcical, nonsensical nature of a state of affairs in which class, race, and gender are taken to be secondary aspects of an *individualized*, disembodied subjectivity. The Negresses are likened to carved statues suddenly come to life. They wear the very satin that envelops the bodies of their superiors, but it is nonetheless red (I am tempted to say "read"), thereby broadcasting the fact of their profligacy and sensuality. And if the reader has difficulty with these all too obvious clues, he is immediately confronted with the specter of Haydee, Haiti, the monstrous presence that would undue the racial common sense on which civilization had been constructed, the very presence that aids in a process by which the markers of white, male, subjectivity (passport and money) are thrown into the (Oriental) ottoman while the newly vulnerable white body is tied to a bed produced by racially suspect Italians. Von Sacher-Masoch creates the monstrous, black presence of the Negresses as diametrically opposed to the possibility of patriarchal order, an order that somehow has been short-circuited in Severin.

He drives this point relentlessly forward, bringing the Negresses back for a number of Severin's beatings and even allowing them to use him as a work animal whom they hitch to a plow and drive through the fields, thereby forcing him even more deeply into his own body while denying their own. Moreover, when these wildly incongruous Negresses (the action takes place, after all, in nominally white Europe) are not present they are very often replaced by racially and nationally ambiguous Jews. A Jew finds Severin the photograph that initiates his obsession with the figure of Venus. A Jew sells him the second-hand books that start him, as a university student, on the road to supersensuality. His first real love is stolen away from him by a rich Jew. A Jewish coachman delivers Wanda and Severin to the train that eventually deposits them in Italy, where they will act upon their perverse contract. On the way, Severin shares his third-class compartment with greasy-haired Jews. And of course, his object of desire is identified herself as Wanda von Duna*jew*. The racialism here is impossible to ignore. The Jew is monstrous. He is that which is both ancient and modern, yet not of the nation in which he resides. The logic of individualism, however, would have us not consider the fact that he is decidedly and unalterably a Jew, a thing that must be kept apart even as it constantly asserts and inserts its messy, sticky subjectivity.[9] When Wanda finally does find a lover to replace Severin, thereby restoring patriarchal normality, his virility is figured as exactly a factor of his race consciousness. She asks,

> "Is he very young?"
>
> "Scarcely older than you. They say he was educated in Paris and that he is an atheist. He fought the Turks at Candia and is said to have distinguished himself no less by his race-hatred and cruelty than by his bravery."
>
> "A man, in fact," she exclaimed, her eyes gleaming." (von Sacher-Masoch [1870] 1991, 248)

Here, then, is von Sacher-Masoch's conception of a proper modernity succinctly stated. Wanda finally encounters a man *in fact* versus a "man" produced through the emasculating fiction of the (sentimental) contract. And, yes, he is given to excess. He is an atheist, a believer in the conceited, if decidedly modern, notion of his own self-creation. Yet he maintains ancient prejudices, murdering idolatrous, almost Negro Turks with impunity. His race hatred becomes, then, both a means by which to temper his individuality (he may not believe in the Christian god, but this does not stop him from killing infidels) and a vehicle to displace his natural tendency toward violence. When Wanda finally tricks Severin into receiving a whipping from her new lover, she undoubtedly saves herself from an already well-established viciousness. Moreover, as von Sacher-Masoch struggles assiduously to demonstrate, this viciousness is absolutely necessary to deter the more profound violence sure to follow the dissolution of boundaries between races, classes and genders.

Yellow Desire

> *Lonely Mag Smith! See her as she walks with downcast eyes and heavy heart. It was not always thus. She had a loving, trusting heart.*[10]

With these brief lines Harriet Wilson began what is undoubtedly one of the most provocative rescriptings of sentimentalism to have been produced in this country. Mag Smith comes to us as a character almost ready-made for one of the popular domestic dramas of the 1850s. She has been robbed of her parents. Alone and penniless, she is pursued by an older, wealthier man, her own Mr. B. But unlike Pamela, she *does* succumb, she submits to the "pleasures" of the flesh. Hers is not a story in which a barrage of words and texts, as in Pamela's endless letters, constantly work to defer the consummation of the (illegitimate) union between master and servant. Instead, her existence as a creature of text, of literature, is incredibly short-lived, ending after only two brief chapters. To put it bluntly, Mag comes to us as a creature who exists solely in the body and, therefore, outside even the semblance of sentimentality.

Strangely enough, then, Mag reproduces in her person the very logic of individuality on which notions of modern domesticity had been constructed. She is, in many ways, one of the most truly *individuated* characters to have been produced within antebellum American literature. She is utterly alone, utterly independent, living on the social and geographic outskirts of the community in which she was once a member. She is also a white woman who takes a black husband, a rare enough figure in the latter part of the twentieth century, much less the nineteenth. Wilson, like von Sacher-Masoch, produces this individuality as a factor of Mag's faulty body and not a set of sentimental contracts. Her marriage and the children it brings lead her into the desperate situation that Wilson narrates. Moreover, as a character whose body dictates the course that her life takes, Mag disallows the mythology surrounding the marriage contract. What affection she holds for Jim, her husband, is absolutely mediated through the reality of physical degradation. "Well, Mag . . . you's down low enough. I don't see but I've got to take care of ye. 'Sposin' we marry!" (Wilson [1859] 1983, 12) The effect is to remind us that the marriage relation is at its core a social *and* economic reality, a factor of sentiment *and* corporeality, one that thrives on the inability of women to gain presence, voice, and independence in the public sphere. Moreover, it suggests that Mag, outside of a sentimentalized white domesticity, is no white at all but "down low enough" to be marriageable within a black community.

> He prevailed; they married. You can philosophize, gentle reader, upon the impropriety of such unions, and preach dozens of sermons on the evils of amalgamation. Want is a more powerful philosopher and preacher. Poor Mag. She has sundered another bond which held her to her fellows. She has descended another step down the ladder of infamy. (Wilson [1859] 1983, 13)

Want, the reality of physical need, is placed in diametric opposition to sentiment, the purview of philosophers and preachers. Wilson produces, then, a version of the logic that we saw in von Sacher-Masoch. Sentiment cannot domesticate a body under extreme pressure. In the absence of societal pressures, in the absence of (domestic) violence, the body comes to speak and act for itself, oftentimes violently disrupting societal norms.

When Jim dies, after the couple has lived together in relative happiness and comfort, producing two young children in the process, Mag is not consumed by the relentlessly hot anger and longing that would have worked, even if in vain, to turn the narrative toward some sort of recognizable sentimentalism. Instead, a "feeling of cold desolation" comes over her as she turns from her husband's grave (Wilson [1859] 1983, 15). It is almost as if with the scandal of her marriage to a black man no longer apparent, Mag starts to slip away from her body, to leave it behind as a cold shell waiting to be reanimated. She wastes almost no time in reestablishing her pariah status, this time marrying Jim's business partner, Seth. "Her will made her the wife of Seth," we are told, alerting us both to the self-interested versus romantic nature of all her actions and to the fact that there is a will, a desire for self-preservation and self-definition that remains separate from the strictures of sentimentalism (Wilson [1859] 1983, 16).

The fact of Mag's awkward body, or, rather, the fact that her body is in a constant state of becoming, does not preclude her from gaining public presence. It simply ensures that that presence cannot be sentimentalized. Mag's ability to be seen—at first by Jim and then by the rest of the community—is precisely a factor of her withdrawal from the norms of (sentimental) society. When she and Seth decide to leave their community, taking only one of the children with them and leaving the other, Frado, at the home of the Bellmont family, they pass by a group of vicious schoolchildren. "Black, white and yeller! Black, white and yeller," the children scream, but still Mag does not flinch. "She did not even turn her head to look at them. She had passed into an insensibility no childish taunt could penetrate, else she would have reproached herself as she passed familiar scenes, for extending the separation once so easily annihilated by steadfast integrity" (Wilson [1859] 1983, 21).

Mag has given up the option of speech, of self-representation. Instead, she allows herself to be defined solely by the children's taunts. In the process, however, she does gain a place, if a terribly uncomfortable one, within the extant systems of public discourse. She is a creature beyond reason yet she is, as a consequence, seen. This simple calculus, this drawing together of abuse with publicity, abjection with presence, is a matter that will be taken up at length in the next chapter. We have seen already, however, that sentimentality tends to produce blacks and would-be blacks as at best antecedents to a white supremacist narrative of domesticity that is so well established that it can never be breached by the specter of interracialism. The black is always "unbound" in the sentimental narrative and encouraged to move outside of white familiarity. Uncle Tom goes to Heaven. Liza, Harry, and George escape to Canada and then Africa. Alternatively, a black sentimentalism can be enacted in proximity to its white counterpart as long as it is not marred by racial ambiguity, as long as the racially ambiguous character does not actually speak a desire that exists outside the racial common sense.

As Frado enters the Bellmont household, however, she never fully embraces either of these options. She does not run nor does she ever successfully establish herself as a thing apart from the white family with whom she lives. She never normalizes her awkward, ambiguous, body. This is not a clean narrative. Instead, Wilson has written a novel that is similar to *Venus in Furs* in that it warps the logic of sentimentalism so that the black—through the vehicle of violence—appears as a permanent and significant fixture within the white home even though the bonds of affection and consanguinity are never wrapped about her. The sheer desperateness of her situation, however, forces the matter of her publicity. Her mother was so abused that she produced a black daughter. The daughter was so despised that she was delivered into the hands of a white sadist. The sadist was so startled by the fact of her victim's humanity, her seemingly endless capacity for suffering, that she built a wall of violence against recognition and empathy. However, this publicity, this presence and voice, cannot be properly labeled black. Instead the great feat, or failure (depending on the state of one's own racial consciousness), of *Our Nig* is that it allows the narration of desire that is so pure, so simply and inevitably of the body, that it exists outside even the logic of racial distinction. I would argue, then, that Frado's race is never fully established. On the contrary, Frado is unlike every other protagonist in early Black American literature in that she is not only mixed race, not only yearns for intimacy with whites, for a place within the logic of sentimentality, but also refuses to deny this yearning or to allow it to kill her. The Garies, Clotel, Tom, Little Eva, and a host of other interracialists die in the course of their respective narratives at a rate that is directly proportionate to the amount of their racial mixing. This is not true for Frado, who survives her ordeal, if in a highly fractured state. More shocking still, she also has the audacity to announce her desire for both whites and whiteness, marking her own "yellowness" in the process. Though Frado's body is worked on diligently by Mrs. Bellmont, among others, it is ultimately never raced in any acceptably sentimental fashion.

Wilson's particular genius is that she makes so sharply explicit the very conceptual problematic with which we have been concerned throughout *Conjugal Union*. The same body that must act as the emblem of blackness is itself always a promiscuous, desirous entity, one that has a history and logic that predates the formal literary strategies for marking its existence. Moreover, the fact that Frado's body is yellow suggests that she is no more the sister of her "colored brethren" than she is of the sadistic Mrs. B. Wilson is unlike Webb, then, in that she never fully establishes control over the unfaithful, racially ambiguous body of her protagonist. Instead, that body is in a state of rebellion that results in its crippling, but that nonetheless forces recognition of its individuality. Frado comes to us as fully formed and independent, very unlike the awkwardly two-dimensional characters we examined in *The Garies.*

The title, *Our Nig; or, Sketches from the Life of a Free Black, in a Two-Story White House, North*, immediately forces one to the recognition that the blackness of the text is something that is contested, not quite the property of the protagonist. Moreover, it is intimately associated with the white domestic sphere of the antebellum North. Indeed, the title, in its two parts, demonstrates the very interplay between body and house with which we have been concerned. The black, *Our* Nig, exists both as property, a thing, *not* unto itself, and as a free individual with a life of her own. The suggestion is, of course, that what we see is a dialectic in which the black proceeds from its status as a thing and toward status as a subject in much the same manner as the slave narrators, the two-story white house acting as the vehicle by which racial ambiguity is turned to racial distinctiveness. And yet this line of thinking cannot explain fully the fact of the considerable formal and narrative contradiction that is apparent in *Our Nig.* The text is nothing like Frederick Douglass's *Narrative* in its graceful prose and compelling story of enlightenment and escape. Instead, *Our Nig* proceeds by fits and starts, never really establishing the stable black individuality and noble black community that crown earlier works. The blackness of this "Black American" text is a long time in making itself apparent. Instead, we are treated to a narrative in which the local dramas of an ostensibly white family are most often on display.

"I don't mind the nigger in the child. I should like a dozen better than one," Mrs. Bellmont announces when she is confronted with the prospect of keeping Frado in her home. "If I could make her do my work in a few years, I would keep her. I have so much trouble with girls I hire, I am almost persuaded if I have one to train up in my way from a child, I shall be able to keep them awhile" (Wilson [1859] 1983, 26). Without the problem of Frado, the problem of the "black" who is in the household, but not of the family, the Bellmonts might have enacted a proper sentimental drama in their own right. The sadistic mother and her copycat daughter, Mary, stand alongside Susan, the semi-invalid child who must choose between money and love; Jack, the young ambitious son; and James, the older, more spiritual brother whom Nig comes to love passionately. They are rounded out by Mr. Bellmont, the stern, if somewhat ineffectual father, and his spinster sister, Aunt Abby. And indeed the family does produce its share of domestic crises. Still, there is a difference. There is always Nig and the fact that she threatens not only racial purity but also the transparency of racial purity. She makes apparent the fiction of whiteness.

What Mrs. Bellmont despises in the girl, then, is not the fact of her blackness but that it is so obviously apparent that the girl's race is not a fact at all. Mrs. Bellmont cannot mind the nigger in the girl because there is no nigger there to mind. The nigger must be produced. Rather, the Bellmonts must produce a sort of homespun discourse of the nigger. Frado is counted as a commodity, as chattel. Her value lies, not in sentiment, but in some nonspecific utility that Mrs. Bellmont is eager to beat out of her. Any nigger will do. A dozen are better than one. And yet Mrs. Bellmont unknowingly acknowledges the problematic toward which her beatings are actually directed. She intends to train Frado up from a child, to keep her close by in order to distance her. She makes the common mistake of assuming that one can bring oneself into intimate proximity with the dirty servant and yet keep all dirt at bay. She forgets that Frado has her own will and her own power. She has a body that cannot simply be beaten into narrative stability.

That Frado's body cannot be trusted to reproduce the racialist logics in which the novel is enmeshed is demonstrated very early and reiterated throughout. "Frado is such a wild, frolicky thing, and means to do jest as she's a mind to; and she won't go if she don't want to," Mag comments fretfully as she and Seth prepare to deliver the girl to the Bellmont home (Wilson [1859] 1983, 18). And she does have reason to fear, for Frado is always a likely runaway. Mag and Seth look up "to find Frado missing" just as they are discussing their plans for the girl's betrayal. We soon find that she has only gotten herself lost, but this desire to remove herself, to escape not only the various spheres of domesticity in which she has been inserted but also the body the text claims is hers, is demonstrated continually. When Frado realizes that she has definitely been left at the Bellmonts and as the beating, kicking, lashing, and gouging are about to begin in earnest, she weighs the respective merits of domesticity versus running:

> Frado lay, revolving in her little mind whether she would remain or not until her mother's return. She was of wilful, determined nature, a stranger to fear, and would not hesitate to wander away should she decide to. She remembered the conversation of her mother with Seth, the words "given away" which she heard used in reference to herself; and though she did not know their full import, she thought she should, by remaining, be in some relation to white people she was never favored with before. So she resolved to tarry, with the hope that mother would come and get her some time. (Wilson [1859] 1983, 28)

The passage brims with the complexity of the philosophical and social quandary confronted by Frado. With a willful, strong nature and no fear or hesitation she can, if she will, turn from the Bellmont household, from the site of torture, to become a creature unto herself, a subject produced out of the void where family and home should stand.

It is important to note, however, that Frado cannot resort to the modes of escape that had been so ably narrativized in the novels and narratives of other black antebellum writers. She is already in the "free" North. Moreover, there is no loving Black American community, as in *The Garies*, to which she might retreat. Frado can gain only the relative freedom of a Mag Smith, the freedom of a pariah, a creature who can run because there is no one to chase her and no place to go. When Frado relinquishes her escape option, when she turns over her body to the Bellmont's, allows her own commodification in order to gain some new relation(s), to touch whiteness, she disavows the very logic of black community and black literature out of which and against which Wilson attempts to piece together her narrative. She holds out for an already disavowed interracial domesticity, a realm of affection and right feeling that does not necessarily exclude the "black." "She thought she should, by remaining, be in some relation to white people she was never favored with before." This dream can never be brought to fruition, however. The journey that Frado makes in the course of the novel is one in which she comes to understand that sentimentalism and interracialism are antithetical. Any affection she receives from the Bellmonts must work either to demean her or to destroy the positive relations that she is able to establish. She mistakes the open, cheerful nature with which Jack pronounces her "Nig" as evidence of a sentimental relationship that exists outside of the contract of ownership. She will find that she has been horribly mistaken as the relentless tortures of Mrs. Bellmont work to rob her of both health and spirit.

The fact that Frado does not marry James, even though the logic of sentimentality dictates as much, demonstrates of course the deferred nature of her authority, her femininity. I am not claiming, however, that her desire was somehow deferred as well. The problem with Frado is that she can never corral that desire, never put it to the service of either running or producing a proper black domesticity. That Frado's desire for James bleeds into her religious desire, her desire for Christ, actually announces it as a thing apart from both the strictures of sentimentalism and the strictures of American racialism. "*He* was the attraction. Should she want to go there [heaven] if she could not see him" (Wilson [1859] 1983, 100). Her passion for James—and his in return—becomes so intense that the two quite literally begin to speak across the specter of profligacy that their mutual desire conjures. As James lay dying, a sign itself of a consuming and extinguishing perversity, the couple enacts a ritual of affection that firmly establishes the desire shared between the young people, as well as the necessity of its deferral. "My Heavenly Father is calling me home. Had it been his will to let me live I should take you to live with me; but, as it is, I shall go and leave you. But, Frado, if you will be a good girl, and love and serve God, it will be but a short time before we are in a *heavenly* home together" (Wilson [1859] 1983, 95).

The ideological work accomplished by James's dying is altogether different from what we saw with the passing of Clarence Garie and his mother. Here, the death does not represent a renormalization of the racial common sense. Instead, by running from the body, from corporeality, James is finally able to speak a desire that is released from its racial moorings. Importantly, his wife figures as an altogether peripheral figure throughout the text, disappearing from the sick room the moment Frado arrives. James asks, "Are you afraid to stay with me alone, Frado?" reminding us that the powers of the flesh become heightened at precisely the moment of its dissipation.

It is this perverse desire—this desire for James, yes, but also for a domesticity that is not disabled by white supremacy—that Frado confesses in *Our Nig.* She works to explain how her own individual desire, a yellow desire that precedes her domestication, forces her to remain the prisoner of the Bellmonts when she might have chosen otherwise. It is my contention, in fact, that Wilson's essentially confessional apparatus works to demonstrate that desire is always enacted in relation to the logics of race and racialism, but that it does not necessarily conform to the same. Frado does not want Jack in spite of his whiteness but because of it. Her connection to him demonstrates the "new relation to white people" that was the promise of her contract. Yet her body is never so easily domesticated, so securely raced. If Wilson had constructed Frado as a clearly defined black character, then the desire between Frado and James could never have been articulated so fully. As Frado turns from James's lifeless body, she also turns from the promise of a virile, supraracialist America, an America that had been disallowed already.

This is where Wilson's critique of the sentimental becomes most blistering. Again and again, Frado announces a desire to be accepted, to be taken in by the community in which she is ostensibly a member. At every turn, however, she is confronted by the fact that that community has produced itself as white while stridently endeavoring to produce Frado as black. Every act of intimacy and affection is always an act of racial demarcation. After ridiculing her, the fellow scholars at Frado's school began to take her into their hearts. "Day by day there was a manifest change of deportment towards 'Nig' " (Wilson [1859] 1983, 32). Yes, then, there is "real" affection for the girl, but only insofar as it does not challenge the logic of racial difference and white supremacy. Nig is loved. Frado is not.

Here is where one begins to understand why the actions of Mrs. Bellmont are never checked by the men who surround her, particularly her husband. One is all but forced to ask why the tormenter in this novel is not Mr. B., as it is in Richardson's *Pamela*, and instead his wife. It would be incorrect to assume that what Wilson was after was a simple demonstration of the inefficacy of the northern patriarchal and sentimental enterprises. I would suggest, in fact, that Wilson does not recognize that enterprise as inefficacious at all. Instead, she understands it as driven by a logic of white supremacy that she confronts in the course of her novel. Mr. B. cannot be the character who pursues Frado's body because, in the logic of both slave narratives and sentimental literature, he is very likely to gain it, thereby destabilizing again the necessary racial purity of sentimental domesticity. Mrs. Bellmont's actions short-circuit this possibility, thereby leaving the racial purity of the domestic union in tact.

Our Nig is not, then, a Masochistic novel in that it does not represent the triumph of the female over the male within the domestic contest. Instead, Mr. Bellmont and his sons are implicated in Frado's abuse at least insofar as they never use their authority to bring the women in their family into order. They work only to ameliorate Frado's misery and then only occasionally. When Mr. Bellmont and Aunt Abby come upon Mrs. Bellmont beating and kicking Frado, the girl uses the opportunity to run from the house. Mr. Bellmont comments that he hopes she will never return.

> "I do mean it. The child does as much work as a woman ought to; and just see how she is kicked about!"
>
> "How do you have it so, John?" asked his sister.
>
> "How am I to help it? Women rule the earth, and all in it."
>
> "I think I should rule my own house, John,"—
>
> "And live in hell meantime," added Mr. Bellmont. (Wilson [1859] 1983, 44)

The ingenuousness of Bellmont's protestations are almost too obvious to note. The family lives in a house and on a farm that is completely owned by him. Moreover, on those occasions when he does decide to protect Frado we see clearly that Mrs. Bellmont cannot resist his orders. We find that he is a man whose "word once spoken admitted of no appeal" (Wilson [1859] 1983, 31), while Mrs. B. "feared to oppose where she knew she could not prevail" (Wilson [1859] 1983, 68).

Mrs. Bellmont and Mary provide a much needed service to their household when they beat Frado. By abusing her they help to maintain the illusion that the whites are the absolute rulers of the world, as demonstrated by their absolute rule over the body of this "black" girl. Frado's beatings become the material markers of the very complex ideological structure that holds together slavery, domesticity, and American racialism. She is the figure who marks the possibility of an interracial, even raceless America, a possibility that must be avoided at all costs. We are given clues throughout the text to prove just this point. Frado is indeed a character who in Cuba or Haiti might have been successfully integrated into the family, if only as a subordinate, and Mrs. Bellmont is exceptionally aware of just this fact. "She was not many shades darker than Mary now; what a calamity it would be ever to hear the contrast spoken of. Mrs. Bellmont was determined the sun should have full power to darken the shade which nature had first bestowed upon her as best befitting" (Wilson [1859] 1983, 39). Again and again, Mrs. Bellmont returns to Frado's body in order to assure herself that there is some reality to race that might be accessed through the corporeal. In doing so, she does not destabilize the patriarchal order of bourgeois domesticity but, rather, strengthens it, keeping her husband and sons away from the desirous Negro who would mar their myths of purity.

Still, though the beatings help to establish the stability of the Bellmont's "whiteness," Frado's blackness is never so fully established nor, as I will demonstrate below, is the "blackness" of Wilson's text. After a particularly vicious attack by Mrs. Bellmont, Frado again runs from the Bellmont household, only to be found through the assistance of the family dog, Fido. When the disheveled and nearly hysterical girl is brought home and comforted by her friend, James, she confronts the inevitability of racial distinction.

> "Did God make you?"
> "Yes."
> "Who made Aunt Abby?"
> "God."
> "Who made your mother?"
> "God."
> "Did the same God that made her make me?"
> "Yes."
> Well, then, I don't like him."
> "Why not?"
> "Because he made her white, and me black. Why didn't he make us *both* white?" (Wilson [1859] 1983, 51)

Frado is finally forced to understand that racial distinction is god-given, inevitable. Indeed, as a part of God's creation it ought to be celebrated instead of shunned. What Mrs. Bellmont really lashes out against when she strikes the girl, then, is not so much the fact of her blackness as the fact that the girl does such a sloppy job of inhabiting that blackness. Frado refuses to stay with—or within—her race. As a consequence, she marks the site of dangerous ambiguity, a place at which the logic of both patriarchy and sentimentalism has been thrown into disarray.

I ask that we remember that *Our Nig* is not only the narrativization of the painful realities of one woman's life. Instead this novel, like all the novels that we examine in *Conjugal Union*, represents an attempt to produce an at least nominally Black American literature. "I sincerely appeal to my colored brethren universally for patronage, hoping they will not condemn this attempt of their sister to be erudite, but rally around me a faithful band of supporters and defenders" (Wilson [1859] 1983, 3). Yet I would maintain that even though Wilson understands her work as part of the myriad efforts at Black American community development, she ultimately does not succeed in establishing a stable—and loyal—blackness within her text. The novel, precisely because of its erudition, always has the rankness of the runaway about it. The "black" family is almost completely absent while the themes of bondage, escape, and community renewal are never so severely rendered as in, say, Henry Bibb's narrative. For much of the work, moreover, Frado is intent upon inserting herself more securely within the (white) family romance. It takes some time before she learns that there is no escaping the strictures of American racialism. It takes some time before she reaches maturity and leaves the Bellmont household. It takes some time before her bond with James is broken. It takes some time before she finally finishes her round of live-in situations with sympathetic whites. It takes some time before she finds herself in the county home, existing as something other than white, but not quite black.

Tellingly, Wilson does not release Frado after she reaches her majority, delivering her into the redeeming hands of God, or at least some local black community. Instead, Frado continues as the only "black" character in the novel until near its conclusion, when in a few short pages we are introduced to her husband and child, neither of whom is ever developed and one of whom, the husband, dies within the course of the narrative. The whole matter of a distinct black community and black domesticity is treated, in fact, as a sort of farce. "A few years ago, within the compass of my narrative, there appeared often in some of our New England villages, professed fugitives from slavery, who recounted their personal experience in homely phrase, and awakened the indignation of non-slaveholders against brother Pro" (Wilson [1859] 1983, 126).

It is impossible to miss the sarcasm with which Wilson has constructed this passage and thus her representation of the black community. We are shown only professed fugitives whose homely phrase might rightly be thought of in the same vein as the minstrel performance that so captured the attention of antebellum Americans. Wilson all but insists, in fact, that the black community that she briefly establishes is produced precisely through performance, a spectacle of blackness, that reflects more the racialist fantasies of whites than the realities of her own "black" life.

When Frado finally marries the "fugitive," Samuel, he never brings the subject of his former status as an enslaved person into the intimate confines of their marriage. Through his character, however, we are for the first time given the hope that perhaps Frado might experience her body as something other than a vehicle of violence and remorse, that she might access fully its "blackness," thereby allowing for the joys inherent within a properly constituted (black) domesticity.

> [W]as it strange that she should attract her dark brother; that he should inquire her out; succeed in seeing her; feel a strange sensation in his heart towards her; that he should toy with her shining curls, feel proud to provoke her to smile and expose the ivory concealed by thin, ruby lips; that her sparkling eyes should fascinate; that he should propose; that they should marry? (Wilson [1859] 1983, 126)

Frado's body is finally not only understood as attractive, a thing for which one can openly yearn, but also as black, or at least somewhat black. Was it strange that she should attract her dark brother? Yes it was, given that her body has only attracted violence, or at best the tortured, other-worldly affections of James. The body on display here, however, is all shining curls, winning smiles, rows of ivory, ruby lips, and sparkling eyes—all mundane attributes of Frado's appearance that had never been presented to us. More to the point, this decidedly purplish prose demonstrates the sentimentalized blackness so apparent in the works of both Frank Webb and Harriet Beecher Stowe. One should remember that previously it was enough to know that Frado was yellow, between black and white, and handsome, thereby creating her as a possible threat to racial purity. Still, Frado does marry. She does bind her own newly valued (black) body with that of her dark brother, finally establishing the peculiar black domesticity that would allow this work to establish its claims on the sentimental.

And yet this fiction had necessarily to unravel. Samuel is indeed running, but not from the horrors of slavery. On the contrary, what Samuel is running from are the horrors of domesticity. Frado has met her own doppelgänger, the husband who actualizes her own tendencies toward flight, her own desire to give up a sentimentalized version of domesticity that led her into a life of systematic violence and torture. From the very beginning, in fact, the reader is led to understand that Samuel is not to be trusted, that his efforts to produce black family and community are not genuine, but instead some sort of highly charged minstrel performance. His story of bondage and escape continues only on the level of the performative, with the supposed fugitive leaving periodically to "lecture," presumably to appreciative white audiences. It is hardly a surprise, then, when we learn that Samuel was never a slave and, more important, that he is incapable of maintaining even the fiction of companionate marriage that would have acted as a proper conclusion to an ostensibly sentimental novel. "He left her to her fate—embarked at sea, with the disclosure that he had never seen the South, and that his illiterate harangues were humbugs for hungry abolitionists" (Wilson [1859] 1983, 127–128).

Frado's pregnancy is announced at just the moment when the "real" Samuel is revealed. Frado learns that she must care for herself and her child alone, just as she comes to understand that her husband is a runner, that even his nominal marriage to her is not enough to tie him to one place. The fact that Samuel dies in New Orleans of yellow fever comes not only as no surprise but almost as an absolute requirement. The symptoms of Samuel's fever had been apparent from the very first moment he was introduced. He refused to establish himself as a stable black character in a stable black community. Instead, he plays with the expectations of whites as surely as he plays with the affections of Frado, refusing in either case to give in to the pressures of normalization, to form a properly black conjugal union. Frado returns, then, to the very state in which both she and her mother began. The world may be populated by blacks and whites, but she is herself, "yeller."

I would like to dwell for a moment on the well-known fact that *Our Nig* did not become an accepted part of the lexicon of early Black American fiction until it was republished in 1983. It did not come to pass that Wilson received the patronage of any of her brethren, colored or otherwise. This was while Americans witnessed during the 1850s not only an incredible boom in the production of all American literatures but also and importantly a great flowering of work by Black Americans. Frederick Douglass, William Wells Brown, Martin Delany, and Henry Bibb were all supporting themselves, more or less successfully, through writing and lecturing. Black and abolitionist newspapers were cropping up throughout the North and West. A number of fine slave narratives had been published, or were about to be published, including Harriet Jacobs's *Incidents in the Life of a Slave Girl*, with which *Our Nig* has much in common. Given the fact that the gauntlet had long since been thrown down for Black American writers, challenging them to prove their humanity through the production of eloquent prose, it is stunning that Wilson's fine novel would have been left to molder.

In briefly addressing this dilemma, I will again make the claim that Wilson might have produced within her novel the same sentimentalized black domesticity that we saw in *The Garies and Their Friends*. Her novel, like *The Garies*, begins with a set of seemingly insurmountable obstacles to the production of a peculiar black domesticity, obstacles that are overcome when the interracialist Garies are removed from the text and that Frado seemingly overcomes with her marriage to Samuel. Yet this marriage does not last. Where much within Webb's novel was taken up with demonstrating the viability of the black family and the black community, only a few pages are given over to these themes in *Our Nig*. Though Wilson does expend some energy attempting to mark her novel as black, she does not do so successfully. The preface in which she specifically hails a Black American community, and the supporting documents of the appendix addressed to "the friends of our dark-complexioned brethren and sisters," do little to reestablish the fidelity of this text not only to the cause of abolition but also to the development of a discrete black community.

What I would like to focus on, in these final comments, is the fact that Wilson is never able to get Frado to relinquish hold on her alternative narratives of domesticity and corporeality. Frado never ceases to express a desire that precedes directly—and unapologetically—from her own peculiar, supra-racial, nonsentimental sense of self and community. As I have argued throughout, we might think of Mrs. Bellmont's beatings as a response to the fact that the girl refuses to stop her peculiar not white, not black modes of discourse. On her first full day at the Bellmonts she is beaten for weeping. Moreover, there are any number of scenes in which Frado must suffer violence, not because she speaks out of turn or in a disrespectful manner, but because she speaks the truth. This is just the case when Mary accuses Frado of having thrown her into a pond. When Frado denies the act and Mr. Bellmont defends her, we find again that what Mrs. Bellmont despises in the child is not the fact of her "blackness" but the fact that her speech never adequately represents that blackness.

> "Will you sit still, there, and hear that black nigger call Mary a liar?"
>
> "How do we know but she has told the truth? I shall not punish her," he replied, and left the house, as he usually did when a tempest threatened to envelop him. No sooner was he out of sight than Mrs. B. and Mary commenced beating her inhumanly; then propping her mouth open with a piece of wood, thrust her up in a dark room, without any supper. (Wilson [1859] 1983, 35–36)

The abuse that Mrs. Bellmont metes out in this passage is itself an emblem of the racialist logic that would make all black speech false. She beats Frado, not because she knows the girl is lying, but because she knows that she is not. The fact that Frado tells the truth suggests that she is something other than black, something that exists outside of the logics of racialism and white supremacy altogether. Mrs. Bellmont forces Frado's mouth open while she beats her on at least two more occasions, while on a third she threatens to cut the girl's tongue out should she report her actions to James and the others. I would argue again, then, that what Mrs. Bellmont is after is somehow stopping the evidence of Frado's humanity, evidence that freely flows from the girl's mouth, evidence that might help establish a public presence for Frado.

Mrs. Bellmont attacks Frado's ability to communicate because she knows that the girl can never communicate the white supremacist notions of family and community on which she has established her own twisted subjectivity. Frado triumphs over this state of affairs, however, by having her story become *the* defining story within the variety of domestic dramas to which we have been introduced. At the same time, however, once the plug has been removed from her mouth, once she is allowed to speak whatever she will, we find that she cannot be counted on to produce the stable narrative of black subjectivity to which those who read Douglass, Bibb, or Webb had come to expect. She never quite makes the move from yellow to black that we saw with young Emily Garie. When Frado speaks her message remains as yellow as her skin. She never really moves beyond an interstitial status. Instead, she continues as a creature that exists outside community—and race—even as Wilson struggles awkwardly to create her as black. Frado is precisely where Mag Smith began. She is alone, penniless, existing as a character who is fully integrated in neither the black or white communities, one who continues, in fact, to yearn for an interracial domesticity that already has been disallowed in the text. The very last words of the novel find her still pining for the Bellmonts even though they are long since gone. "Frado has passed from their memories, as Joseph from the butler's, but she will never cease to track them till beyond mortal vision" (Wilson [1859] 1983, 131). It is for this betrayal, for escaping both black and white peculiarity, that Frado—and Wilson—suffered the most unthinkable of critical insults. They were ignored.

Five • CONJUGAL UNION

> The consummation of conjugal union is the best security for political relations, and he who is incapable of negotiating to promote his own personal requirements might not be trustworthy as the agent of another's interest; and the fitness for individuals for positions of public import, may not be misjudged by their doings in the private affairs of life.
>
> —*Martin Delany*

> In the mythology of the modern world, the quintessential protagonist is the bourgeois, Hero for some, villain for others, the inspiration or lure for most, he has been the shaper of the present, the destroyer of the past.
>
> —*Immanuel Wallerstein*

In each of the readings I have offered thus far I have tried to be sensitive to the manner in which the American modes of corporeality and domesticity with which I have been concerned are themselves tied to projects of bourgeois political, economic, and social hegemony. Still, I have not attempted to suggest that what we see represented in antebellum Black American literature is simply an attempt on the part of Black American writers to construct themselves and their literature as bourgeois. As Wallerstein reminds us, the bourgeois is an essentially disembodied subject, the quintessence of the modern world's mythologies. It is, in fact, just this reality that makes practices of bourgeois figuration problematic for projects of black subject formation. Antebellum intellectuals consistently rejected efforts aimed at producing a black subjectivity and black literature that did not reference a *literal* black body that, in turn, referenced a *peculiar* black household. Even William Wells Brown and Harriet Wilson attempt to salvage—through killing off Clotel and marrying off Frado—some sort of normative modality for black corporeality and familiarity. Thus, the very fact of the bourgeois's universality, the fact of his disembodiment, produced him as at best an awkward model for the project of black subjectification.[1]

And yet this figure could not be ignored if the black was to gain access to the widest avenues of public life, much less the narrative strategies of domestic literatures. The figure of the bourgeois was absolutely necessary to the project of Black American cultural production if only because it stood so firmly against the figures of master and slave. That is to say, the bourgeois's presence counterbalanced the grotesque and erotically charged interdependency of the master/slave dyad, an interdependency that posed a serious threat to the economic, political, familial, and emotional independence thought necessary for the proper functioning of a "free" nation.[2] Martin Delany writes:

> We want business men and women among us and must have them in every place. We have been heretofore taught that these things were unfit for us, as they interfered with our prospects of heaven. This our oppressors taught us to prevent us from competing with them in business; and being ignorant, we believed it. Let this henceforth be no longer the case. Industry as much belongs to us, as to them. Surely if we can work for them, and do their drudgery—go at their bidding, and come at their command—spend our money with them in buying from them; if they can advise with us in religion, in medicine, and law, then may we also, if we only determined that it shall be so, sell to them as well as buy from them; give advice to them in matters of religion, medicine, and law, as well as receive advice from them in all these matters. But we must qualify ourselves for these various departments first, which is comparatively an easy matter. We must have farmers, mechanics, and shopkeepers generally among us. By these occupations we make money—these are the true sources of wealth. Give us wealth, and we can obtain all the rest.[3]

We see succinctly stated, then, the common sense of bourgeois hegemony. Gain wealth, produce oneself as an equal in business, in the market, and all the rest will come in time. Delany makes it painfully obvious, moreover, that what keeps blacks from taking these first nascent steps toward economic and political independence is an enervating "domestic economy," a childish, slavish dependence on whites that keeps blacks away from more noble and rewarding pursuits.

The problem, of course, is that once the black gains bourgeois status, a feat that Delany imagines as a fairly easy matter, what is to stop him from losing his grip on the logic of racial specificity, returning to the very domestic interracialism that Delany decries? By the end of the passage we see Delany all but turning again to a sort of black/white interdependency. As the black doctor counsels the white patient and the minister comforts the supplicant, what is to stop fragile racial distinctions from falling by the wayside? In briefly addressing this matter I would point to the fact that Delany is meticulous in structuring his prose so that black and white are always figured in a sort of syntactical opposition. There is never a single moment in which black and white are imagined with anything approaching complexity. Instead, when the white is active the black is passive; when the black comes forward the white falls back. In all the giving and receiving that Delany imagines the black and the white always continue on opposite sides of the gesture. Thus Delany avoids, however awkwardly, the quandary of bourgeois figuration. He utilizes the bourgeois as a ready-made weapon in the struggle against the blurring of black and white subjectivities while nonetheless avoiding the difficulties of disembodiment that much within early Black American literature was so eager to counteract.

I have opened these matters in order to address more cogently the aesthetic and discursive strategies within Delany's work, particularly his socioeconomic treatise, *The Condition, Elevation and Emigration and Destiny of the Colored People of the United States,* and his novel, *Blake, or the Huts of America.* Therein, Delany produces a proper bourgeois, or proto-bourgeois subject who is constantly juxtaposed with subjects established through a promiscuous corporeality. Weak, submissive, and complicitous slaves stand alongside violent, debased, and parasitic masters. Throughout his various narratives, Delany emphasizes the interdependency of the pair on one another, repeatedly remarking a necessary physical, social, and economic intimacy between master and slave. He suggests, in fact, that the violence between master and slave works ultimately to draw the two more closely together so that the presence of this dyad, even as it is marked by violent struggle, belies any sense of a normative black subjectivity. In doing so he disallows any sustained consideration of the "problem of disembodiment" as enacted by the figure of the bourgeois by creating a spectacular apparatus around the figures of master and slave. Delany's often violent imagery works, then, not only to demonstrate the barbarism of slavery but also to enact a new set of possibilities in which neither racial ambiguity nor disembodiment is necessary to the production of a postslavery, post–white supremacist society. Instead he, like Frank Webb, privileges the properly constituted black character, proper in that he is decidedly, peculiarly black while nonetheless remaining bourgeois and, therefore, not "of the master."

It is this understanding that led me in an earlier version of this work to label Delany's aesthetic sadomasochistic, suggesting that torture and suffering operate in dialectical relation to one another, thereby complicating Hegel's master/slave narrative precisely by eroticizing it, by insisting upon struggle as itself an enactment of desire, at once a clash between men and a lover's embrace.[4] Since the publication of that essay, however, I have been troubled by Gilles Deleuze's forceful observation that the overlap of morphologies on display in Sade and von Sacher-Masoch's philosophical and aesthetic practices does not mean that they necessarily speak to the same concerns. Von Sacher-Masoch is obsessed with the way in which the marriage contract enervates patriarchy and allows the production of a sentimental domesticity. Sade, on the other hand, enacts a logic that is precisely antisocial. The world that he visions in his literature is always sealed off, always established apart, a subject of its own rituals. As Barthes eloquently reminds us, Sade works most assiduously to establish a formal language in which there are only classes of actions, not classes of people.[5] Von Sacher-Masoch, meanwhile, was concerned to maintain just these social distinctions.

Following these observations, I will amend my earlier argument to suggest Delany's aesthetic as drawn from two distinct philosophies of corporeal existence in which, on the one hand, violence stands against the body in order to enact a fantastic universe, a world outside the world, while on the other, it works to maintain prior social distinctions, particularly distinctions between bodies. I choose not to label this aesthetic sadomasochistic because I agree that there is no necessary union between the philosophical traditions articulated by Sade and von Sacher-Masoch. Instead, I suggest that Delany's work might be best understood as both Sadian and Masochistic, in that it privileges both "the black fantastic," as well as a sociologically demonstrable black body, black household and black community. Unlike von Sacher-Masoch and Sade, however, Delany is not particularly concerned with producing that black utopia through reference to a body ensnared. Instead, he consistently turns to the image of the body in flight, the body that gives definition to community by remaining distinct from community, the body that can never be recognized as unreal precisely because it is never available for examination, never verified by touch.

It is an easy enough matter to demonstrate that Delany's partnership with Douglass in the early years of the *North Star*'s publication, particularly his travel to and examination of far-flung stretches of Black America, represents a beginning point in the development of an aesthetic practice that would privilege both abstraction and the physical body, the figure of the runner and the figure of the domesticated, tortured slave. Douglass and Delany reveled in the production of a cosmopolitan flavor for the paper that in any issue might feature foreign reports, sketches of John Quincy Adams, Alexander Dumas, or Toussaint L'Ouverture; news items on the Mexican-American war; features on blind sculptors, the Crafts' tour of Germany; and the development of telescopes and microscopes, as well as extensive reporting on the abolitionist movement and the state of the free black community.[6] Yet the necessity of grounding the paper in some sense of black—versus abolitionist—specificity was paramount to the editors. Douglass writes,

> Hitherto the immediate victims of slavery and prejudice, owing to various causes, have had little share in this department of effort: they have frequently undertaken, and almost as frequently failed. This latter fact has often been urged by our friends against our engaging in the present enterprise; but, so far from convincing us of the impolicy of our course, it serves to confirm us in the necessity, if not the wisdom, of our undertaking. That others have failed is a reason for our earnestly endeavoring to succeed. Our race must be vindicated from the embarrassing imputations resulting from former non-success. We believe that what *ought* to be done *can* be done. We say this in no self-

> confident or boastful spirit, but with the full sense of our weakness and unworthiness, relying upon the Most High for wisdom and strength to support us in our righteous undertaking.[7]

Even so, Douglass and Delany continued to face the assumption that there was no specificity to black genius. That the black was literate, that he could successfully publish a newspaper, might act as proof of some nebulously defined equality, but it did nothing to help establish some field of knowledge to which black subjects had privileged access. Once the vindication of the race was accomplished why indeed should "black subjects" continue to be taken up exclusively by black people?

The answer that Douglass and Delany embed in the very structure of *The North Star* turned on the same Herderian notions of national culture that influenced generations of students of so-called national character.[8] The culture of the black may be disseminated by the intellectual in the metropolis, but it is produced by the folk in the hinterland. Thus, the role of the black intellectual necessarily involves travel, shuttling back and forth between the roots of the culture and the means of that culture's representation.[9] The very fact that Delany is absent is what makes him vital to the functioning of the *North Star*. It suggests, moreover, how deeply implanted within Delany's aesthetic practice the trope of running actually was. In particular, it provides a way to understand why Delany, especially in *The Condition,* was so concerned with the notion of black emigration or, rather, the aesthetic and sociological schematization of this same running motif. Delany offers a quite compelling argument for mass expatriation, citing the 1851 Fugitive Slave Act itself as proof of the disdain and contempt of the United States government for its black subjects. He concludes that Black Americans should not expect justice within the confines of the United States and offers a number of sites as possible locations for black resettlement, especially Central and South America.[10] Thus, Black America can be actualized once she runs from herself, moves away from the very realities out of which she has been produced.

Yet very few have recognized the obvious philosophical impasse embedded within Delany's emigrationism. His understanding that the black must run in order to establish himself as a modern subject stems from a more basic belief that black subjectivity must not come at the expense of normative modes of black corporeality. One had always to drag one's body along on any foray into civic life. He writes, "Nor was it, as is frequently very erroneously asserted, by colored as well as white persons, . . . on account of hatred to the African, or in other words, on account of hatred to his color, that the African was selected as the subject of oppression in this country" (Delany [1852] 1988, 21). He argued instead that it was the very fact of the Black American's obvious degradation that constructed him as a social pariah, *not* the fact of his black body. Thus, in resisting their exploitation, Black Americans did not have to deny their color, as it were. Instead, they had literally to recapture black bodies from white households. Thus, Delany is eager to see the black disavow his status as body servant, a proto-subject brought into existence only through intimate physical contact with white masters.[11] What we see in Delany, then, is an attempt to abstract blackness from certain (embodied) realities precisely to give definition to a "real" blackness, one distinct from the enervating interracialism of American slavery.

I would ask the reader to consider the fact that, as Doris Sommer has pointed out, the development of discourses on nationalism coincided in the West with both the development of pro-bourgeois economic discourses *and* discourses on sexuality. She suggests that in the production of a national subject, bourgeois universalism had always to be paired with a real and embodied desire, one that would establish a national specificity within modes of bourgeois figuration. Sommer writes, "sex was forced into a productive economy that distinguished a legitimate realm of sexuality inside a clearly demarcated conjugal relationship and 'banished' the casual pleasures of polymorphous sexuality."[12] Bourgeois subjectivity did not, therefore, become absolutely unified within the modern period. Instead, I read both Sommer and Foucault as specifically refusing the assumption that "polymorphous sexuality" ever came to be fully repressed within the narratives—and the narrative strategies—that they examine. There is always a desirous, unstable body threatening to breach the very borders that have been produced to manage it. The pleasure of Delany's texts lies, then, in their insistence that knowledge is produced through the interplay of normative, binaristic modes of corporeality, the repression of competing modes, and the transcendence of that repression.

I would point to the constant calls by antebellum Black American intellectuals for blacks to give up their relatively relaxed attitudes toward sexuality and to sever their sexual, romantic, and familial ties to whites. I suggest that these calls were themselves proof of the fact that these same intellectuals always understood their work as both challenged and supported by an untameable black body.[13] In the specific case of Martin Delany his particular genius was his ability to narrativize the repression of this (black) body while continuing to privilege it as a site of meaning. The attempt by black antebellum intellectuals to encourage, or perhaps to enforce, a "respectable" sexual practice was not only an act of acquiescence to bourgeois norms, not only a rather self-conscious attempt to sever ties to that which smacked of slavery, to squelch sexual—and racial—liberality, but also an attempt to reference a pristine blackness, a clean racial difference, even while anxiously attempting to suggest that racial difference was not all important in public life. Take these lines drawn from an 1855 exposé of the Liberian colony:

> A large number of the colonist women have been reduced to the extremity of marrying, or taking up with naked native men, and are living with them in shameless co-habitation; and to estimate this degradation properly, it is necessary to know, that nothing can exceed the supreme contempt with which the colonists always regard the natives.[14]

> One colonist named Early . . . abandoned his wife, bought ten native wives, seven of whom had children by him, set up a town for himself, and became a great man there. (Miller 1859, 57)

What is so remarkable about these passages is the fact that bodies are centered in our gaze even and especially when the effects of these bodies are bemoaned. Contempt for the anti-African, pro-colonial, pro-slavery sentiment of the American Colonization Society, the organization primarily responsible for the erection and maintenance of Liberia, is conflated with distaste for female degradation, the dissolution of marriage, *and* profligate sexuality—all the while black bodies are demonstrated in a manner that suggests their absolute necessity in any narrative of black subjectivity. It is true. Remove a Black American to the continent and she behaves like a native. Leave a black man under the hot, bewitching African sun and he will leave his wife, take ten native women, and set himself up as a king. Thus race, gender, and sexuality, the discourses of this body, enabled the manipulation of notions of a universal bourgeois subjectivity for the local project of establishing a specifically Black American sense of national belonging precisely by pointing to presumably natural—and racial—desires upon which that body is always at risk of acting.

This is all by way of my attempting to establish Delany's aesthetic practices as emblematic of those deployed by early national and antebellum Black American writers in their production of Black American literature and culture. The title of this book, *Conjugal Union*, is itself taken from Delany's attempt to narrate the proper relation of body, community, and subjectivity—one in which the marriage relation is understood to bring together individuals precisely through ministration to bodies. Thus, I have privileged the term *conjugal* versus *marriage* because I want always to be cognizant of the fact that the domestic is itself established on a complex understanding of the body that renders it both product and producer of that same domesticity.

I place Delany's literature at the very pinnacle of antebellum Black American writing precisely because it expresses so vividly the complicated process of establishing a black public presence, a black subject, who can be seen, not in spite of, but because of his body, because of the fact that he has been "worked" already, produced in private as rational, representative, *and* black. Delany better than almost all his peers was able to imagine a world in which the emphasis was placed squarely on the body, in which a man might literally grab hold of his destiny, his subjectivity, and make something of them, something that could be touched. The workings of this particular discursive project are made most apparent in Delany's novel *Blake, or the Huts of America.*

The novel's action follows Henrico "Henry" Blacus's attempt to reunify and avenge his family or, rather, to pull together the pieces of his family, both literal and figurative, after the onset of the white man's degradations. Henry, later known as Blake, is described as "a black—pure Negro—handsome, manly and intelligent," thereby referencing the dark skin and presumably unadulterated

Africanity of Delany himself and, more important, the Toussaintesque masculinity thought so necessary for the production of conjugal union.[15] Blake's wife, the "mulatto" daughter of the slave master, is "true to her womanhood" (Delany 1970, 8). Indeed, she has been sold because of her refusal to succumb to the sexual advances of her master and father, Colonel Franks. As a consequence, Blake flees the plantation, taking his infant son and several others with him. The remainder of the novel is taken up with his attempt to find his wife, reunify his family, and avenge their wrongs. In the process, he travels throughout the slave South, then to Cuba and Africa, all along providing sketches of "the Black American People." He has intelligence, skill, capital, and a loving wife and child to boot. And yet the novel insists on the fact that he is unfailingly black, his name itself all but announcing this reality.

Blake, as one might guess, has been immersed fully in the gospel of capital accumulation—financial, cultural, and otherwise. He admonishes slaves throughout the text to get money at all costs, arguing that it is money that opens the door to freedom. He believes, moreover, that petty moral or philosophical concerns should not deter the nascent bourgeois from his task:

> Keep this studiously in mind and impress it as an important part of the scheme of organization, that they must have money, if they want to get free. Money will obtain them everything necessary by which to obtain their liberty. The money is within all of their reach if they only knew it was right to take it. God told the Egyptian slaves to "borrow from their neighbors"—meaning their oppressors—"all their jewels;" meaning to take their money and wealth wherever they could lay hands upon it and depart from Egypt. So you must teach them to take all the money they can get from their masters, to enable them to make the strike without a failure. (Delany 1970, 43)

Delany gives credence not only to the particularly American idea that the only acceptable distinctions between men are ones of individual merit, not inherited social rank but also that one's worth might not be misjudged by one's ability to accumulate capital. Blake defends the fact that he has "stolen" money from his master by pointing out the hypocrisy of the slaveowning aristocrat's monopolization of wealth that he has not produced. "I'm incapable of stealing from any one, but I have, from time to time, taken by littles, some of the earnings due me for the more than eighteen years service to this man Franks. . . . 'Steal' indeed! I would that when I had an opportunity, I had taken fifty thousand instead of two" (Delany 1970, 31).

Perhaps even more to the point, Delany works to establish not only the slave's essential degradation but the master's enfeeblement as well. The master, in Delany's social schema, becomes so alienated from the production of goods and services that he loses all knowledge of the process by which he himself is reproduced. Even the master who has taken the first halting steps toward establishing bourgeois status has somehow lost control over his body, such that he must literally consume the body of the slave in order to reproduce himself.

In a conversation between Judge Ballard, a Yankee entrepreneur who has traveled recently to the South to purchase a cotton plantation, and Major Armsted, a southerner well versed in the intricacies of plantation economies, we find that the judge has a distaste for Negroes. The major points out, however, that it is these very Negroes who produce the commodities that sustain them.

> "Did ever it occur to you that black fingers made that cigar, before it entered your white lips! . . . and very frequently in closing up the wrapper, they draw it through their lips to give it tenacity."
>
> "The deuce! Is that a fact, Major!"
>
> "Does that surprise you, Judge? I'm sure the victuals you eat is cooked by black hands, the bread kneaded and made by black hands, and the sugar and molasses you use, all pass through black hands, or rather the hands of Negroes pass through them; at least you could not refrain from thinking so, had you seen them as I have frequently, with arms full length immersed in molasses."
>
> "Well Major, truly there are some things we are obliged to swallow, and I suppose these are among them." (Delany 1970, 62–63)

Delany eloquently demonstrates both the ignorance of the would-be master and his vulnerability. Without the assistance of the Negro he literally cannot eat. The hypocrisy of the slaver's claim that he has produced his own wealth and that the exigencies of this particular social formation require the separation of the races is made evident. Delany places into the slaver's mouth, as it were, the ultimate indictment of his parasitical relationship to the slave. The slave has become part of the cigars and molasses that the master consumes. The master has become so alienated from his own body that he needs the Negro as a sort of prosthetic. Hence, the life of the Negro becomes one not only with the "life" of the commodity but with the life of the master as well. What the judge is really obliged to swallow is not simply the knowledge of the always already of interracial intimacy but also the very lives, indeed the bodies, of the slaves whom he presumably detests.

At the same time, we see Delany naming the black body's tendency toward abstraction. He works, in fact, to demonstrate that the slaver's obsession with the body of the black works ultimately to produce it as a fiction, even and especially when violence presumably marks its ineffacable "realness." Delany's thinking in these matters is made explicit in a scene that has been placed directly at the center of the narrative. The chapter "Solicitude and Amusement" opens innocently enough. The reader is led to believe that, apart from the matronly concern of Mrs. Franks for the recently sold Maggie, this chapter will operate as a rather pedestrian description of the social lives of southern planters. Judge Ballard and Major Armsted are invited by their host, Colonel Franks, to "see the sights" at the nearby plantation of Mr. Grason. The visit is designed as the initiation of Judge Ballard into southern life. Grason fetes his guests with food and brandy, boasting "I've got a *queer* animal here; I'll show him to you after dinner" (emphasis mine).

Dinner over, the gentlemen walked into the *pleasure grounds*, in the rear of the mansion.

"Nelse, where is Rube? Call him!" said Grason to a slave lad, brother to the boy he sent for.

Shortly there came forward, a small black boy about eleven years of age, thin visage, projecting upper teeth, rather ghastly consumptive look, and emaciated condition. The child trembled with fear as he approached the group. "Now gentlemen," said Grason, "I'm going to show you a sight!" having in his hand a long whip, the cracking of which he commenced, as a ring-master in the circus. . . . "Wat maus gwine do wid me now? I know wat maus gwine do," said this miserable child, "he gwine make me see sights!" when going down on his hands and feet, he commenced trotting around like an animal.

"Now gentlemen, look!" said Grason. "He'll whistle, sing songs, hymns, pray, swear like a trooper, laugh, and cry, all under the same state of feelings."

With a peculiar swing of the whip, bringing the lash down upon a certain spot on the exposed skin, the whole person being prepared for the purpose, the boy commenced to whistle almost like a thrush; another cut changed it to a song, another to a hymn, then a pitiful prayer, when he gave utterance to oaths which would make a Christian shudder, after which he laughed outright; then from the fullness of his soul he cried:

"O maussa, I's sick! Please stop little!" casting up bogs of hemorrhage.

Franks stood looking on with unmoved muscles. Armsted stood aside whittling a stick; but when Ballard saw, at every cut the flesh turn open in gashes streaming down with gore, till at last in agony he appealed for mercy, he involuntarily found his hand with a grasp on the whip, arresting its further application.

"Not quite a southerner yet Judge, if you can't stand that!" said Franks on seeing him wiping away the tears. (Delany 1970, 66–67)

After the men have consumed food and brandy, all presumably produced by slave hands, they proceed to abuse the slave in a manner that is clearly intended to express their own omnipotence in relation to the slave's absolute helplessness. I would ask, however, that we shake off the stunning effects of this passage long enough to consider its formal complexities. The whip works to establish not only a brutish and grotesque white subjectivity but also a sort of black fantastic through access to a real black body. The torture of the boy allows the release of a language of the body that exists absolutely apart from the efforts of the white slavers. The boy's own ritualistic submission comes on cue: "Wat maus gwine do wid me now? I know wat maus gwine do." "O maussa, I's sick! Please stop little!" Even as his humanity is squelched and his body is decimated, he comes to move beyond the limits of blackness to access universalistic, presocial discursive modes that do not and cannot reference any sort of black physical or communal normativity. With the swing of the lash the master reduces the boy to his basic elements while also cracking open the mask, the studied art of dissimulation, to reveal an essential and transcendent humanity, an at once embodied and *dis*embodied genius: "the boy commenced to whistle almost like a thrush; another cut changed it to a song, another to a hymn, then a pitiful prayer, when he gave utterance to oaths which would make a Christian shudder."[16]

I will turn for a moment to the work of Julia Kristeva to suggest that what we witness during the beating of the young slave is the revelation of the possibilities inherent in violence, and in particular that violence that allows us access to the abject. The very process by which the humanity of the black subject is denied, the violence by which the distinction between the human and the animal/object gives way, can lead to an awareness of the "possibilities just beyond our grasp." The slave, at the point of his whipping, at the moment of his death, behaves as neither recognizable subject nor object. He is a *queer* animal, existing outside of the subject/object binarism altogether.[17]

Kristeva argues that the borderline subject brings into play "contents" that are *normally* absent within rational thought, thought that maintains the I/Other, Inside/Out binarism. She also suggests that these contents represent a "sublimating discourse," one that stresses the aesthetic and the mystical over the scientific and the rational, that does not recreate the bifurcation of body and subjectivity. I would argue, therefore, that as the boy whistles, sings, prays, and makes oaths, all under the same state of feelings, he creates an index of black humanity that finds its efficacy precisely in the fact that it refuses rationalist modes of thought and expression. This is, however, precisely why he is such an improper figure, one who had to be at once celebrated and extricated. We should remember that Delany is not after any old universalism, but instead one that can be properly embodied, properly domesticated, properly figured as black. The boy's abjection leads us toward a fantastic world that must be rejected even before it is attained, precisely because it is a world without substantive black subjectivity.[18] Delany's deployment of spectacular violence works, therefore, both as a mimetic device in the articulation of the violence inherent in the denial of (black) humanity and rationality and as a means by which to make way for a new logic of subjectivity—one that, however liberating, must be immediately turned toward the specificities of bourgeois universalism and black corporeality.

The spectacle of the boy's ritualistic whipping is anticipated when Delany places Blake himself on the auction block. As Blake ascends the platform on which the worth of his humanity is to be judged, he occupies the space of the feminine, the homosexual, the abnormative. The eyes of the *male* crowd are on him, stripping him to essentials, creating him as dominated, exploited, and vulnerable.[19]

> "Come up here my lad!" continued the auctioneer, wielding a long red rawhide. "Mount this block, stand beside me, an' let's see which is the best looking man! We have met before, but I never had the pleasure of introducing you. Gentlemen one and all, I take the pleasure in introducing to you Henry—pardon me, sir—Mr. Henry Holland, I believe—am I right, sir?—Mr. Henry Holland, a good looking fellow you will admit.

> "I am offered one thousand dollars; one thousand dollars for the best looking Negro in all Mississippi! If all the negro boys in the state was as good looking as him, I'd give two thousand dollars for 'em all myself!" This caused another laugh. "Who'll give me one thousand five—"
>
> Just then a shower of rain came on. (Delany 1970, 26)

This passage is, of course, filled with double entendres that reveal the full scope of the white men's "insult." The auctioneer holds his *long red rawhide* as he invites Blake to *mount* the block. Several references are made to Blake's good looks, looks that increase his worth, much as good looks and fair skin suited many female slaves for the lucrative New Orleans sex markets. Just when the men have worked themselves into a frenzy, moreover, it rains, or a shower *comes*, as it were, thereby dissipating the sexual tension the passage works to build. The more significant insult, however, is the assertion that the black body, and in particular the black male body, can never adequately contain the universalist pretensions that Blake displays. The joke turns upon the fact that no black can ever attain status as a public subject, as mister, because of the fact that his body can never be overlooked. Instead, it is always tied to a "master" narrative that he never controls. Moreover, the black (man's) body is such an unstable thing that even gender cannot be firmly secured, thus the obvious feminization of Delany as he mounts the auction block. When we finally arrive at the scene of the boy's whipping and murder, the novel is rife with body violations: black becomes white, man becomes woman, master turns to slave, and so forth. Delany must work, therefore, to reestablish (black) normativity. In particular, he must recreate the unity between black corporeality and bourgeois universalism with which he is obsessed without again enacting the breaches that he finds so shocking.

Significantly, Blake receives his manhood immediately after the young slave's death. It is within the very next chapter, "Henry At Large," that Blake with "speed unfaltering" and "spirits unflinching" makes his final break with slavery. Only after the death of the pitiful youth is Blake able to call out to God and be heard.

> "Arm of the Lord, awake! Renew my faith, confirm my hope, perfect me in love. Give strength, give courage, guide and protect my pathway, and direct me in my course!" Springing to his feet as if a weight had fallen from him, he stood up a new man. (Delany 1970, 69)

I submit that the death of the youth is a sacrifice, of sorts. His passing allows both Blake and the white slavers to negotiate the slippery and treacherous terrain of the crossroads. The recognition of their own vulnerability, the knowledge of their own lack, is temporarily abated as the boy stands in for all that is, on the one hand, weak, innocent, and feminine and, on the other, dirty, promiscuous, and undisciplined. Christlike, he dies for the sins of "his" people so that they might become "new men." His death is absolutely necessary, therefore, for the further development of the narrative, in that it allows Delany a means by which to confront the work's many contradictions. As the boy dies Blake becomes the perfect hero. Not only is he manly, strong, and oh so embodied, oh so black, but he also manages somehow to exist beyond that body, so much so that he is able to escape slavery, travel the world, and foment an (inter)national revolution of slaves and free blacks in just a few hundred pages.

Blake sets on a journey immediately after the death of the boy in which he shuttles easily across the geographic, cultural, linguistic, political, and historical expanses that separate Africa from the Americas, the "mulatto" from the "pure," the Anglo from the Hispanic, rich from poor, even as his name changes from Henrico to Henry, from Blacus to Blake, depending on the particular configuration of cultures in which he finds himself. Again, I would argue that as Blake runs, as he removes his body from the possibility of close consideration, he establishes unity between a real black body and representative, universalist modes of bourgeois figuration. In the process he is able to produce a black (national) presence that is so real, so natural that even,

> the trees of the forest or an orchard illustrate it; flocks of birds or domestic cattle, fields of corn, hemp, or sugar cane; tobacco, rice, or cotton, the whistling of the wind, rustling of the leaves, flashing of lightning, roaring of thunder, and running of streams all keep it constantly before their eyes and in their memory, so that they can't forget it if they would. (Delany 1970, 39)

Blake becomes, then, both the perfect sociological organism and the vehicle of its abstraction. His trip to the farthest reaches of "New Africa" was accomplished with the greatest of ease as he shed and reconstructed his various identities, all the while spreading the twin gospels of nationalism and capitalism. His adventures, however, were not simply ones of exploration but also of conquest. Blake's work is to define the contours of the new Black (American) community, but the process of this definition necessarily involves the "domestication" of many parts of the African diaspora and the excision of others. Blake should be understood, then, not only as a device through which the various elements of the nation are illustrated but also and significantly the line along which the inside is separated from the out, the national from the foreign. His job becomes one of banishing from vision the tensions that disallow the fulfillment of the nationalist project while simultaneously fashioning the "excrescences" that are the constant result of this task into mythology, art, history, culture. Throughout, Blake initiates thinly veiled rituals of dominance that parallel, I believe, the torture of the young boy, but Delany is never obliged to acknowledge them as sadistic. He has projected all profligate aggressiveness onto his debased white subjects while simultaneously ridding himself—and the narrative—of the twin specters of weakness and culpability.

In the chapter following Blake's rebirth as a "new man," he happens upon a group of handsome young slave women whose loose clothing hangs upon them in tatters, but who nevertheless *instinctively* "drew their garments around and about them" when they noticed Blake's approach. Their lives are full of pain. They work from sunrise to sunset, seven days a week, with little to eat, dressed only in frocks made of coarse tow linen. Yet when asked which they prefer—the backbreaking toil of the fields or the less demanding work of the cotton gin, where Blake first encounters them—they choose the fields, for in the more public space of the gin "so many ole white plantehs come an' look at us, like we was show!" (Delany 1970, 77). Once again, Delany pulls our attention back to the notion of the black as (sexual) spectacle, the word *show* already having been overlain with erotic meaning. It is at this point that suddenly we are introduced to Blake's alter ego, who has returned once again from the realm of the unthinkable. Blake asks the women upon hearing that they are threatened sexually, "Who sees that the tasks are all done in the field?" They answer that it is Jerry, the black driver, and add that he mercilessly beats them. Blake assures them that "he'll never whip another" and then moves immediately back to the issue at hand, the leering white planters and the threat to newly established notions of racial distinction that they represent. He counsels the young women, "die before surrendering to such base purposes" and exits, telling them that his name is "Farewell" (Delany 1970, 79).

The almost gratuitous manner in which the bad black man is introduced in this passage, sandwiched between condemnations of lecherous white masculinity and complicitous or even treacherous black femininity, strikes me as significant because it represents such a glaring moment of awkwardness and uncertainty in the narrative. Here we have the performance of the black obscene. The black brute himself metes out the terror that engenders these young women's vulnerability, yet he is not depicted as some lurking, menacing threat whom the women must constantly avoid and outwit. Instead, he is almost an afterthought. Following Blake's exit we are casually informed that Jerry, the driver, "was missed, and never after heard of." What we see, then, is a return to the very problematic that has driven much of this discussion. The moment that Delany is able to establish securely the unity between the black body and black (bourgeois) universalism, he is forced to confront the fact of the body's profligacy. Rather, he must confront that which was revealed through the boy's torture. The body has its own logic that, once released, can be counted on to spoil our expectations. The black man in his black body may be the noble Blake. He may just as readily, however, be the abusive Jerry. Delany is almost forced to get rid of this paradox, even if in doing so he produces an unsightly tear in his narrative. In the process Blake is able to force recognition of himself, or the masculine, aggressive, and spotlessly moral aspects of himself, without having to ever acknowledge any unseemly needs and desires, the awkwardness of his own body.

Once this process has taken place, Delany produces what is fully the most joyous and sentimental moment in the text, the moment when finally all distinctions between body and community, body and the representation of the body, are disallowed, the moment when Blake becomes one with his (literary) alter ego, Placido. The "real" Placido was a black Cuban revolutionary and poet who was executed in Havana in 1844, some fifteen years before the first instalment of *Blake*.[20] Delany's Placido is described as a person of "slender form, lean and sinewy, rather morbid, orange-peel complexion, black hair hanging lively quite to the shoulders, heavy deep brow and full moustache, with great expressive black piercing eyes" (Delany 1970, 192–193). This description corresponds neatly with the thin, sickly slave youth. Yet there is a difference: this time we are encountering a man. The delicate poet is filled out with a deep brow and full moustache and most especially those great piercing eyes. He greets Blake sternly, not offering him a chair but commanding, "Be seated sir!" Moreover, Blake is connected intimately to this man, who we quickly discover is his cousin. It seems that finally Blake/Delany has found that other part of himself, that which is sensitive and creative but nevertheless virile. All boundaries break down as the two men recognize in one another an awareness of "self" and nation that ties them together into an indissoluble unity. It is as if Delany sets the feeble, effeminate youth free when he sacrifices him at the white slavers's altar and then sends Blake to find him, or rather the new, improved, masculine him. He erupts, "I am the lost boy of Cuba," as he rushes into Placido's arms, body and mind finally becoming one (Delany 1970, 193).

Delany never finished his novel, never demonstrated the pan-African revolt to which the work alludes, never set down in detail the contours of the government he envisioned. He did, however, accomplish his task. He created a model for how the many disparate peoples of the African diaspora might be produced as black, or more parochially as Black American. Cubans join hands with Africans while Henry Blake crosses continents and cultures to be reunited with Henrico Blacus. Moreover, he does so by establishing a union of mind and body, one that could be recreated through proper domestic relations.

Here, however, is where the decidedly masculinist tenor of Delany's black bourgeois nationalist project becomes most apparent. Even at the ultimate moment of bourgeois nationalist triumph, the meeting of the Grand Council in which the thorny details of black solidarity are to be worked through, the subjects, in the persons of Blake and Placido, exercise explicit dominance over a potentially unruly other, the "misses," who are admitted only through the men's courtesy (Delany 1970, 257). It is here that we see the performance of the pan-Africanism that earned for Delany the title, "father of black nationalism."[21] "Delegates" from the United States, Cuba, and Africa are present. They are rich and poor, black and mulatto, Protestant, Catholic, and (formerly) pagan. There are no divisions here. The previously omnipresent weakness and vulnerability of the black subject are no where to be found.

Still the "misses" resist, refusing to leave good enough alone. Their girlish—and disruptive—chatter gives way to the pointed questions of the aristocratic Madame Cordora, who takes Blake and Placido to task for the content, if not the form, of their prayers and exhortations. She asks, "Can we as Catholics, with any degree of propriety consistently with our faith, conform to those [nationalistic quasi-religious] observances?" Blake offers the quintessential bourgeois response, "No religion but that which brings us liberty will we know; no god but He who owns us as his children will we serve" (Delany 1970, 257). Madame Cordora continues with an even more difficult issue, "The poet [Placido] in his prayer spoke of Ethiopia's sons; are not some of us left out in the supplication, as I am sure, although identified together, we are not all Ethiopians." Placido responds, "How are the mixed bloods ever to rise? The thing is plain; it requires no explanation. The instant that an equality of the blacks with the whites is admitted, we being the descendants of the two, must be acknowledged the equals of both" (Delany 1970, 260–261).

It is striking that this interchange, for all its fanfare, boils down to an intellectual contest between Madame Cordora and the combined figures of Blake and Placido. The single and somewhat ignorant female confronts the male couple whose logic seems insurmountable. We are not even constrained by the knowledge that the real Placido's revolutionary ardor was cooled at the end of the executioner's noose. Actual black bodies, at least the bodies of black misses, can never be trusted to act properly, to allow themselves to be placed securely in the service of black nationality. It is necessary, therefore, that at least one more system of control, one more moment of violence, be enacted.

It should come as no surprise that the text comes to a close in a fit of marriages. Blake is reunited with Maggie, about whom we have heard almost nothing since the beginning of the text. Gofer Gondolier marries Abyssa Soudan, while Juan Montego catches Madame Cordora herself, thereby giving credence to the assertion that "the consummation of conjugal union is the best security for political relations" (Delany 1970 275). Conjugality not only steers us away from the fact of the palpable homoeroticism that the combined figures of Blake and Placido reflect but also helps settle the issue of how one might wed a peculiarly Black American body to the principles of (black) bourgeois universalism. Marriage does not, however, stop the process of resistance and domination that I explicated above. On the contrary, it simply reasserts the actors's commitment to this same process, creating them all as a species of loyal opposition. The fairly simplistic resolution that the marriages offer is possible only because much of the reality of black experience already has been denied so forcefully. These marriages, with their promise of black autonomy, nobility, and invulnerability, are only possible because the difficult and problematic aspects of the Black American community have been suppressed already. Yet the very rushed and rather pedestrian manner in which the "courtships" and marriages are rendered belies the notion of permanency. One might argue, in fact, that Delany's novel remains "unfinished" precisely because the process of nationalization that he describes is so obviously unstable and in need of constant reworking. The revolution that they plan is never enacted because the fantastic world, the black utopia that the revolution would have presaged, was not quite available to Delany or his contemporaries. It is in this sense that the questions of ambiguity with which we have been concerned throughout this book have not been resolved, but simply sewn more deeply into the narrative. As Delany points the accusing finger at the aristocratic master and the "helpless" slave, he also draws himself—and his narrative—into the very (violent) processes that he so loathes. At the same time, the abuse that we witness in the text allows for the articulation of a counterlogic, one that both precedes and transcends the rational discourse that Delany attempts to manipulate. Thus, even as Delany constructs a unified black (bourgeois) subject and black (bourgeois) literature, one can assume that this unity is ephemeral, fleeting. Like the footprints of the fugitive, the evidence of blackness can never stand by itself, but always must be measured, recorded, produced as abstraction, if its reality is to be established.

EPILOGUE

> The poor bondman lifts up a smiling face above the surface of a sea of agonies, hoping on, hoping ever. His tawny brother, the Indian, dies, under the flashing glance of the Anglo-Saxon. Not so the negro; civilization cannot kill him. He accepts it—becomes a part of it. In the church, he is an uncle Tom, in the state he is the most abused and least offensive. All the facts in his history mark out for him a destiny, united to America and Americans.
>
> —*Frederick Douglass*

> Up from this slavery gradually climbed the Free Negro with clearer, modern expression and more definite aim long before the emancipation of 1863. His great effort lay in his cooperation with the Abolition movement. He knew he was not free until all Negroes were free. Individual Negroes became the exhibits of the possibilities of the Negro race, if once it was raised above the status of slavery. Even when, as so often, the Negro became Court Jester to the ignorant American mob, he made his plea in songs and antics.
>
> —*W. E. B. Du Bois*

I will say again what I said at the outset. This book has been most concerned with questions of history *and* questions of historical representation. I ask not only who is the Black American but also how has the Black American come to be established, what technologies allow for the articulation of a seamless unity between the black body and black subjectivity? In my attempts to address these matters I have turned to the dynamic years immediately prior to the Civil War, when free blacks worked assiduously to establish a black public presence, an embodied and properly domesticated black self. As I hope my readings indicate, however, this process was hardly even or uncontested. Instead, much of the dynamism of early Black American literature stems from the fact that even as its architects made a concerted effort to announce the blackness of their work, they had to do so through media that could never—and can never—fully articulate the "fact" of racial peculiarity. Moreover, they were always aware of competing modes of corporeality that called into question normative modes of American racialism.

At the same time, I want to short-circuit the idea that what I have demonstrated in *Conjugal Union* is a literary and historical drama that remained essentially isolated within antebellum America. On the contrary, I suggest that the antebellum period was but the starting point in the very project of (re)constructing black subjectivity in which this study itself takes part. The insistence on conjugal union, the tying together of black bodies, black domesticities, and black (bourgeois) notions of universalism, has been and continues to be articulated within even the more rarefied precincts of American cultural and intellectual life. Moreover, the difficulties, the half starts, and the solipsisms of this project are as apparent today as they were in the 1850s. Thus, I invoke Du Bois in the same breath as Douglass, not to mark the peculiarity, the genius, of either man, but because I understand them as central figures in the production of just these peculiar forms of American corporeality.

Indeed, the force of Du Bois's argument in *Black Reconstruction* lies in his contention that enslaved persons were already prepared for the conflagration of the Civil War, not prepared by it. The close of slavery may have marked a definitive moment in the production, the articulation of the Black American, but it did not mark her origin.[1] The work of establishing an embodied black presence had been under way from some time before Lee's surrender at Appomattox. One of Du Bois's many gifts to American culture, then, is the fact that he so steadfastly refused the lie that the black vernacular, if you will, only began to announce itself in the twentieth century, particularly with the advent of the Harlem Renaissance. Instead, he insisted throughout his career that there was a (real, ancient) blackness to which one could gain access through recourse to the black body.

To put the matter in the most basic terms, Du Bois's struggle was to reconcile what Ronald Judy has called the negativity of the black subject with political and social exigencies that necessitated—and necessitate—the articulation of a real black body.[2] As Anthony Appiah, Paul Gilroy, Henry Louis Gates, and a spate of others have argued, blackness as a conceptual category has its origins in Enlightenment ideals of the sublime and transcendent, in which the black represented not simply that which was base and ugly but, more to the point, that which was the very antithesis of subjectivity. In this way, one might argue that the black does not reference the African per se, but instead a sort of conceptual void around which the ideological structures of white supremacy have been moored. As a consequence, Du Bois, as both philosopher and scientist, was left in the unenviable position of having to construct out of nothing, as it were, an identity, an ontological base for a modern black subjectivity, where presumably none existed before.

I would proceed even further in this vein by suggesting that the rather tired narrative in which Du Bois's elitism is juxtaposed with Booker T. Washington's accommodationism is inadequate because it does not take into account the fact that both men were concerned first and foremost with erecting structures by which black subjectivity might be articulated within modern society, structures that repeatedly turned to the black body as a means by which to secure unstable black ontology. It is important to note in this regard that, like Du Bois's Fisk, Washington's Tuskeegee was designed with the specific intent of training teachers through particular reference to this body, a body that presumably linked them to the students to whom they would minister. The work that was performed at Tuskeegee almost never included instruction or practice in the type of skilled labor that would suit students to take advantage of the new opportunities opening up in industry and agriculture. Instead, the often backbreaking toil was designed specifically to train a black elite (or perhaps to train the bodies of a black elite) in a manner that would suit them as agents of a compliant work ethic, in which blacks would accept—and indeed support—their relegation to the bottom rungs of the class and caste ladders. One might argue, then, that the cultural work that was being accomplished was, in a sense, the reestablishment of the black's presence within his body, even and especially as the fact of that body's peculiarity was brought most into question.[3]

It is this understanding, this sense of the complex question of the black body's relation to black ontology, that leads me to reject Cornel West's typification of Du Bois's aesthetic as essentially Arnoldian, a heavy-handed rearticulation of Victorian notions of an educated elite standing in contradistinction to the vulgar and anarchistic working masses.[4] Instead, I would argue that Du Bois's thinking was much more in line with Raymond Williams's notion of the cultural as the will (within industrial society) to maintain a nominally separate moral and intellectual universe that nonetheless works to mediate human interaction.[5] I leave you, then, with the understanding that Black American intellectuals have enacted just such a separate universe through constant reference to a black body that is itself mediated through domesticity, though households. Moreover, I must point out the fact that the image of the black family constantly bedeviled by the black runaway is hardly new, but comes to us from deep within the ideological structures through which American notions of racial distinctiveness have been constructed. At the same time, I heartily concur with those who would argue that there is much to be celebrated in the Black American fascination with our bodies and our homes. Still, I must ask, as we approach the millennium, how much longer can this particular set of ideological and discursive strategies serve our interests, especially in the face of the constant reports of black bodies and households under siege? What is to be gained in the often precious manner in which we cherish the common sense of black ontology? What worlds will collide if black bodies continue their promiscuous, self-interested longing? What catastrophes await the erection of improper households? What more is to be achieved through this union?

NOTES

Introduction

1. Here I draw directly on the work of Henry Louis Gates Jr., who demonstrates a significant shift in the genealogy of Black American literature during the antebellum period in which Wheatley's role as exemplar of the nascent Black American writing tradition was taken over by Frederick Douglass. See Henry Louis Gates Jr., "From Wheatley to Douglass: The Politics of Displacement," in Eric J. Sundquist, ed., *Frederick Douglass: New Literary and Historical Essays* (Cambridge: Harvard University Press, 1990): 47–65.

2. Wheatley writes,

> To show the lab'ring bosom's deep intent,
> And thought in living characters to paint,
> When first thy pencil did those beauties give,
> And breathing figures learnt from thee to live,
> How did those prospects give and my soul delight,
> A new creation rushing on my sight!
> Still, wondrous youth! each noble path pursue;
> On deathless glories fix thine ardent view:
> Still may the painter's and the poet's fire,
> To aid thy pencil and thy verse conspire!
> And may the charms of each seraphic theme
> Conduct thy footsteps to immortal fame!
> High to the blissful wonders of the skies
> Elate thy soul, and raise thy wishful eyes.
> Thrice happy, when exalted to survey
> That splendid city, crowned with endless day,
> Whose twice six gates on radiant hinges ring:
> Celestial Salem blooms in endless spring.
> Calm and serene thy moments glide along,
> And may the muse inspire each future song!
> Still, with the sweets of contemplation blessed,

May peace with balmy wings your soul invest!
But when these shades of time are chased away,
And darkness ends in everlasting day,
On what seraphic pinions shall we move,
And view the landscapes in the realms above!
There shall thy tongue in heavenly murmurs flow,
And there my muse with heavenly transport glow;
No more to tell of Damon's tender sighs,
Or rising radiance of Aurora's eyes;
For nobler themes demand a noble strain,
And purer language on the etherial plain.
Cease, gentle Muse! the solemn gloom of night
Now seals the fair creation from my sight.

"To S. M., A Young African Painter," in Phillis Wheatley, *Poems of Phillis Wheatley, A Native African and a Slave* (1838; reprint, Bedford, Mass.: Applewood Books, 1969).

3. I am certainly not the first to point out that, though persons of African descent were hardly understood as equal within colonial and antebellum America, the assumption of a solid bifurcation between black and white developed only by fits and starts and was not wholly available to American intellectuals until well into the nineteenth century. See, for example, George M. Frederickson, *The Black Image in the White Mind: The Debate on Afro-American Character and Destiny, 1817–1914* (New York: Harper and Row, 1971); Dana D. Nelson, *The Word in Black and White: Reading "Race" in American Literature 1638–1867* (New York: Oxford University Press, 1992); Frank Shuffleton, ed., *A Mixed Race: Ethnicity in Early America* (New York: Oxford University Press, 1993); Mechal Sobel, *The World They Made Together: Black and White Values in Eighteenth Century Virginia* (Princeton: Princeton University Press, 1987); and Jean Fagan Yellin, *The Intricate Knot: Black Figures in American Literature, 1776–1863* (New York: New York University Press, 1972).

4. Sterling Stuckey, *Slave Culture: Nationalist Theory and the Foundations of Black America* (New York: Oxford University Press, 1987). See also William L. Andrews, *To Tell a Free Story: The First Century of Afro-American Autobiography, 1760–1865* (Chicago: The University of Illinois Press, 1986); R. J. M. Blackett, *Beating Against the Barriers: Biographical Essays in Nineteenth-Century Afro-American History* (Baton Rouge: Louisiana State University Press, 1986); John Ernest, *Resistance and Reformation in Nineteenth-Century African-American Literature: Brown, Wilson, Jacobs, Delany, Douglass and Harper* (Jackson: University Press of Mississippi, 1995); James Oliver Horton and Lois E. Horton, *In the Hope of Liberty: Culture, Community and Protest Among Northern Free Blacks, 1700–1860* (New York: Oxford University Press, 1997); Frankie Hutton, *The Early Black Press in America, 1827–1860* (Westport, Conn.: Greenwood Press, 1993); Leon Litwack, *North of Slavery: The Negro in the Free States, 1790–1860* (Chicago: The University of Chicago Press, 1961).

5. See Penelope Bullock, *The Afro-American Periodical Press, 1838–1909* (Baton Rouge: Louisiana State University Press, 1981); Frances Smith Foster, *Written by Herself: Literary Production by African American Women, 1746–1892* (Bloomington: Indiana University Press, 1993); Garland I. Penn, *The Afro-American Press and Its Editors* (1891; reprint, New York: Arno Press, 1969).

6. The reference is, of course, to William Wells Brown's 1853 novel, *Clotel, or the President's Daughter* (1853; reprint, New York: University Books, 1969).

7. See Karen Sanchez-Eppler, *Touching Liberty: Abolition, Feminism and the Politics of*

the Body (Berkeley: University of California Press, 1993). See also Sharon Cameron, *The Corporeal Self: Allegories of the Body in Melville and Hawthorne* (Baltimore: Johns Hopkins University Press, 1981); Hortense Spillers, "Mama's Baby, Papa's Maybe: An American Grammar Book." *Diacritics* 17.2 (1987). I will attempt to maintain throughout *Conjugal Union* a critical distinction between corporeality as an ideological process and the body as a physical fact. This is while I have been influenced by Judith Butler's astute observation that "real bodies" are always produced through discursive processes so that it is impossible to separate the physical "fact" of the body from our various methods of narrating that fact. See Judith Butler, *Bodies That Matter: On the Discursive Limits of "Sex"* (New York: Routledge, 1993).

8. This work grows out of a yet developing theoretical tradition in which the body is said to be primary within the project of establishing ontological stability, particularly with regards to race and nation. Nonetheless, that body is always understood as itself a fiction, a site of varying discursive strategies that produce what we might call the effect of corporeality. As Fanon has pointed out, our understanding of the black always begins at the level of the corporeal. The black is at once raw sex, physical labor, and chattel property. The fact of blackness can never be erased, even and especially because it is so obsessively referenced in the production of modern subjectivities. The white child references a real blackness, "Mama see the Negro, I'm frightened," even as that reference is always already an act of projection. Frantz Fanon, *Black Skin, White Masks* (New York: Grove Press, 1967). See also Mary Douglas, *Purity and Danger: An Analysis of Concepts of Pollution and Taboo* (New York: Frederick A. Praeger Publishers, 1966); Elaine Scarry, *The Body in Pain: The Making and Unmaking of the World* (New York: Oxford University Press, 1985); Peter Brooks, *Body Work: Objects of Desire in Modern Narrative* (Cambridge: Harvard University Press, 1993); Laura Doyle, *Bordering on the Body* (New York: Oxford University Press, 1994); Robyn Wiegman, *American Anatomies: Theorizing Race and Gender* (Durham: Duke University Press, 1995); George Mosse, *Nationalism and Sexuality: Middle Class Morality and Sexual Norms in Modern Europe* (Madison: The University of Wisconsin Press, 1985); and Jane Gallop, *Thinking Through the Body* (New York: Columbia University Press, 1988).

9. *Memoir of Phillis Wheatley*, in Phillis Wheatley, *Poems of Phillis Wheatley, A Native African and a Slave* (1838; reprint, Bedford, Mass.: Applewood Books, 1969). 81–100.

10. In advancing these arguments I will borrow liberally from Nancy Armstrong's powerful discussion of the role of domesticity in the production of modern subjectivity. I am largely convinced by her use of Foucault to suggest that the British middle classes should not be seen as the antecedents of their representation, but instead as the products of that representation. I hope that it is obvious that I am attempting a similar procedure in relation to Black Americans and the cultural products that have come to be known as Black American. Where my work diverges from Armstrong's, however, is in my emphasis on the historical specificities of antebellum America. I insist upon the understanding that the domestic institutions of the early national and antebellum periods had necessarily to encompass the realities of slavery, racial mixing, and racial intimacy. In order to establish the bourgeois codes of domesticity that Armstrong illuminates, American writers, black and otherwise, had somehow to rescue the family from the messy domesticity engendered by slavery; earlier, more flexible notions of familial investiture, and of course the shocking examples of interracial conjugality so apparent just across U.S. borders. One had somehow to establish a logic of corporeality that worked to define which

bodies could produce—and be produced by—which households. Thus, I must necessarily push beyond Armstrong's work to reveal how the domestic negotiates and constitutes not only class and gender identity but race as well. Rather, I demonstrate throughout *Conjugal Union* that discourses of the body (including race) and discourses of domesticity are mutually constitutive. There can be no household in the mid-nineteenth century that is not already a racialized household. Indeed, households, as we will see especially in chapter 2, are specifically produced as defining agents within American racialist discourse. In this way my work builds upon the small, if impressive, body of literature, especially that produced by Hazel Carby, Carla Peterson, and Claudia Tate, that seriously challenges the "race neutral" narratives of domesticity articulated by Nancy Armstrong and Mary Kelley, among others. See Nancy Armstrong, *Desire and Domestic Fiction: A Political History of the Novel* (New York: Oxford University Press, 1987); Mary Kelley, *Private Woman, Public Stage: Literary Domesticity in Nineteenth Century America* (New York: Oxford University Press, 1984). Hazel Carby, *Reconstructing Womanhood: The Emergence of the Afro-American Woman Novelist* (New York: Oxford University Press, 1987); Carla Peterson, *"Doers of the Word": African American Women Speakers and Writers in the North (1830–1880)* (New York: Oxford University Press, 1995); Claudia Tate, *Domestic Allegories of Political Desire: The Black Heroine's Text at the Turn of the Century* (New York: Oxford University Press, 1992).

11. There is, of course, already a well-developed literature rigorously asserting the centrality of writing and print culture to the production of public subjectivities. It is true that few of these works manage sustained discussions of either race or the vigorous efforts of blacks within the contexts and communities that they describe. Still, I want not only to announce the presence of blacks within antebellum and early national American literary culture but also to suggest that as the sense of a specifically American literary project developed, blackness became in many respects the cipher that allowed an apparent disembodiment of "the American subject," a disembodiment that was essential to the production of a disinterested American citizenship. The fact of the black body, the fact of blackness, allowed for the production of a transcendent and transparent whiteness while precluding the production of a public "black" subjectivity. See Cathy N. Davidson, *Revolution and the Word: The Rise of the Novel in America* (New York: Oxford University Press, 1986); Christopher Looby, *Voicing America: Language, Literary Form, and the Origins of the United States* (Chicago: The University of Chicago Press, 1996); Jane Tompkins, *Sensational Designs: The Cultural Work of American Fiction, 1790–1860* (New York: Oxford University Press, 1985); Michael Warner, *The Letters of the Republic: Publication and the Public Sphere in Eighteenth-Century America* (Cambridge: Harvard University Press, 1990); Michael Warner, "The Mass Public Sphere and the Mass Subject," in Craig Calhoun, ed., *Habermas and the Public Sphere* (Cambridge: The MIT Press, 1992), 377–402; and Larzer Ziff, *Literary Democracy: The Declaration of Cultural Independence in America* (New York: Viking Press, 1981).

12. Jean Fagan Yellin, *Women and Sisters: The Antislavery Feminists in American Culture* (New Haven: Yale University Press, 1989). The historical literature clearly indicates not only a fair amount of sexual contact between black and white persons during the nineteenth century but also regular incidents of black/white cohabitation. See Martha Elizabeth Hodes, *White Women, Black Men: Illicit Sex in the Nineteenth Century South* (New Haven: Yale University Press, 1997). I am also eager to stress the fact that even though this study is an exclusively American affair, I am altogether mindful of the reality that the

production of America was and is a transnational endeavor. This is readily apparent in any examination of the country's incredible fear that foreign racialisms might insert themselves into the American common sense. See especially Paul Gilroy, *The Black Atlantic: Modernity and Double Consciousness* (Cambridge: Harvard University Press, 1993); and Anne McClintock, *Imperial Leather: Race, Gender and Sexuality in the Colonial Contest* (New York: Routledge, 1995).

13. I am strongly influenced in this regard by Bakhtin. While I cannot take up a full-scale treatment of his incredible contributions to literary and cultural study, I would at least like to make the point that I was partially driven to undertake this project by the fact that in Bakhtin's explorations into literary form, in *The Dialogic Imagination* and especially within *Rabelais and his World*, he is so very insistent on recognition of the body's place in the production of meaning, or rather the manner in which a sort of excessive mechanics of embodiment is indispensable to the production of modern narrative. Mikhail M. Bakhtin, *The Dialogic Imagination: Four Essays*, trans. by Michael Holquist and Caryl Emerson, ed. by Michael Holquist (Houston: University of Texas Press, 1981); Mikhail M. Bakhtin, *Rabelais and His World*, trans. by Helene Iswolsky (Cambridge: MIT Press, 1968).

14. Though I emphasize the work of Black American novelists, journalists, and political writers largely because that work has been almost completely ignored in American literary scholarship, I am wholly aware of the fact that the rhetoric of blackness, if you will, was hardly exclusive to Black American individuals and communities. Eric Lott, Alexander Saxton, and David Roediger, among others, have shown that "the black" figured centrally in the production of American (white) culture in the antebellum period and beyond. See Eric Lott, *Love and Theft: Blackface Minstrelsy and the American Working Class* (New York: Oxford University Press, 1993); David Roediger, *The Wages of Whiteness: Race and the Making of the American Working Class* (New York: Verso, 1991); Alexander Saxton, *The Rise and Fall of the White Republic: Class Politics and Mass Culture in Nineteenth-Century America* (New York: Verso, 1990); Eric J. Sundquist, *To Wake the Nations: Race in the Making of American Literature* (Cambridge: Belknap Press of Harvard University Press, 1993); Kenneth Warren, *Black and White Strangers: Race and American Literary Realism* (Chicago: The University of Chicago Press, 1993).

15. At the Library Company of Philadelphia there is a very interesting 1858 travel narrative by David F. Dorr entitled *A Colored Man Round the World*, which is fairly unremarkable as a piece of literature except for the fact that in his travels, his running, he is constantly beset both by the fact of his own black body and by the technologies that work to establish competing ideologies of corporeal existence in the various cultures that he traverses. In speaking of a veiled woman whom he encounters, he writes, "I looked at her one hour, and she at me, through her eyelits. I would have given five pds. to lift her veil; I know she was pretty, her voice was so fluty, and her hands so delicate, and her feet so small and her dress so gaunty [*sic*]; she was like an eel. I do not believe she had any loves in her. I asked the guide if there was no way in the world to get acquainted with her, and he said, none under heaven." David F. Dorr, *A Colored Man Round the World* (Printed for the author, 1858). For a discussion of running and migration in Black American literature and culture, see Farah Jasmine Griffin, *"Who SetYou Flowin'": The African American Migration Narrative* (New York: Oxford University Press, 1994); and Phillis Klotman, *Another Man Gone: The Black Runner in Contemporary Afro-American Fiction* (Port Washington, N.Y.: Kennikat Press, 1977).

Chapter 1

1. See, for example, Bernard W. Bell, *The Afro-American Novel and Its Traditions* (Amherst: The University of Massachusetts Press, 1987); and especially Sterling Stuckey, *Slave Culture: Nationalist Theory and the Foundations of Black America* (New York: Oxford University Press, 1987).

2. David Walker, *Appeal to the Coloured Citizens of the World, But in Particular, and Very Expressly, to Those of the United States of America*, intro. by Charles M. Wiltse (1829; reprint, New York: Hill and Wang, 1965).

3. The origins, or perhaps the originality, of the black body were still being rigorously debated in the antebellum era. Take, for example, these lines from an 1854 pamphlet on race science.

> Some, in direct opposition to scripture, have asserted that these distinct tribes and nations, so diverse in stature, in colour, in language, and in physical conformation, could not all have descended from one common parent—that the peculiarities now observable in the structural anatomy of the different human races, have always existed, and separated those races as distinctly as one tribe of animals is divided from another. Climate and circumstances are not believed to have had any influence on these matters, and yet the very author who advances this opinion tells us afterwards that race is permanent, only so long "as the existing media and order of things prevail." What are we to understand by this, if not that climate and circumstances *have* power to affect changes in the human frame, and to produce all those diversities of character and conformation now observable in the great divisions of the family of man? We merely mention this to show the inconsistencies into which scientific men are often led, when in pursuit of a favourite theory, the more especially when that theory is at variance with the revealed truth; and to show also that those who contend for a natural and unchangeable inferiority of race, are not altogether so perfect in their wisdom, that we should listen to them in preference to the word of God, who tells us that He hath "made of one blood all the nations of men, to dwell upon the face of the earth." Is it not plain from this declaration, that all men are brothers—children of one common parent, aye, of one *earthly* parent?

See H. G. Adams, ed., *God's Image in Ebony: Being a Series of Biographical Sketches, Facts, Anecdotes, etc., Demonstrative of the Mental Powers and Intellectual Capacities of the Negro Race* (London: Partridge and Oakey, 1854). See also William Stanton, *The Leopard's Spots: Scientific Attitudes Toward Race in America, 1815–59* (Chicago: The University of Chicago Press, 1960).

4. Thomas Jefferson, *Notes on the State of Virginia* (1788; reprint, New York: Norton, 1954), 138.

5. Samuel Stanhope Smith, *An Essay on the Cause of the Variety of Complexion and Figure in the Human Species*... (Philadelphia: Robert Aitken, 1787).

6. Mrs. Maria W. Stewart, *Productions of Mrs. Maria W. Stewart* (1831), reprinted in Susan Houchins, *Spiritual Narratives* (New York: Oxford University Press, 1988), 20.

7. Tellingly, this speech was given as Stewart's farewell to public life. Responding to the prejudices against women's publicity, she mounted this one gallant attempt to defend herself, then left Boston and her life as a "public intellectual."

8. Robyn Wiegman, *American Anatomies: Theorizing Race and Gender* (Durham: Duke University Press, 1995), 64.

9. Nancy Armstrong, *Desire and Domestic Fiction: A Political History of the Novel* (New York: Oxford University Press, 1987), 9.

10. F. J., "Speak To That Young Man," *The Colored American*, 18 April 1840: 1.

11. See Jane H. Pease and William H. Pease, *They Who Would Be Free: Blacks' Search For Freedom, 1830–1861* (Urbana: University of Illinois Press, 1974).

12. William D. Piersen, *Black Yankees: The Development of an Afro-American Sub-Culture in New England* (Amherst: The University of Massachusetts Press, 1988).

13. James Oliver Horton, *Free People of Color: Inside the African American Community* (Washington, D.C.: Smithsonian Institution Press, 1993).

14. Henry Nbele, "Stanzas," *Freedom's Journal*, 23 March 1827: 8.

15. Henry Bibb, *Narrative of the Life and Adventures of Henry Bibb, An American Slave, Written by Himself* (1850; reprint, New York: Negro Universities Press, 1969), 33.

16. Angela Davis, "Reflections on the Black Woman's Role in the Community of Slaves," *Black Scholar* 3.4 (December 1971): 2–15.

17. John Jolliffe, "Dissolving the Union," *The Weekly Anglo-African*, 24 November 1860: 1.

18. "The Old Maid's Diary," *Freedom's Journal*, 2 November 1827: 134. "A Bachelor's Thermometer," *Freedom's Journal*, 9 November 1827: 137.

19. Take, for example, this passage: "[S]orry as we are to utter any thing which may tend to damp the hopes of or cloud the prospects of a fair lady, truth compels us to say that when once she has passed THE LINE . . . the chances are fearfully against the probability of her obtaining a husband, even of the sedate age of forty or fifty. If she pass many degrees beyond the line, her state becomes almost hopeless, nay, desperate, and she may reconcile herself to live and die as an old maid." "Chances of Marriage," *Freedom's Journal*, 29 September 1828: 21.

20. "To Our Patrons," *Freedom's Journal*, 16 March 1827: 1.

21. "Married," *Black Republican and Office Holders Journal*, August 1865: 2.

22. "Particular Notice," *Black Republican and Office Holders Journal*, August 1865: 3–4.

23. Frederick Douglass, *Narrative of the Life of Frederick Douglass, An American Slave*, in Michael Meyer, ed., *Frederick Douglass: The Narrative and Selected Writings* (1845; reprint, New York: Random House, 1984), 73.

24. This at least partially explains Henry Louis Gates's success at neatly schematizing the binary oppositions in Douglass's narrative. See Henry Louis Gates, Jr *Figures in Black: Words, Signs and the "Racial" Self* (New York: Oxford University Press, 1987).

25. Deborah McDowell offered one of the earliest and still most insightful discussions of the structures of gender within both Douglass's literature and the critical apparatuses that developed around it. See Deborah McDowell, "In the First Place: Making Frederick Douglass and the Afro-American Tradition," in William Andrews, ed., *Critical Essays on Frederick Douglass* (Boston: G. K. Hall, 1991); see also George Cunningham, "Called Into Existence: Desire, Gender and Voice in Frederick Douglass's *Narrative* of 1845," *differences* 1.3 (1989): 108–135; Jenny Franchot, "The Punishment of Esther: Frederick Douglass and the Construction of the Feminine," in Eric J. Sundquist, ed., *Frederick Douglass: New Literary and Historical Essays* (New York: Cambridge University Press, 1990), 141–165.

26. Gayle Rubin, "The Traffic in Women: Notes on the 'Political Economy' of

Sex," in Rayner Reiter, ed., *Toward an Anthropology of Women* (New York: Monthly Review Press, 1975).

Chapter 2

1. Lydia Maria Child, "The Quadroons," in Lydia Maria Child, *Fact and Fiction: A Collection of Stories* (New York, 1846); William Craft, *Running a Thousand Miles for Freedom, or the Escape of William and Ellen Craft From Slavery* (1860; reprint, Salem, N.H.: Ayer Publishers, 1991).

2. Addison Gayle, *The Way of the New World: The Black Novel In America* (Garden City, N.Y.: Anchor Press/Doubleday, 1975); Bernard W. Bell, *The Afro-American Novel and Its Traditions* (Amherst: The University of Massachusetts Press, 1987); Blyden Jackson, *The History of Afro-American Literature*, Vol. 1 (Baton Rouge: Louisiana State University Press, 1989). For more general discussions of Brown and his work, see William Edward Farrison, *William Wells Brown: Author and Reformer* (Chicago: The University of Chicago Press, 1969); J. Noel Heermance, *William Wells Brown and Clotelle: A Portrait of the Artist in the First Negro Novel* (Hamden, Conn.: Archon Books, 1969).

3. Brown's talents are not properly measured, therefore, by his abilities at sensitive and finely rendered revelations of the black idiom, especially given his willingness to borrow heavily, sometimes verbatim, from a promiscuous group of sources, including the minstrel stage. Moreover, as John Ernest has observed, Brown never celebrates the fact of his novel's singularity. That it was the first novel written by a Black American was a matter that received no comment at all from Brown in its first edition, nor did it cause him to regard the work as precious, or "finished." Though scant critical attention has been paid to them, Brown did publish two other versions of the work: *Clotelle: A Tale of the Southern States* and *Clotelle, or, The Colored Heroine*, in 1864 and 1867, respectively. There is some significant change between the versions, and Brown does not flinch at reworking the "facts" of his narrative to fit contemporary realities. In each of the novels, moreover, Brown makes abundantly apparent the work's embeddedness within the textual and graphic archives of American and European abolitionist culture. See John Ernest, *Resistance and Reformation in Nineteenth-Century African-American Literature: Brown, Wilson, Jacobs, Delany, Douglass and Harper* (Jackson: University Press of Mississippi, 1995).

4. My thinking on these issues has been greatly influenced by the work of Hazel Carby, who breaks with many other critics of Black American literature and culture in that she eschews the task of explicating the "tragic" dimensions of the mulatto figure in nineteenth-and early-twentieth-century Black American women's literature for an examination of the ideological function of these same elements: "the mulatta figure allowed for movement between two worlds, white and black, and acted as a literary displacement of the actual increasing separation of the races. The mulatta figure was a recognition of the difference between and separateness of the two races at the same time as it was a product of a sexual relationship between white and black." Hazel Carby, *Reconstructing Womanhood* (New York: Oxford University Press, 1987), 90. See also Werner Sollors, *Neither Black Nor White Yet Both: Explorations of Interracial Literature* (New York: Oxford University Press, 1997).

5. William Wells Brown, *St. Domingo: Its Revolutions and Its Patriots. A Lecture Delivered Before the Metropolitan Atheneum, London, May 16 and at St. Thomas' Church, Philadelphia, December 20, 1854* (Boston: Bela Marsh, 1855).

6. Stuart Hall, "The After-life of Frantz Fanon: Why Fanon? Why Now? Why

Black Skin, White Masks?," in Alan Read, ed., *The Fact of Blackness: Frantz Fanon and Visual Representation* (Seattle: Bay Press, 1996).

7. William Wells Brown, *Narrative of the Life and Escape of William Wells Brown*, in William Wells Brown, *Clotel, or the President's Daughter*, intro. by William Edward Farrison (1853; reprint, New York: University Books, 1969), 17.

8. As Guy Debord argues, "what the spectacle gives us is the total practice of one particular economic and social formation: it is, so to speak, that formation's *agenda.* It is also the historical moment by which we happen to be governed." Guy Debord, *The Society of the Spectacle*, trans. by Donald Nicholson-Smith (New York: Zone Books, 1994), 15.

9. Peter Brooks, *Body Work: Objects of Desire in Modern Narrative* (Cambridge: Harvard University Press, 1993).

10. William Wells Brown, *A Description of William Wells Brown's Original Panoramic Views of the Scenes in the Life of an American Slave, From His Birth in Slavery to His Death or His Escape to His First Home of Freedom on British Soil* (London: Charles Gilpin, n.d.), iii.

11. This fascination with the figure of the enslaved white was indeed a constant in abolitionist literature. Take, for example, these lines from *The North Star.*

> A white boy was taken from Virginia to South Carolina at the age of seven, and thence to Georgia and sold to Col. B. His daughter, the lady of a lawyer, related to me the fact, saying that the little fellow used to tell the story to their children and weep. His tale was this, that his mother was very poor, and at the time when she was sick, he was placed in a "Negro quarter," in the care of a Negro woman, and at night a man came and tied his feet and hands and took him on horseback.—He wept, and tried to scream, but the wretch placed his hands over his mouth. Col. B.'s wife prohibited his telling the story to the children, because it made them weep and unhappy. "Wash" died the slave of Col. B., at the age of 22.
>
> Another—Eliza was the offspring of parents in Virginia, in high life; but to conceal their guilt, their child, when an infant, was placed with a nurse at the "Negro quarters," and there raised. She was a few years ago sold, and is now owned by Mr. P., in a Southern city. She is white, and has no Negro blood in her composition, and has raised up a family of colored children. She is very badly treated. . . .
>
> Still Another—A few years ago, a "Negro trader" exchanged a colored slave for a little girl. On his arrival in Alabama, two or three slave holders protested that the child was white, and finally paid $400 for her, and returned her to Georgia, where it was ascertained that her parents died poor, and that she was sold into slavery. The gentlemen sent her to her kindred in North Carolina. The lady who told me this story says she saw the little girl, and she was a most beautiful child. "White Slavery," *The North Star*, 10 March 1848: 3

12. I borrow this notion of black Jeremiad from Wilson Moses. Wilson J. Moses, *Black Messiahs and Uncle Toms: Social and Literary Manipulations of a Religious Myth* (University Park: Pennsylvania State University Press, 1982).

13. Henry Louis Gates Jr., *Figures in Black: Words, Signs and the "Racial" Self* (New York: Oxford University Press, 1987); Robert Stepto, *From Behind the Veil: A Study of Afro-American Narrative* (Urbana: University of Illinois Press, 1979); Robert Stepto, "Narration, Authentication, and Authorial Control in Frederick Douglass' *Narrative* of 1845," in Wil-

liam L. Andrews, ed., *African American Autobiography: A Collection of Critical Essays* (Englewood Cliffs, N.J.: Prentice Hall, 1993), 26–35.

14. See Claudia Tate, *Domestic Allegories of Political Desire* (New York: Oxford University Press, 1992).

15. See Eve Sedgwick, *Between Men: English Literature and Male Homosocial Desire* (New York: Columbia University Press, 1985); Eve Sedgwick, *Epistemology of the Closet* (Berkeley: The University of California Press, 1990).

16. See Deborah M. Garfield and Rafia Zafar, eds., *Harriet Jacobs and Incidents in the Life of a Slave Girl: Critical Essays* (New York: Cambridge University Press, 1996).

17. Harriet Jacobs, *Incidents in the Life of a Slave Girl* (Cambridge: Harvard University Press, 1987), 5.

18. Frederick Douglass, *The Heroic Slave* in Michael Meyer, ed., *Frederick Douglass: The Narrative and Selected Writings* (1853; reprint, New York: Modern Library, 1984), 301.

19. For a very interesting discussion of the question of disembodiment in Douglass's writing, see Ben Slote, "Revising Freely: Frederick Douglass and the Politics of Disembodiment," *A/B: Autobiography Studies* 11:1 (Spring 1996): 19–37.

20. Ned, "Original Communications," *Freedom's Journal*, 4 May 1827: 2.

21. "Female Scandal," *Freedom's Journal*, 4 April 1828: 10.

22. This scandal matter was a regular subject of black antebellum journalism.

> Yes, you pass it along, whether you believe it or not—that one-sided whisper against the character of a virtuous female. You don't believe it, but you will use your influence to bear up the false report, and pass it on the current. Strange creatures are mankind. How many reputations have been lost by surmise—how many hearts have bled by whisper—how many benevolent deeds have been chilled by the shrug of the shoulder—how many individuals have been shamed by a gentle, mysterious hint—how many chaste bosoms have been [beset] with grief at a single nod—how many graves have been dug by false report? Yet you will pass the slander along. You will keep it above water with the wag of your tongue when you might sink it forever. Destroy the passion for tale-telling, we pray. List not a word that may injure the character of another, and as far as you are concerned, the slander will die. But tell it once, and it will go on the wings of the wind, increasing with each breath, till it has circulated through the state and has brought to the grave, one who might have been a blessing to the whole world. "Slander," *Mirror of the Times*, 12 December 1857: 2. See also Patricia Meyer Spacks, *Gossip* (New York: Knopf, 1985).

23. The name is taken from William Craft, who with his wife Ellen escaped from slavery in just this manner. See William Craft, *Running a Thousand Miles for Freedom, or the Escape of William and Ellen Craft from Slavery* (1860; reprint, Salem, N.H.: Ayer Publishers, 1991).

24. William Wells Brown, *My Southern Home: or, The South and Its People*, in William L. Andrews, ed., *From Fugitive To Free Man: The Autobiographies of William Wells Brown* (1880; reprint, New York: Mentor, 1993), 191–192.

25. Brown's fascination with the art of dissimulation is demonstrated further in his political and travel writing, especially in his treatment of the figure of Joseph Jenkins, a former slave, whom he encountered in London. Brown treats Jenkins extensively in the

1855 memoir of his European adventures, *Sketches of People and Places Abroad*, and again in his 1865 compilation of biographies, *The Black Man*, in which he describes Jenkins as the greatest genius he had met in Europe because he had become so adept at switching from one identity to the next. He was variously a handbill distributor in Cheapside, a crosswalk sweeper in Chelsea, a religious tract salesman in Kensington, a minister, and a band leader, as well as "Selim, the African Prince," who performed *Othello* in local saloons. See William Wells Brown, *The Black Man, His Antecedents, His Genius, and His Achievements* (1865; reprint, Salem, N.H.: Ayer Publishers, 1992), 259–265; William Wells Brown, *Sketches of People and Places Abroad; The American Fugitive in Europe* (1855; reprint, Freeport, N.Y.: Books for Libraries Press, 1970), 268–275.

26. This is where I must distinguish my work from Marjorie Garber's exceptional study of transvestism, *Vested Interests.* Therein she suggests that the transvestite operates as a third figure who exists, not between the poles of male and female, but as "a mode of articulation, a way of describing a space of possibility." Even though Garber's thinking goes a long way toward ridding us of simplistic notions of transvestism that reduce it to simple masquerade, I have chosen not to privilege the "crisis" of Clotel's transvestism because I am eager to place Brown's work within a historical context in which the mulatto exists, not as a figure, "a mode of articulation," within the production of a Black American literature, but instead as an actual historical agent. Brown's use of the spectacle of transvestism, then, is properly understood as an attempt to refract the *reality* of the mulatto's presence and agency instead of some half-defined status as a rhetorical or discursive device. See Marjorie Garber, *Vested Interests: Cross-Dressing and Cultural Anxiety* (New York: Routledge, 1992).

Chapter 3

1. My understanding of the interplay between market and household has been greatly influenced by the work of Gillian Brown. See Gillian Brown, *Domestic Individualism: Imagining Self in Nineteenth-Century America* (Berkeley: The University of California Press, 1990).

2. For more on the trope of cleanliness within American culture, see Suellen Hoy, *Chasing Dirt: The American Pursuit of Cleanliness* (New York: Oxford University Press, 1995).

3. Peter Stallybrass and Allon White, *The Politics and Poetics of Transgression* (Ithaca: Cornell University Press, 1986).

4. Frank J. Webb, *The Garies and Their Friends*, introduced by Robert F. Reid-Pharr (1857; reprint, Baltimore: Johns Hopkins University Press, 1997), 100.

5. See Stewart R. King, "Blue Coat or Lace Collar?" Military and Civilian Free Coloreds in the Colonial Society of Saint-Domingue," Ph.D. diss., Johns Hopkins University, 1997).

6. For more on the complex interaction between notions of the grotesque and (American) notions of racial distinction, see Leonard Cassuto, *The Inhuman Race: The Racial Grotesque in American Literature and Culture* (New York: Columbia University Press, 1997).

7. See especially "Domestic Politics in Uncle Tom's Cabin," in Gillian Brown, *Domestic Individualism: Imagining Self in Nineteenth-Century America* (Berkeley: The University of California Press, 1990), 13–38.

8. Zygmunt Bauman, *Modernity and Ambivalence* (Ithaca: Cornell University Press, 1991). I discuss the phobia within certain precincts of African-American nationalism

regarding third parties, or unclean interlopers, in Robert F. Reid-Pharr, "Speaking Through Anti-Semitism: The Nation of Islam and the Poetics of Black (Counter) Modernity," *Social Text* 14.4 (Winter 1996): 132–147.

9. The repeated occurrences of yellow fever in the United States during both the eighteenth and nineteenth centuries created such panic that normal modes of behavior were thrown unceremoniously by the wayside. Bodies remained unburied. The sick were not attended. More important, the social intercourse of blacks and whites was for a time radically altered. Persons of African descent were imagined to be less vulnerable to the effects of fever because of their supposedly increased ability to fight off tropical disease. As a consequence, blacks at times played prominent roles in the management of yellow fever outbreaks. This was particularly true of the infamous Philadelphia epidemic of 1793, during which African Americans volunteered to bury the dead and care for the dying while whites kept their distance for fear of becoming infected. "When the yellow fever raged in Philadelphia . . . and the whites fled . . . the colored people volunteered to do that painful and dangerous job. . . . It is notorious that many whites who were forsaken by their own relations and left to the mercy of this fell disease, were nursed gratuitously by the colored people." Thus in this appeal to the citizens of Philadelphia directed at securing black political rights we find a writer explicitly making the connection between [a] peculiar black body (the presumed immunity to yellow fever) and the fitness of blacks for positions within social and political life. See Robert Purvis, *Appeal of Forty Thousand Citizens, Threatened with Disfranchisement, to the People of Pennsylvania* (Philadelphia: Merrihew and Gunn, 1838), 13–14. See also Absalom Jones and Richard Allen, *A Narrative of the Proceedings of the Black People. During the Late Awful Calamity in Philadelphia, in the Year 1793: and a Refutation of Some Censure Thrown Upon Them in Some Late Publications* (Philadelphia: William W. Woodward, 1793); Benjamin Banneker, *Banneker's Almanac for the Year 1795: Being the Year After the Third Leap Year Containing (Besides Everything Necessary in an Almanac.) An Account of the Yellow Fever Lately Prevalent in Philadelphia; With the Number of those Who have Died. From the Fifth of August Till the Ninth of November, 1793* (Philadelphia: William Young Bookseller, 1795); and William Coleman, *Yellow Fever in the North: The Methods of Early Epidemiology* (Madison: The University of Wisconsin Press, 1987).

10. James Oliver Horton and Lois E. Horton, *In Hope of Liberty: Culture, Community and Protest Among Northern Free Blacks, 1700–1860* (New York: Oxford University Press, 1997).

11. Ira Berlin, *Slaves Without Masters: The Free Negro in the Antebellum South* (New York: The New Press, 1974).

12. Quoted in C. L. R. James, *The Black Jacobins: Toussaint L'Ouverture and the San Domingo Revolution* (New York: Vintage, 1963), 364.

13. Eric Lott, *Love and Theft: Blackface Minstrelsy and the American Working Class* (New York: Oxford University Press, 1993). Robert Levine also points to the 1842 attack on the Moyamensing Temperance Society as an important source for the riot scene. See Robert Levine, "Disturbing Boundaries: Temperance, Black Elevation, and Violence in Frank J. Webb's *The Garies and Their Friends*," *Prospects* 19 (1994): 349–374. See also Robert Levine, *Martin Delany, Frederick Douglass and the Politics of Representative Identity* (Chapel Hill: The University of North Carolina Press, 1997).

14. See James Oliver Horton, *Free People of Color: Inside the African American Community* (Washington, D.C.: Smithsonian Institution Press, 1993).

15. Paul Hoch's early discussion of the necessity of the black beast to the produc-

tion of white male identity has yet, in my opinion, to be eclipsed. See Paul Hoch, *White Hero, Black Beast: Racism. Sexism and the Mask of Masculinity* (London: Pluto, 1979).

16. The notion of the strange figure who acts as the spoiler of modern conceptions of community and identity has been developed by a number of scholars. See especially Julia Kristeva, *Strangers to Ourselves*, trans. by Leon S. Roudiez (New York: Columbia University Press, 1991); and Rene Girard, *The Scapegoat*, trans. by Yvonne Freccero (Baltimore: The Johns Hopkins University Press, 1986).

Chapter 4

1. Arlene Elder writes,

> The literary models chosen by nineteenth-century African American novelists were those of white sentimental and propaganda fiction and, to a lesser degree, Black American anti-slavery oratory and autobiographical narrative. The sentimental novel, which had been popular in America since the publication of *The Power of Sympathy* in 1789, was embraced wholeheartedly, even though melodramatic techniques shrouded these books in a romantic haze and riddled them with unreal characters and incredible incidents.

Arlene Elder, *"The Hindered Hand": Cultural Implications of Early African American Fiction* (Westport, Conn.: Greenwood Press, 1978), 3. See also Claudia Tate, "Allegories of Black Female Desire; or, Rereading Nineteenth-Century Sentimental Narratives of Black Female Authority," in Cheryl A. Wall, ed., *Changing Our Own Words: Essays on Criticism, Theory, and Writing by Black Women* (New Brunswick: Rutgers University Press, 1989), 98–126; Catherine Elizabeth O'Connell, "Chastening the Rod: Sentimental Strategies in Three Antebellum Novels by Women," Ph.d. diss., University of Michigan, 1992.

2. See Houston A. Baker Jr., *Long Black Song: Essays in Black American Literature and Culture* (Charlottesville: The University Press of Virginia, 1972); Houston A. Baker Jr., *The Journey Back: Issues in Black Literature and Criticism* (Chicago: The University of Chicago Press, 1980); Barbara Christian, *Black Women Novelists: The Development of a Tradition, 1892–1976* (Westport, Conn.: Greenwood Press, 1980); Barbara Smith, "Toward a Black Feminist Criticism," 1977. Reprinted in Angelyn Mitchell, ed. *Within the Circle: An Anthology of African American Literary Criticism From The Harlem Renaissance To The Present* (Durham: Duke University Press, 1994), 410–427. Robert Stepto, *From Behind the Veil: A Study of Afro-American Narrative* (Urbana: The University of Illinois Press, 1979).

3. The texts that I have most in mind are Henry Louis Gates Jr., *The Signifying Monkey: A Theory of African-American Literary Criticism* (New York: Oxford University Press, 1988); and Houston A. Baker Jr., *Blues, Ideology, and Afro-American Literature: A Vernacular Theory* (Chicago: University of Chicago Press, 1985). It is telling that both men, whose careers have in many ways paralleled the development of Black American literary and cultural study, subsequently produced significant contributions within the practice of (black) feminist and "woman-centered" criticism. See Henry Louis Gates Jr., ed., *Reading Black, Reading Feminist: A Critical Anthology* (New York: Meridian, 1990); Houston A. Baker Jr., *Workings of the Spirit: The Poetics of Afro-American Women's Writing* (Chicago: The University of Chicago Press, 1991).

4. See David Reynolds, *Beneath the American Renaissance: The Subversive Imagination in the Age of Emerson and Melville* (New York: Knopf, 1988).

5. Frederick Engels, *The Origin of the Family, Private Property and the State in Light of the Researches of Lewis H. Morgan* (1884; reprint New York: International Publishers, 1942), 64.

6. Of course, this insistence on the primacy of the body in the production of human subjectivity can easily turn toward just the types of racialism that Engels evinces with his reliance on Morgan and those telltale native American skulls.

7. I am building here on the very interesting observations made by Cynthia J. Davis. See Cynthia J. Davis, "Speaking the Body's Pain: Harriet Wilson's *Our Nig*," *African American Review* 27:3 (Fall 1993): 391–404. Saidiya Hartman's *Scenes of Subjection* had only just been published as I was completing this study. I would like to take this opportunity, however, to reiterate her observation that processes of black subjectification have been altogether caught up in a variety of forms of violent subjugation, as well as the various resistances to them. See Saidiya V. Hartman, *Scenes of Subjection: Terror, Slavery and Self-Making in Nineteenth-Century America* (New York: Oxford University Press, 1997).

8. Leopold von Sacher-Masoch, *Venus in Furs*, in *Masochism* (New York: Zone Books, 1991), 222–223.

9. For more on the notion of the Jew as interloper, see Zygmunt Bauman, *Modernity and Ambivalence* (Ithaca: Cornell University Press, 1991); Sander Gilman, *Difference and Pathology* (Ithaca: Cornell University Press, 1985).

10. Harriet Wilson, *Our Nig; or, Sketches From the Life of a Free Black* (1859; reprint, New York: Vintage Books, 1983), 5.

Chapter 5

1. Frederick Douglass offers a very interesting gloss on this matter in a defense of "colored newspapers," in which he comments at length on the disjuncture between the black's desire for recognition as a figure indistinguishable from other (bourgeois) figures and the concomitant will to be recognized—and heard—as black. He argues that the black's body always stands prior to his modes of representation. Thus, the idea that black newspapers continue practices of racial distinction is rendered preposterous.

> They are sometimes objected to, on the ground that they serve to keep up an odious and wicked distinction between white men and colored persons and are a barrier to that very equality which we are wont to advocate. We have sometimes, heard persons regret the very mention of color, on this account, and to counsel its abandonment. We confess to no such feelings: we are in no wise sensitive on this point. Facts are facts: white is not black and black is not white. There is neither good sense, nor common honesty, in trying to forget this distinction. So far from the truth is the notion that colored newspapers are arriving to keep up that cruel distinction, the want of them is the main cause of its continuance. The distinction which degrades us is not that which exists between a *white* man and a black man. They are equal men, the one is white and the other is black; but both are men, and equal men. The white man is only superior to the black man, when he outstrips him in the race of improvement; and the black man is only inferior, when he proves himself incapable of doing just what is done by his white brother. In order to remove this odious distinction, we must do just what white men do. It must be no longer white lawyer, and black wood sawyer,—white editor, and black

> street cleaner: it must be no longer white, intelligent, and black, ignorant; but we must take our stand side by side with our white fellow countrymen, in all the trades, arts, profession [sic.] and callings of the day.

Frederick Douglass, "Colored Newspapers," *The North Star*, 7 January 1848: 2.

2. For an excellent discussion of the tendency to blur the distinction between master and slave in antebellum political discourse, see Eric Foner, *Politics and Ideology in the Age of the Civil War* (New York: Oxford University Press, 1980).

3. Martin R. Delany, "Domestic Economy" *The North Star*, 20 April 1849: 2.

4. See Robert F. Reid-Pharr, "Violent Ambiguity: Martin Delany, Bourgeois Sadomasochism, and the Production of a Black National Masculinity," in Marcellus Blount and George Cunningham, eds., *Representing Black Men* (New York: Routledge, 1996), 73–94.

6. Barthes writes,

> In the scene, all functions can be interchanged, everyone can and must be in turn agent and patient, whipper and whipped, coprophagist and coprophagee, etc. This is a cardinal rule, first, because it assimilates only Sadian eroticism into a truly formal language, where there are only classes of actions, not groups of individuals, which enormously simplifies its grammar: the subject of the action (in the grammatical sense) can just as readily be a libertine, an assistant, a victim, a wife; second, because it keeps us from basing the grouping of Sadian society on the particularity of sexual practices (just the opposite of what occurs in our own society; we always wonder whether a homosexual is "active" or "passive"; with Sade, sexual preference never serves to identify a subject.

Roland Barthes, *Sade/Fourier/Loyola*, trans. by Richard Miller (Baltimore: Johns Hopkins University Press, 1976), 30.

6. This gloss details the contents of *The North Star* for the 28 April 1848 issue.

7. Frederick Douglass, "Our Paper and Its Prospects," *The North Star*, 3 December 1847: 2.

8. As I hope is apparent by now, this study is very much informed by a well-developed literature on theories of nationalism that have long since moved beyond the notion of folk culture as the basis for national culture. See Benedict Anderson, *Imagined Communities: Reflections on the Origin and Spread of Nationalism* (New York: Verso, 1983); Ernest Gellner, *Nations and Nationalism* (Ithaca: Cornell University Press, 1990); Paul Gilroy, *There Ain't No Black in the Union Jack: The Cultural Politics of Race and Nation* (1987; reprint Chicago: The University of Chicago Press, 1991); Eric J. Hobsbawm, *Nations and Nationalism Since 1780: Programme, Myth, Reality* (New York: Cambridge University Press, 1990); Eric Hobsbawm and Terrence Ranger, *The Invention of Tradition* (New York: Cambridge University Press, 1983); Hans Kohn, *Nationalism: Its Meaning and History* (Malabar, Fla: Robert E. Krieger Publishing Co., 1982); Hugh Seton-Watson, *Nations and States: An Enquiry in the Origins of Nations and the Politics of Nationalism* (Boulder, Colo.: Westview Press, 1977).

9. I am indebted here to Raymond Williams's intriguing schematization of the movement between metropolis and hinterland in the production of modern culture. See Raymond Williams, *The Country and the City* (New York: Oxford University Press, 1973).

10. Martin R. Delany, *The Condition, Elevation, Emigration, and Destiny of the Colored People of the United States* (1852; reprint, Salem, N.H.: Ayer Publishers, 1988). This nation-

alist aesthetic reaches its zenith when Delany travels to West Africa in order to secure land for Black American expatriation. See Martin Delany, *Official Report of the Niger Valley Exploring Party* (1861), reprinted in Wilson Jeremiah Moses, ed., *Classical Black Nationalism: From the American Revolution to Marcus Garvey* (New York: New York University Press, 1996).

11. Delany writes,

> How do we compare with them? Our fathers are their coachmen, our brothers their cookmen, and ourselves their waiting-men. Our mothers their nurse-women, our sisters their scrub-women, our daughters their maid-women, and our wives their washer-women. Until colored men, attain to a position above permitting their mothers, sisters, wives, and daughters, to do the drudgery and menial offices of other men's wives and daughters; it is useless, it is nonsense, it is pitiable mockery, to talk about equality and elevation in society.

Like Frank Webb, Delany is almost obsessively concerned with pulling the black servant out of the white household, out of physical intimacy with racially distinct masters. He insists that this interracial intimacy is antithetical to a stable black domesticity. Fathers, mothers, brothers, sisters and daughters are degraded within the white bourgeois domestic sphere, a situation that seems altogether too similar to slavery. The implication is that white men are able to gain status as gentlemen through the degradation of black families. White wives and daughters are spared menial drudgery and the badge of inferiority that it confers through the interposition of black wives and daughters. Black fathers and sons, on the other hand, are themselves degraded, even feminized, because of their inability to throw up protective boundaries around the black family (Delany [1852] 1988, 21).

12. Doris Sommer, *Foundational Fictions: The National Romances of Latin America* (Berkeley: The University of California Press, 1991), 37.

13. See John Blassingame, *Slave Community: Plantation Life in the Antebellum South* (New York: Oxford University Press, 1972). More revealing still is the rather didactic writing of antebellum journalists, much of which was designed to stop the practice of African or slave-based rituals. Take, for example, this passage from the pages of *Freedom's Journal*:

> [W]e feel it our imperious duty to offer our protest against all public processions. No good can possibly arise from them but on the contrary much loss of time and expense. The brain of many a sensible man has often been so intoxicated on these occasions, that it required one week or more to convince him that he was still an inhabitant of this world of cares and perplexities. . . .

In short, the goal is to shape the prerational, sensual slave into the logical, economical, and obedient industrial worker. As a consequence, Black American intellectuals were trapped within a rather suffocating paradox, hoping, on the one hand, to bind the community together while, on the other, attempting to empty this same community of some of the attributes that helped define it. Editorial, *Freedom's Journal*, 30 March 1827.

14. Armistead Miller, *Liberia Described. A Discourse Embracing a Description of the Climate, Soil, Productions, Animals, Missionary Work, Improvements, etc. with a Full Description of the Acclimating Fever* (Philadelphia: Joseph M. Wilson, 1859), 48.

15. Martin Delany, *Blake, or The Huts of America* (Boston: Beacon Press, 1970), 16.

16. Strangely enough, I was made even more suspicious of my earlier arguments by a note I received from Lynn Chancer, whose *Sadomasochism in Everyday Life* inspired

much of my thinking on these matters. Graciously responding to an early draft of that essay Chancer wrote,

> It may be important, if difficult, to clarify the point about the slave being in the sadomasochistic dynamic: clearly, the slave has no choice (like the young boy—does Blake/Delany see him as compliant in your example) and yet somehow and just as obviously can never be entirely devoid of agency and possessed by another (does Blake/Delany therefore blame him, explaining why the assertive masculine Blake comes into being after the youth's death)? So my general point here is that this issue of the masochist/slave having agency and yet being in a situation of compulsion could be clarified a bit in your paper, lest you seem to be theoretically setting up a choice between *either* blaming the victim *or* untruthfully denying that victim some existential freedom no matter what the situation. (Letter to the author dated November 15, 1993)

I believe now, as I reread Chancer's critique, that I was too enamored with the gracefulness of the traditional Freudian account of violence and sexual perversion that suggests Sadism and Masochism as but two different aspects of the same pathology, the inability to gain recognition and community from/with another through normative modes of engagement. At this juncture and following Deleuze, I want to suggest that the Sadian and the Masochistic actually represent divergent philosophical tendencies in the schematization of the subject's relation to society, with Sade as radical and von Sacher-Masoch as hyperconservative. By insisting upon the disunion of the two traditions I am better able to focus on the fact that the site of their overlap is precisely the body. My argument here, however, is that this fact actually does not prove the unity of the two traditions, but the fact of the body's essential disunity, the fact that it is at once the emblem of a stable (black) society, the evidence of an obvious and irrefutable blackness, *and* the site at which this blackness is most often brought into question, the site of flight. Thus, it follows that the young slave's body can be both a site of agency and a site of dispossession. See Lynn Chancer, *Sadomasochism in Everyday Life: The Dynamics of Power and Powerlessness* (New Brunswick, N.J.: Rutgers University Press, 1992).

17. Kristeva writes,

> Owing to the ambiguous opposition I/Other, Inside/Outside—an opposition that is vigorous but pervious, violent but uncertain—there are contents, "normally" unconscious in neurotics, that become explicit if not conscious in "borderline" patients' speeches and behaviours. Such contents are often openly manifested through symbolic practices, without by the same token being integrated into the judging consciousness of those particular subjects. Since they make the conscious/unconscious distinction irrelevant, borderline subjects and their speech constitute propitious ground for a sublimating discourse ("aesthetic" or "mystical," etc.) rather than a scientific or rationalist one.

Julia Kristeva, *Powers of Horror: An Essay on Abjection* (New York: Columbia University Press, 1982), 7.

18. I am supported in this claim by the work of Henry Louis Gates Jr., particularly his *Figures in Black: Words, Signs and the "Racial" Self.* Therein he argues that from its very inception, Black American literature has contested and signified upon a modernist discourse that posits the black as cultureless and subhuman, a subhumanity that is demonstrated by the black subject's supposed lack of a tradition of letters. In the process,

the black becomes the very marker of the limits of culture and humanity, the awkwardly defined outsider who gives definition to universalist fantasies. As a consequence, the spectacle of the literate black worked as a refutation not only of racist notions regarding black intellect but of the entire project of post-Enlightenment rationality, at least insofar as that project disallowed recognition of the unity between black corporeality and universalist notions of rationality. The black writer had to create, then, a literature that both produced him as an insider, a rational subject, and concurrently critiqued and transcended this same Inside/Outside binarism that was itself produced via the *de*humanization of the black. Henry Louis Gates Jr., *Figures in Black: Words, Signs, and the "Racial" Self* (New York: Oxford University Press, 1987).

19. See Laura Mulvey, *Visual and Other Pleasures* (Bloomington: Indiana University Press, 1989).

20. For a very interesting discussion of the role of Placido in the Cuban national imaginary, see Vera Kutzinski, *Sugar's Secrets: Race and the Erotics of Cuban Nationalism* (Charlottesville: The University of Virginia Press, 1993). Also, it is important to note that Cuban politics and culture were significant concerns of Delany long before the publication of *Blake*. See Martin R. Delany, "The Annexation of Cuba," *The North Star*, 27 April 1849: 2.

21. This understanding has made me a bit slow to take up fully Paul Gilroy's reevaluation of Martin Delany. Specifically, I believe that in his celebration of Delany's pan-Atlanticism, Gilroy misses the fact that national boundaries crumble in Delany's literature only as gender boundaries are more firmly established. See Paul Gilroy, *The Black Atlantic: Modernity and Double Consciousness* (Cambridge: Harvard University Press, 1993). See also Robert F. Reid-Pharr, "Engendering the Black Atlantic," *Found Object* 4 (Fall 1994): 11–16.

Epilogue

1. W. E. B. Du Bois, *Black Reconstruction in America, 1860–1880*, intro. by David Levering Lewis (1935; reprint, New York: Simon and Schuster, 1992).

2. Ronald Judy, *(Dis)forming the American Canon: African-Arabic Slave Narratives and the Vernacular*, intro. by Wahneema Lubiano (Minneapolis: University of Minnesota Press, 1993).

3. See James D. Anderson, *The Education of Blacks in the South, 1860–1935* (Chapel Hill, N.C.: The University of North Carolina Press, 1988).

4. West writes:

> Just as Arnold seeks to carve out discursive space and a political mission for the educated elite in the British Empire somewhere between the arrogance and complacency of the aristocracy and the vulgarity and anarchy of the working classes, DuBois wants to create a new vocabulary and social vocation for the black educated elite in America somewhere between the hatred and scorn of the white supremacist majority and the crudity and illiteracy of the black agrarian masses. Yet his gallant efforts suffer from intellectual defects and historical misconceptions.

Cornel West, "Black Strivings in a Twilight Civilization," in Henry Louis Gates Jr. and Cornel West, *The Future of the Race* (New York: Knopf, 1996), 67. Du Bois's emphasis on an embodied cultural practice is demonstrated in the particular cases of *Dark Princess* and *John Brown* through his obsessive concern with demonstrating how bodies always can be turned to in our efforts to establish subjectivity. I am reminded of the scene in the Brown biography in which Du Bois recounts in detail Brown's insistence that his errant son whip him in order that he might, through his suffering, redeem the son in the eyes of god and man. Moreover, in *Dark Princess*, Du Bois's favorite work, the logic of the narrative turns on the notion that nobility is indeed an embodied trait, so much so that when the princess, Kautilya, meets the black American (proto)revolutionary, David, they are represented as examples of the always already, creatures whose destiny is to mate and pass on the truths that they *literally* embody.

5. In this way I continue the critique offered by Anthony Appiah some years ago of Du Bois's "Conservation of Races" essay, in which he argues that Du Bois does not give up on biological models of race in his efforts to modernize thinking on the matter. Unlike Appiah, however, I do not treat Du Bois's desire to continue notions of racial specificity as a disability, but instead as an appropriate, perhaps inevitable, response to the fact that blackness and subjectivity were always already incommensurate. Anthony Appiah, "The Uncompleted Argument: Du Bois and the Illusion of Race," *Critical Inquiry* 12.1 (Autumn 1985): 21–37.

BIBLIOGRAPHY

Newspapers

The Black Republican, 15 April 1865–20 May 1865
Black Republican and Office Holder's Journal August 1865
The Colored American, 7 March 1840–13 March 1841
Freedom's Journal, 16 March 1827–28 March 1829
Mirror of the Times 1855–1857?
The North Star, 3 December 1847–17 April 1851
The Northern Star and Freemen's Advocate, 3 February 1842–2 January 1843
The Rights of All, 29 May 1829–9 October 1829
The Weekly Anglo-African, 24 November 1860–12 January 1861

Articles and Monographs

Adams, H. G., ed. *God's Image in Ebony: Being a Series of Biographical Sketches, Facts, Anecdotes, etc., Demonstrative of the Mental Powers and Intellectual Capacities of the Negro Race.* London: Partridge and Oakey, 1854.

Ahmad, Aijaz. *In Theory: Classes, Nations, Literatures.* New York: Verso, 1992.

Althusser, Louis. *Lenin and Philosophy, and Other Essays.* New York: Monthly Review Press, 1971.

Anderson, Benedict. *Imagined Communities: Reflections on the Origin and Spread of Nationalism.* New York: Verso, 1983.

Anderson, James D. *The Education of Blacks in the South, 1860–1935.* Chapel Hill: The University of North Carolina Press, 1988.

Andrews, William L. *To Tell a Free Story: The First Century of Afro-American Autobiography, 1760–1865.* Chicago: The University of Illinois Press, 1986.

Andrews, William L., ed. *African American Autobiography: A Collection of Critical Essays* Englewood Cliffs, N.J.: Prentice Hall, 1993.

Andrews, William., ed. *Critical Essays on Frederick Douglass.* Boston: G. K. Hall, 1991.

Andrews, William L., ed. *From Fugitive to Free Man: The Autobiographies of William Wells Brown* New York: Pengiun, 1993.

Appiah, Kwame Anthony. *In My Father's House: Africa in the Philosophy of Culture*. New York: Oxford University Press, 1992.

———. "The Uncompleted Argument: Du Bois and the Illusion of Race." *Critical Inquiry* 12.1 (Autumn 1985): 21–37.

Armstrong, Nancy. *Desire and Domestic Fiction: A Political History of the Novel.* New York: Oxford University Press, 1987.

Armstrong, Nancy, and Leonard Tennenhouse, eds. *The Violence of Representation: Literature and the History of Violence*. New York: Routledge, 1989.

Awkward, Michael. *Negotiating Difference: Race, Gender, and the Politics of Positionality*. Chicago: The University of Chicago Press, 1995.

Baker, Houston A. Jr. *Blues, Ideology, and Afro-American Literature: A Vernacular Theory*. Chicago: The University of Chicago Press, 1985.

———. *The Journey Back: Issues in Black Literature and Criticism*. Chicago: The University of Chicago Press, 1980.

———. *Long Black Song: Essays in Black American Literature and Culture*. Charlottesville: The University Press of Virginia, 1972.

———. *Workings of the Spirit: The Poetics of Afro-American Women's Writing*. Chicago: The University of Chicago Press, 1991.

Baker, Houston A., Manthia Diawara, and Ruth H. Lindeborg, eds. *Black British Cultural Studies: A Reader* Chicago: The University of Chicago Press 1996.

Bakhtin, Mikhail M. *The Dialogic Imagination: Four Essays*. Translated by Michael Holquist and Caryl Emerson. Edited by Michael Holquist. Houston: University of Texas Press, 1981.

———. *Rabelais and His World.* Translated by Helene Iswolsky. Cambridge: MIT Press, 1968.

Balibar, Etienne, and Immanuel Wallerstein. *Race, Nation, Class: Ambiguous Identities*. New York: Verso, 1991.

Banneker, Benjamin. *Banneker's Almanac for the Year 1795: Being the Year After the Third Leap Year Containing (Besides Everything Necessary in an Almanac,) An Account of the Yellow Fever Lately Prevalent in Philadelphia; With the Number of Those Who Have Died, From the Fifth of August Till the Ninth of November, 1793*. Philadelphia: William Young Bookseller, 1795.

Banton, Michael. *Racial Theories*. New York: Cambridge University Press, 1987.

Barnard, F. M. "National Culture and Political Legitimacy: Herder and Rousseau." *Journal of the History of Ideas* 44.2 (April–June 1983) 231–253.

Barthes, Roland. *Sade/Fourier/Loyola*. Translated by Richard Miller. Baltimore: Johns Hopkins University Press, 1976.

Bauman, Zygmunt. *Modernity and Ambivalence*. Ithaca: Cornell University Press, 1991.

Baym, Nina. *Novels, Readers and Reviewers: Response to Fiction in Antebellum America*. Ithaca: Cornell University Press, 1984.

Bell, Bernard W. *The Afro-American Novel and Its Traditions*. Amherst: The University of Massachusetts Press, 1987.

Berlin, Ira. *Slaves Without Masters: The Free Negro in the Antebellum South*. New York: The New Press, 1974.

Berlin, Ira, and Ronald Hoffman, eds. *Slavery and Freedom in the Age of the American Revolution*. Chicago: The University of Chicago Press, 1983.

Bhabha, Homi K. *The Location of Culture* New York: Routledge, 1994.

———, ed. *Nation and Narration*. New York: Routledge, 1990.

Bibb, Henry. *Narrative of the Life and Adventures of Henry Bibb, An American Slave, Written by Himself.* 1850. Reprint, New York: Negro Universities Press, 1969.

Blackett, R. J. M. *Beating Against the Barriers: Biographical Essays in Nineteenth-Century Afro-American History.* Baton Rouge: Louisiana State University Press, 1986.

———. *Building an Antislavery Wall: Black Americans in the Atlantic Abolitionist Movement, 1830–1860.* Ithaca: Cornell University Press, 1983.

Black Public Sphere Collective. *The Black Public Sphere.* Chicago: The University of Chicago Press, 1995.

Blassingame, John. *Slave Community: Plantation Life in the Antebellum South.* New York: Oxford University Press, 1972.

Blight, David W. *Frederick Douglass' Civil War: Keeping Faith in Jubilee.* Baton Rouge: Louisiana State University Press, 1989.

Brawley, Benjamin Griffith. *Early Negro American Writers.* Chapel HIll: University of North Carolina Press, 1935.

Bromell, Nicholas Knowles. *By the Sweat of the Brow: Literature and Labor in Antebellum America.* Chicago: The University of Chicago Press, 1993.

Brooks, Peter. *Body Work: Objects of Desire in Modern Narrative.* Cambridge: Harvard University Press, 1993.

Brown, Gillian. *Domestic Individualism: Imagining Self in Nineteenth-Century America.* Berkeley: The University of California Press, 1990.

Brown, William Wells. *The Black Man, His Antecedents, His Genius, and His Achievements.* 1865. Reprint, Salem, N.H.: Ayer Publishers, 1992.

———. *Clotel, or the President's Daughter.* 1853. Reprint, New York: University Books, 1969.

———. *Clotelle: or the Colored Heroine A Tale of the Southern States.* 1867. Reprint, Miami, Fla.: Mnemosyne Publishing, 1969.

———. *A Description of William Wells Brown's Original Panoramic Views of the Scenes in the Life of an American Slave, From his Birth in Slavery to His Death or His Escape to his First Home of Freedom on British Soil* (London: Charles Gilpin, n.d.)

———. *Narrative of William Wells Brown, a Fugitive Slave.* 1848. In *From Fugitive to Free Man: The Autobiographies of William Wells Brown,* edited by William L. Andrews, Reprint, New York: Mentor, 1993.

———. *My Southern Home: or, The South and Its People.* 1860. In *From Fugitive to Free Man: The Autobiographies of William Wells Brown,* edited by William L. Andrews, 1993. Reprint, New York: Mentor, 1993.

———. *St. Domingo: Its Revolutions and Its Patriots. A Lecture Delivered Before the Metropolitan Atheneum, London, May 16 and at St. Thomas' Church, Philadelphia, December 20, 1854.* Boston: Bela Marsh, 1855.

———. *Sketches of People and Places Abroad; The American Fugitive in Europe.* 1855. Freeport, N.Y.: Books for Libraries Press, 1970.

Bullock, Penelope. *The Afro-American Periodical Press, 1838–1909.* Baton Rouge: Louisiana State University Press, 1981.

Butler, Judith. *Bodies That Matter: On the Discursive Limits of "Sex."* New York: Routledge, 1993.

———. *Gender Trouble: Feminism and the Subversion of Identity.* New York: Routledge, 1990.

Calhoun, Craig, ed. *Habermas and the Public Sphere.* Cambridge: MIT Press, 1992.

Cameron, Sharon. *The Corporeal Self: Allegories of the Body in Melville and Hawthorne.* Baltimore: Johns Hopkins University Press, 1981.

Carby, Hazel. *Reconstructing Womanhood: The Emergence of the Afro-American Woman Novelist.* New York: Oxford University Press, 1987.

Cassuto, Leonard. *The Inhuman Race: The Racial Grotesque in American Literature and Culture.* New York: Columbia University Press, 1997.

Chancer, Lynn. *Sadomasochism in Everyday Life: The Dynamics of Power and Powerlessness.* New Brunswick, N.J.: Rutgers University Press, 1992.

Child, L. Maria. *An Appeal in Favor of that Class of Americans Called Africans.* 1836. Reprint, New York: Arno Press and the New York Times, 1968.

———. "The Quadroons." In *Fact and Fiction: A Collection of Stories*, by Lydia Maria Child, 61–76. New York: 1846.

Christian, Barbara. *Black Feminist Criticism: Perspectives on Black Women Writers.* New York: Pergamon Press, 1985.

———. *Black Women Novelists: The Development of a Tradition, 1892–1976.* Westport, Conn. Greenwood Press, 1980.

Coleman, William. *Yellow Fever in the North: The Methods of Early Epidemiology.* Madison: The University of Wisconsin Press, 1987.

Cooper, Frederick. "Elevating the Race: The Social Thought of Black Leaders, 1827–1850." *American Quarterly* 24 (December 1972): 604–625.

Craft, William. *Running a Thousand Miles for Freedom, or the Escape of William and Ellen Craft from Slavery.* 1860. Reprint, Salem, N.H.: Ayer Publishers, 1991.

Cunningham, George. "Called Into Existence: Desire, Gender and Voice in Frederick Douglass's *Narrative* of 1845." *differences* 1.3 (1989): 108–135.

Davidson, Cathy N. *Revolution and the Word: The Rise of the Novel in America.* New York: Oxford University Press, 1986.

Davis, Angela. "Reflections on the Black Woman's Role in the Community of Slaves." *Black Scholar* 3.4 (December 1971): 2–15.

Davis, Cynthia J. "Speaking the Body's Pain: Harriet Wilson's *Our Nig.*" *African American Review* 27.3 (Fall 1993): 391–404.

Davis, David Brion. *The Problem of Slavery and Western Culture.* Ithaca: Cornell University Press, 1966.

Debord, Guy. *The Society of the Spectacle.* Translated by Donald Nicholson-Smith. New York: Zone Books, 1994.

Delany, Martin. *Blake, or the Huts of America.* Boston: Beacon Press, 1970.

———. *The Condition, Elevation, Emigration, and Destiny of the Colored People of the United States.* 1852. Reprint, Salem, N.H.: Ayer Publishers, 1988.

———. *Official Report of the Niger Valley Exploring Party* 1861. Reprinted in *Classical Black Nationalism: From the American Revolution to Marcus Garvey*, edited by Wilson Jeremiah Moses, New York: New York University Press, 1996.

Deleuze, Gilles. *Coldness and Cruelty.* In *Masochism.* New York: Zone Books, 1989.

D'Emilio, John, and Estelle B. Freedman. *Intimate Matters: A History of Sexuality in America.* New York: Harper and Row, 1988.

Dorr, David F. *A Colored Man Round the World.* Printed for the Author, 1858.

Douglas, Mary. *Purity and Danger: An Analysis of Concepts of Pollution and Taboo.* New York: Frederick A. Praeger Publishers, 1966.

Douglass, Frederick. *The Claims of the Negro, Ethnologically Considered. An Address Delivered Before the Literary Societies of Western Reserve College, At Commencement, July 12, 1854.* Rochester, N.Y.: Lee, Mann and Long, 1854.

———. *The Heroic Slave.* 1853. In *Frederick Douglass: The Narrative and Selected Writings*, edited by Michael Meyer, 299–348. Reprint, New York: The Modern Library, 1984.

———. *Narrative of the Life of Frederick Douglass, An American Slave.* 1845. In *Frederick Douglass: The Narrative and Selected Writings*, edited by Michael Meyer, 3–127. Reprint, New York: The Modern Library, 1984.

Doyle, Laura. *Bordering on the Body: The Racial Matrix of Modern Fiction and Culture.* New York: Oxford University Press, 1994.

Du Bois, W. E. B. *Black Reconstruction in America, 1860–1880.* Introduction by David Levering Lewis. 1935. Reprint, New York: Simon and Schuster, 1992.

———. *Dark Princess.* Introduction by Claudia Tate. 1928. Reprint, Jackson: University Press of Mississippi, 1995.

———. *John Brown.* Introduction by John David Smith. 1909. Reprint, Armonk, N.Y.: M. E. Sharpe, 1997.

Ducille, Ann. *The Coupling Convention: Sex, Text, and Tradition in Black Women's Fiction.* New York: Oxford University Press, 1993.

Eagleton, Terry. *Ideology: An Introduction.* New York: Verso, 1991.

Eagleton, Terry, Fredric Jameson, and Edward W. Said. *Nationalism, Colonialism and Literature.* Edited by Seamus Deane. Minneapolis: University of Minnesota Press, 1990.

Elder, Arlene. *The "Hindered Hand": Cultural Implications of Early African American Fiction.* Westport, Conn.: Greenwood Press, 1978.

Engels, Frederick. *The Origin of the Family, Private Property and the State in Light of the Researches of Lewis H. Morgan.* 1884. Reprint, New York: International Publishers, 1942.

Ernest, John. *Resistance and Reformation in Nineteenth-Century African-American Literature: Brown, Wilson, Jacobs, Delany, Douglass and Harper.* Jackson: University Press of Mississippi, 1995.

Fanon, Frantz. *Black Skin, White Masks.* New York: Grove Press, 1967.

Farrison, William Edward. *William Wells Brown: Author and Reformer.* Chicago: The University of Chicago Press, 1969.

Fiedler, Leslie. *Love and Death in the American Novel.* New York: Meridian Books, 1960.

Fishkin, Shelley Fisher. *Was Huck Black? Mark Twain and African American Voices.* New York: Oxford University Press, 1993.

Foner, Eric. *Politics and Ideology in the Age of the Civil War.* New York: Oxford University Press, 1980.

Foreman, Gabrielle P. "The Sentimental Subversions: Reading Race and Sexuality in the Nineteenth Century." Ph.D diss., The University of California at Berkeley, 1992.

Foster, Frances Smith. *Written by Herself: Literary Production by African American Women, 1746–1892.* Bloomington: Indiana University Press, 1993.

Foucault, Michel. *Discipline and Punish.* Translated by Alan Sheridan. New York: Vintage, 1979.

———. *The History of Sexuality.* Translated by Mark Hurley. New York: Vintage, 1980.

Franklin, V. P. *Black Self-Determination: A Cultural History of the Faith of the Fathers.* New York: Lawrence Hill, 1984.

Frazier, E. Franklin. *The Negro Family in the United States.* Chicago: The University of Chicago Press, 1948.

Fredrickson, George M. *The Arrogance of Race: Historical Perspectives on Slavery, Racism, and Social Inequality.* Middletown, Conn.: Wesleyan University Press, 1988.

———. *The Black Image in the White Mind: The Debate on Afro-American Character and Destiny, 1817–1914*. New York: Harper and Row, 1971.

Gallop, Jane. *Thinking Through the Body*. New York: Columbia University Press, 1988.

Garber, Marjorie. *Vested Interests: Cross-Dressing and Cultural Anxiety*. New York: Routledge, 1992.

Garfield, Deborah M., and Rafia Zafar, eds. *Harriet Jacobs and Incidents in the Life of a Slave Girl: Critical Essays*. New York: Cambridge University Press, 1996.

Gates, Henry Louis Jr. *Figures in Black: Words, Signs and the "Racial" Self*. New York: Oxford University Press, 1987.

———. *The Signifying Monkey: A Theory of African-American Literary Criticism*. New York: Oxford University Press, 1988.

———, ed. *"Race," Writing, and Difference*. Chicago: The University of Chicago Press, 1985.

———, ed. *Reading Black, Reading Feminist: A Critical Anthology*. New York: Meridian, 1990.

Gates, Henry Louis Jr. and Cornel West. *The Future of the Race*. New York: Knopf, 1996.

Gayle, Addison. *The Way of the New World: The Black Novel in America*. Garden City, N.Y.: Anchor Press/Doubleday, 1975.

Gellner, Ernest. *Nations and Nationalism*. Ithaca: Cornell University Press, 1990.

Gilman, Sander. *Difference and Pathology*. Ithaca: Cornell University Press, 1985.

Gilroy, Paul. *The Black Atlantic: Modernity and Double Consciousness*. Boston: Harvard University Press, 1993.

———. *There Ain't No Black in the Union Jack: The Cultural Politics of Race and Nation*. 1987. Reprint, Chicago: The University of Chicago Press, 1991.

Girard, Rene. *The Scapegoat*. Translated by Yvonne Frecerro. Baltimore: Johns Hopkins University Press, 1986.

Goldberg, David Theo. *Anatomy of Racism*. Minnesota: The University of Minnesota Press, 1990.

Gossett, Thomas F. *Race: The History of an Idea in America*. New York: Oxford University Press, 1963.

Graff, Gerald. *Professing Literature: An Institutional History*. Chicago: The University of Chicago Press, 1987.

Gramsci, Antonio. *Selections From the Cultural Writings*. Edited by David Forgacs. Cambridge: Harvard University Press, 1985.

Griffin, Farah Jasmine. *"Who Set You Flowin'": The African American Migration Narrative*. New York: Oxford University Press, 1994.

Griffith, Cyril. *The African Dream: Martin R. Delany and the Emergence of Pan-African Thought*. University Park: The Pennsylvania State University Press, 1975.

Guillory, John. *Cultural Capital: The Problem of Literary Canon Formation*. Chicago: The University of Chicago Press, 1993.

Gutman, Herbert. *The Black Family in Slavery and Freedom, 1750–1925*. New York: Vintage Books, 1976.

Habermas, Jurgen. *The Structural Transformation of the Public Sphere: An Inquiry Into a Category of Bourgeois Society*. Translated by Thomas Burger with assistance from Frederick Lawrence. Cambridge: MIT Press, 1989.

Hall, Stuart. "The After-life of Frantz Fanon: Why Fanon? Why Now? Why *Black Skin, White Masks?*" In *The Fact of Blackness: Frantz Fanon and Visual Representation*, edited by Alan Read, Seattle: Bay Press, 1996. pp. 12–37

———. "Race, Articulation and Societies Structured in Dominance." 1980. Reprinted in Baker, Houston A. Jr., Manthia Diawara, and Ruth H. Lindeborg, eds. *Black British Cultural Studies: A Reader.* Chicago: The University of Chicago Press, 1996, 16–60.

Hartman, Saidiya V. *Scenes of Subjection: Terror, Slavery and Self-Making in Nineteenth-Century America.* New York: Oxford University Press, 1997.

Heermance, J. Noel. *William Wells Brown and Clotelle: A Portrait of the Artist in the First Negro Novel.* Hamden, Conn.: Archon Books, 1969.

Hobsbawm, Eric J. *Nations and Nationalism Since 1780: Programme, Myth, Reality.* New York: Cambridge University Press, 1990.

Hobsbawn, Eric J. and Terence Ranger. *The Invention of Tradition.* New York: Cambridge University Press, 1983.

Hoch, Paul. *White Hero, Black Beast: Racism, Sexism and the Mask of Masculinity.* London: Pluto, 1979.

Hodes, Martha Elizabeth. *White Women, Black Men: Illicit Sex in the Nineteenth Century South.* New Haven: Yale University Press, 1997.

Holly, Joseph C. *Freedom's Offerings: A Collection of Poems.* Rochester: Chas H. McDonnell, 1853.

Horton, James Oliver. *Free People of Color: Inside the African American Community.* Washington, D.C.: Smithsonian Institution Press, 1993.

Horton, James Oliver, and Lois E. Horton. *In the Hope of Liberty: Culture, Community and Protest Among Northern Free Blacks, 1700–1860.* New York: Oxford University Press, 1997.

Hoy, Suellen. *Chasing Dirt: The American Pursuit of Cleanliness.* New York: Oxford University Press, 1995.

Hutton, Frankie. *The Early Black Press in America, 1827–1860.* Westport, Conn.: Greenwood Press, 1993.

Jackson, Blyden. *The History of Afro-American Literature.* Vol. 1. Baton Rouge: Louisiana State University Press, 1989.

Jacobs, Harriet A. *Incidents in the Life of a Slave Girl, Written by Herself.* 1861. Reprint, Cambridge: Harvard University Press, 1987.

James, C. L. R. *American Civilization.* Edited by Anna Grimshaw and Keith Hart. Cambridge: Blackwell Publishers, 1993.

———. *The Black Jacobins: Toussaint L'Ouverture and the San Domingo Revolution.* New York: Vintage, 1963.

———. *Mariners, Renegades and Castaways: The Story of Herman Melville and the World We Live In.* 1953. Reprint, Detroit: Bewick/ed, 1978.

Jameson, Fredric. *The Political Unconscious: Narrative as a Socially Symbolic Act.* Ithaca: Cornell University Press, 1981.

Jefferson, Thomas. *Notes on the State of Virginia.* 1788. Reprint, New York: Norton, 1954.

Joliffe, John. 1860 Dissolving the Union. *The Weekly Auglo-African*, 24 November.

Jones, Absalom, and Richard Allen, *A Narrative of the Proceedings of the Black People, During the Late Awful Calamity in Philadelphia, in the Year 1793; and a Refutation of Some Censure Thrown Upon Them in Some Late Publications.* Philadelphia: William W. Woodward, 1793.

Judy, Ronald. *(Dis)forming the American Canon: African-Arabic Slave Narratives and the Vernacular.* Introduction by Wahneema Lubiano. Minneapolis: University of Minnesota Press, 1993.

Kelly, Mary. *Private Woman, Public Stage: Literary Domesticity in Nineteenth-Century America.* New York: Oxford University Press, 1984.

King, Stewart R. "Blue Coat or Lace Collar? Military and Civilian Free Coloreds in the Colonial Society of Saint-Domingue." Ph.D. diss., Johns Hopkins University, 1997.

Kinshasa, Kwando Mbiassi. "*Free Blacks' Quest for a National Identity: Debates in the African American Press on Assimilation and Emigration, 1827–1861.*" Ph.D. diss., New York University, 1983.

Klotman, Phillis. *Another Man Gone: The Black Runner in Contemporary Afro-American Fiction.* Port Washington, N.Y.: Kennikat Press, 1977.

Kohn, Hans. *Nationalism: Its Meaning and History.* Malabar, Fla.: Robert E. Krieger, 1982.

Kristeva, Julia. *Powers of Horror: An Essay on Abjection.* New York: Columbia University Press, 1982.

———. *Strangers to Ourselves.* Translated by Leon S. Roudiez. New York: Columbia University Press, 1991.

Kutzkinski, Vera. *Sugar's Secrets: Race and the Erotics of Cuban Nationalism.* Charlottesville: The University of Virginia Press, 1993.

Lacapra, Dominick, ed. *The Bounds of Race: Perspectives on Hegemony and Resistance.* Ithaca: Cornell University Press, 1991.

Lapsansky, Philip S. "Afro-Americana: Frank J. Webb and His Friends." The Library Company of Philadelphia. *The Annual Report of the Library Company of Philadelphia.* Philadelphia: The Library Company of Philadelphia, 1990.

Leverenz, David. *Manhood and the American Renaissance.* Ithaca: Cornell University Press, 1989.

Levine, Robert S. *Martin Delany, Frederick Douglass and the Politics of Representative Identity.* Chapel Hill: The University of North Carolina Press, 1997.

Litwack, Leon. *North of Slavery: The Negro in the Free States, 1790–1860.* Chicago: The University of Chicago Press, 1961.

Litwack, Leon, and August Meier, eds. *Black Leaders of the Nineteenth Century.* Urbana: University of Illinois Press, 1988.

Loewenberg, Bert James, and Ruth Bogin. *Black Women in Nineteenth Century American Life.* Philadelphia: Pennsylvania State University Press, 1976.

Looby, Christopher. *Voicing America: Language, Literary Form, and the Origins of the United States.* Chicago: The University of Chicago Press, 1996.

Lott, Eric. *Love and Theft: Blackface Minstrelsy and the American Working Class.* New York: Oxford University Press, 1993.

Martin, Waldo E. *The Mind of Frederick Douglass.* Chapel Hill: The University of North Carolina Press, 1984.

Matthiessen, F. O. *American Renaissance: Art and Expression in the Age of Emerson and Whitman.* New York: Oxford University Press, 1941.

McClintock, Anne. *Imperial Leather: Race, Gender and Sexuality in the Colonial Contest* New York: Routledge, 1995.

McDowell, Deborah E. *"The Changing Same" Black Women's Literature, Criticism, and Theory.* Bloomington: Indiana University Press, 1995.

McDowell, Doborah E. and Arnold Rampersad, eds. *Slavery and the Literary Imagination.* Baltimore: The Johns Hopkins University Press, 1989.

Meyer, Michael, ed. *Frederick Douglass: The Narrative and Selected Writings* New York: Random House, 1984.

Michaels, Walter Benn. *Our America: Nativism, Modernism, and Pluralism.* Durham: Duke University Press, 1995.

Michael, Walter Benn, and Donald Pease, eds. *The American Renaissance Reconsidered.* Baltimore: Johns Hopkins University Press, 1985.

Miller, Armistead. *Liberia Described. A Discourse Embracing a Description of the Climate, Soil, Productions, Animals, Missionary Work, Improvements, etc. with a Full Description of the Acclimating Fever.* Philadelphia: Joseph M. Wilson, 1859.

Miller, Floyd J. *The Search for a Black Nationality: Black Emigration and Colonization, 1787–1863.* Chicago: The University of Illinois Press, 1975.

Mitchell, Angelyn, ed. *Within the Circle: An Antholog y of African American Literary Criticism From the Harlem Renaissance to the Present* Durham: Duke University Press, 1994.

Morrison, Toni. *Playing in the Dark: Whiteness and the Literary Imagination.* Cambridge: Harvard University Press, 1992.

Moses, Wilson J. *Black Messiahs and Uncle Toms: Social and Literary Manipulations of a Religious Myth.* University Park: Pennsylvania State University Press, 1982.

———. *The Golden Age of Black Nationalism, 1850–1925.* New York: Oxford University Press, 1978.

———. *The Wings of Ethiopia: Studies in African-American Life and Letters.* Ames, Iowa: Iowa State University Press, 1990.

Mosse, George. *Nationalism and Sexuality: Middle Class Morality and Sexual Norms in Modern Europe.* Madison: The University of Wisconsin Press, 1985.

Mulvey, Laura. *Visual and Other Pleasures.* Bloomington: Indiana University Press, 1989.

Nell, William C. *The Colored Patriots of the American Revolution, With Sketches of Several Distinguished Colored Persons: To Which is Added a Brief Survey of the Condition and Prospects of Colored Americans.* 1855. Reprint, Salem, N.H.: Ayer Publishers, 1986.

Nelson, Dana. *The Word in Black and White: Reading "Race" in American Literature, 1638–1867.* New York: Oxford University Press, 1992.

Nicholson, Linda. *Gender and History: The Limits of Social Theory in the Age of the Family.* New York: Columbia University Press, 1986.

O'Connell, Catherine Elizabeth. "Chastening the Rod: Sentimental Strategies in Three Antebellum Novels by Women." Ph.D. diss., University of Michigan, 1992.

Omi, Michael, and Howard Winant. *Racial Formation in the United States From the 1960s to the 1980s.* New York: Routledge, 1986.

Parker, Andrew, Mary Russo, Doris Sommer, and Patricia Yeager, eds. *Nationalisms and Sexualities.* New York: Routledge, 1992.

Paterson, Orlando. *Slavery and Social Death.* Cambridge: Harvard University Press, 1980.

Pease, Jane H., and William H. Pease. *They Who Would Be Free: Bluck's Search For Freedom, 1830–1861.* Urbana: University of Illinois Press, 1974.

Penn, I. Garland. *The Afro-American Press and Its Editors.* 1891. Reprint, New York: Arno Press, 1969.

Peterson, Carla. *"Doers of the Word"; African American Women Speakers and Writers in the North (1830–1880).* New York: Oxford University Press, 1995.

Piersen, William D. *Black Yankees: The Development of an Afro-American Sub-Culture in New England.* Amherst: The University of Massachusetts Press, 1988.

Pinkney, Alphonso. *Red, Black, and Green: Black Nationalism in the United States.* New York: Cambridge University Press, 1976.

Poovey, Mary. *Making a Social Body: British Cultural Formation.* Chicago: University of Chicago Press, 1995.

Preston, Dickson J. *Young Frederick Douglass: The Maryland Years.* Baltimore: The Johns Hopkins University Press, 1980.

Pryse, Marjorie, and Hortense Spillers, eds. *Conjuring: Black Women, Fiction and Literary Tradition*. Bloomington: Indiana University Press, 1985.

Purvis, Robert. *Appeal of Forty Thousand Citizens, Threatened with Disfranchisement, to the People of Pennsylvania*. Philadelphia: Merrihew and Gunn, 1838.

Reid-Pharr, Robert F. "Engendeirng the Black Atlantic." *Found Object* 4 (Fall 1994): 11–16.

———. "Speaking Through Anti-Semitism: The Nation of Islam and the Poetics of Black (Counter) Modernity." *Social Text* 14.4 (Winter 1996): 133–147.

———. "Violent Ambiguity: Martin Delany, Bourgeois Sadomasochism, and the Production of a Black National Masculinity." In *Representing Black Men*, edited by Marcellus Blount and George Cunningham, 73–94. New York: Routledge, 1996.

Reynolds, David. *Beneath the American Renaissance: The Subversive Imagination in the Age of Emerson and Melville*. New York: Knopf, 1988.

Roediger, David. *The Wages of Whiteness: Race and the Making of the American Working Class*. New York: Verso, 1991.

Rollin, Frank A. *Life and Public Service of Martin Delany*. New York: Arno, 1969.

Rubin, Gayle. "The Traffic in Women: Notes on the 'Political Economy' of Sex." In *Toward an Anthropology of Women*, edited by Rayner Reiter, 157–210. New York: Monthly Review Press, 1975.

Sanchez-Eppler, Karen. *Touching Liberty: Abolition, Feminism and the Politics of the Body*. Berkeley: University of California Press, 1993.

Saxton, Alexander. *The Rise and Fall of the White Republic: Class Politics and Mass Culture in Nineteenth-Century America*. New York: Verso, 1990.

Scarry, Elaine. *The Body in Pain: The Making and Unmaking of the World*. New York: Oxford University Press, 1985.

———, ed. *Literature and the Body: Essays on Populations and Persons*. Baltimore: Johns Hopkins University Press, 1986.

Sedgwick, Eve. *Between Men: English Literature and Male Homosocial Desire*. New York: Columbia University Press, 1985.

———. *Epistemology of the Closet*. Berkeley: The University of California Press, 1990.

Seton-Watson, Hugh. *Nations and States: An Enquiry in the Origins of Nations and the Politics of Nationalism*. Boulder, Colo.: Westview Press, 1977.

Showalter, Elaine. *Sexual Anarchy: Gender and Culture at the Fin de Siecle*. New York: Penguin Books, 1990.

Shuffleton, Frank, ed. *A Mixed Race: Ethnicity in Early America*. New York: Oxford University Press, 1993.

Shumway, David R. *Creating American Civilization: A Genealogy of American Literature as an Academic Discipline*. Minneapolis: University of Minnesota Press, 1994.

Slote, Ben. "Revising Freely: Frederick Douglass and the Politics of Disembodiment." *A/B: Autobiography Studies* 11.1 (Spring 1996): 19–37.

Smith, Barbara. "Toward a Black Feminist Criticism." 1977. Reprinted in Mitchell, Angelyn, ed. *Within The Circle: An Anthology of African American Literary Criticism from The Harlem Renaissance to the Present*. Durham: Duke University Press, 1994, 410–427.

Smith, Rev. Samuel Stanhope. *An Essay on the Cause of the Variety of Complexion and Figure in the Human Species to which are added Strictures on Lord Kaim's Discourse, on the Original Diversity of Mankind*. Philadelphia: Robert Aitken, 1787.

Smith, Valerie. *Self-Discovery and Authority in Afro-American Narrative*. Boston: Harvard University Press, 1987.

Sobel, Mechal. *The World They Made Together: Black and White Values in Eighteenth Century Virginia.* Princeton: Princeton University Press, 1987.

Sollors, Werner. *Beyond Ethnicity: Consent and Descent in American Culture.* New York: Oxford University Press, 1986.

———. *Neither Black Nor White Yet Both: Thematic Explorations of Interracial Literature* New York: Oxford University Press, 1997.

Sommer, Doris. *Foundational Fictions: The National Romances of Latin America.* Berkeley: The University of California Press, 1991.

Spacks, Patricia Meyer. *Gossip.* New York: Knopf, 1985.

Spelman, Elizabeth V. *Inessential Woman: Problems of Exclusion in Feminist Thought.* New York: Beacon Press, 1988.

Spillers, Hortense, ed. *Comparative American Identities: Race, Sex and Nationality in the Modern Text.* New York: Routledge, 1991.

———. "Mama's Baby, Papa's Maybe: An American Grammar Book." 1987. Reprinted in Mitchell, Angelyn, ed. *Within the Circle: An Anthology of African American Literary Criticism From the Harlem Renaissance to the Present.* Durham: Duke University Press 1994, 454–481.

Stallybrass, Peter, and Allon White. *The Politics and Poetics of Transgression.* Ithaca: Cornell University Press, 1986.

Stanton, William. *The Leopard's Spots: Scientific Attitudes Toward Race in America, 1815–59.* Chicago: The University of Chicago Press, 1960.

Stepto, Robert. *From Behind the Veil: A Study of Afro-American Narrative.* Urbana: University of Illinois Press, 1979.

———. "Narration, Authentication, and Authorial Control in Frederick Douglass' *Narrative* of 1845." *in African American Autobiography: A Collection of Critical Essays*, edited by William L. Andrews, 26–35. Englewood Cliffs, N.J.: Prentice Hall, 1993.

Sterling, Dorothy. *The Making of an Afro-American: Martin Robinson Delany, 1812–1885.* Garden City, N.Y.: Doubleday, 1971.

———. *We Are Your Sisters: Black Women in the Nineteenth Century.* New York: W. W. Norton, 1984.

Stewart, Maria W. *Productions of Mrs. Maria W. Stewart.* Introduction by Susan Houchins. 1831. Reprint, New York: Oxford University Press, 1988.

Stuckey, Sterling. *Slave Culture: Nationalist Theory and the Foundations of Black America.* New York: Oxford, 1987.

Sundquist, Eric J. *To Wake the Nations: Race in the Making of American Literature.* Cambridge: Harvard University Press, 1993.

———, ed. *Frederick Douglass: New Literary and Historical Essays.* New York: Cambridge University Press, 1990.

Takaki, Ronald. *Iron Cages: Race and Culture in 19th Century America.* New York: Oxford University Press, 1990.

———. *Violence in the Black Imagination: Essays and Documents.* New York: Oxford University Press, 1993.

Tate, Claudia. *Domestic Allegories of Political Desire: The Black Heroine's Text at the Turn of the Century.* New York: Oxford University Press, 1992.

Therborn, Goran. *The Ideology of Power and the Power of Ideology.* New York: Verso, 1980.

Toll, Robert C. *Blacking Up: The Minstrel Show in Nineteenth-Century America.* New York: Oxford University Press, 1974.

Tompkins, Jane. *Sensational Designs: The Cultural World of American Fiction, 1790–1860*. New York: Oxford University Press, 1985.

Ullman, Victor. *Martin R. Delany: The Beginnings of Black Nationalism*. Boston: Beacon Press, 1971.

von Sacher-Masoch, Leopold. *Venus in Furs*. in *Masochism*. New York: Zone Books, 1991.

Wald, Priscilla. *Constituting Americans: Cultural Anxiety and Narrative Form*. Durham: Duke University Press, 1995.

Walker, David. *Appeal to the Colored Citizens of the World, But in Particular, and Very Expressly, to Those of the United States of America*. Introduced by Charles M. Wiltse. 1829. Reprint, New York: Hill and Wang, 1965.

Wall, Cheryl, ed. *Changing Our Own Words: Essays on Criticism, Theory, and Writing by Black Women*. New Brunswick: Rutgers University Press, 1989.

Warner, Michael. *The Letters of the Republic: Publication and the Public Sphere in Eighteenth-Century America*. Cambridge: Harvard University Press, 1990.

———. "The Mass Public and the Mass Subject." In Calhoun Craig, ed. *Habermas and the Public Sphere*. Cambridge: MIT Press, 1992, 377–401.

Warren, Kenneth. *Black and White Strangers: Race and American Literary Realism*. Chicago: The University of Chicago Press, 1993.

Webb, Frank J. *The Garies and Their Friends*. Introduced by Robert F. Reid-Pharr. 1857. Reprint, Baltimore: Johns Hopkins University Press, 1997.

Wheatley, Phillis. *Poems of Phillis Wheatley, a Native African and a Slave*. 1838. Reprint, Bedford, Mass.: Applewood Books, 1969.

Wiegman, Robyn. *American Anatomies: Theorizing Race and Gender*. Durham: Duke University Press, 1995.

Williams, Raymond. *The Country and the City*. New York: Oxford University Press, 1973.

———. *Culture and Society: 1780–1950*. 1958. Reprint, New York: Columbia University Press, 1983.

———. *Marxism and Literature*. New York: Oxford University Press, 1977.

Wilson, Harriet. *Our Nig; or, Sketches From the Life of a Free Black*, In *A Two-Story White House, North* 1859. Reprint, New York: Vintage Books, 1983.

Yellin, Jean Fagan. *The Intricate Knot: Black Figures in American Literature, 1776–1863*. New York: New York University Press, 1972.

———. *Women and Sisters: The Antislavery Feminists in American Culture*. New Haven: Yale University Press, 1989.

Young, Robert. *White Mythologies: Writing History and the West*. New York: Routledge, 1990.

Ziff, Larzer. *Literary Democracy: The Declaration of Cultural Independence in America*. New York: Viking Press, 1981.

INDEX